Karate Jutsu

HISTORY AND EVOLUTION OF THE
OKINAWAN MARTIAL ART

Simon Keegan

New Haven Publishing ltd

Published 2018
NEW HAVEN PUBLISHING LTD
www.newhavenpublishingltd.com
newhavenpublishing@gmail.com

Front cover image credit: Chris Feser
(www.flickr.com/photos/feserc/3542414538/)
via Wikimedia Commons

Cover design © Pete Cunliffe
pcunliffe@blueyonder.co.uk

Contents

Acknowledgements   5
Foreword by Jim Mather 9th Dan   7
Foreword by Fumio Demura 9th Dan   10
Foreword by Steve Rowe 9th Dan   13
Foreword by Terry Wingrove 9th Dan   14
Author's Introduction   16
Special Introduction by Laoshi John Dang   17
Part One: Pre 1700   19
Karate and Yawara: Two trees intertwined   19
Early Records of Karate   32
Buddhist Myths   37
Wutang Myths   40
General Qi: The Kata Innovator   41
The Rise of Karate in the Ryukyu   43
Wang Ji   46
Jigen Ryu: Sword Art of Karate   48
Hama Higa and Takahara Pechin   52
 Part Two: 1700s-1800s   54
The Motobu Family   54
The Five Fists of Hsing-I   61
Satunuku 'Tode' Sakugawa   62
Sakugawa Meets Kushanku   63
Kushanku and Channan   69
Part Three: Shuri Te, Tomari Te and Naha Te   74
Bushi Matsumura   74
Iwah: Quanfa Teacher of Bushi Matsumura   84
Ason: Shorei Ryu Master   89
Naihanchi   91
Shuri Te   92
Tomari Te and Shorin Ryu   99
Shorei Ryu and Naha Te   105
The Bubishi   108
Goju Ryu   110
Feeding Crane and Uechi Ryu   112
Part Four: Karate Jutsu   116
Gokenki and Tang Daiji   116
From Karate Jutsu to Karate Do   118
Karate Jutsu in Kansai 1920-1960   118

Motobu Ryu in Kansai   119
Shito Ryu in Kansai   126
Uechi Ryu in Kansai   129
Kushin Ryu in Kansai   130
Part Five: Karetedo   132
The New Shuri Te, Tomari Te and Naha Te   135
The Dai Nippon Butokukai   139
Kanken Toyama: Godfather of Okinawan Karate   140
Branches of 20th Century Okinawan Schools   142
Japanese Teaching Titles   147
The First Karate Blackbelts   147
The Return of Dai Nippon Butokukai   148
The Renaissance of Okinawan Kobudo   149
Kokusai Budoin   151
Gogen Yamaguchi (10th Dan IMAF)   155
Hironori Ohtsuka (10th Dan IMAF)   157
Shizuya Sato (10th Dan IMAF)   160
Minoru Mochizuki (10th Dan IMAF)   162
The JKA is Formed   163
Hirokazu Kanazawa (10th Dan IMAF)   166
Key JKA Shotokan events   169
Goju Ryu: Miyagi's successors   171
RyuTe   174
Part Six: International Karate   176
Early Karate for the Gaijin   176
Karate in the USA   180
British Martial Arts   184
Karate Jutsu in Kansai 1960-1987   217
Malaysian Budokan Karate   226
British Wado Ryu 1970-1990s: Toru Takamizawa   229
The World Karate Federation and the Olympics   232
Kickboxing and Freestyle Karate   234
Karate and Mixed Martial Arts   238
Epilogue: The Okinawan Karate Kaikan   243
About the Author   245
Index of Karateka   249

Acknowledgements

My wife Sally and children Poppy and Eddy.

My father David Keegan 5th Dan, my first teacher and an expert in Koryu Bujutsu and Classical Chinese martial arts.

Hanshi Terry Wingrove 9th Dan Karate Jutsu and Yawara master of the Nippon Seibukan, for his friendship and teachings and considerable input into this book.

Sifu Steve Rowe 9th Dan of Shikon, expert of Karate, Iaido and Yang style Taijiquan for his constant support and mentorship and help with this book.

Hanshi Jim Mather 9th Dan, head of the United States National Karate Association for his support and friendship.

Shihan Fumio Demura 9th Dan, head of the Genbukai, and Sensei Julian Mallalieu 5th Dan Genbukai for his friendship and insight into Shito Ryu.

Laoshi John Dang and his father Ken, descendants of the Tang family of Canton Tiger Boxers, for help researching Hu Quan and for their support over the years.

Shihan Philip Handyside 9th Dan, headteacher of Shobukan Karate, a friend and mentor.

Renshi Jim Rooney 6th Dan Dai Nippon Butokukai.

Jamie Tozer my first blackbelt in Hakuda Kempo Toshu Jutsu, for the brilliant photography.

All the martial arts teachers I have trained with over the years, especially: Kyoshi Stephen Bullough 8th Dan, my Bushidokan teacher; Kyoshi Bob Carruthers 7th Dan, my Shotokan teacher; Kyoshi Reiner Parsons 7th Dan, my Goju Ryu teacher and his son Renshi Derrick Parsons 6th Dan. Other masters I have been lucky enough to attend training with including Hanshi Tadanori Nobetsu 10th Dan, founder of Nisseikai Goju Ryu and chief director of Kokusai Budoin; the late Hanshi Shizuya Sato 10th Dan Nihon Jujutsu and founding member of Kokusai Budoin; the late Hanshi Allan Tattersall 9th Dan, master of Muso Jikiden Eishin Ryu & Koryu Jujutsu and UK head of the Dai Nippon Butokukai; the late Alan Ruddock 6th Dan, master of Aikido; Hanshi Patrick McCarthy 9th Dan for his pioneering research and generosity with his time and advice.

Renshi Andy Sloane 6th Dan in Okinawa for his contributions on Isshin Ryu; Michael Manning for the insight into early British Karate; Sensei Alfie Lewis 9th Dan for the support and help; Sensei David Castan for the friendship and a Dojo to call home at Circle Martial Arts; Russ Jarmesty, Vic Caldwell and the late Scott Caldwell at Martial Arts Guardian; Michael Day at Ippon magazine; Chris Ratcliffe 6th Dan and Frank Williams 7th Dan for their friendship and support at Red Sun Karate; Steve Brennan, Shoshin Ryu for introducing me to Koryu Uchinadi and Tegumi; Mike Newton 7th Dan for an introduction to Budokan Karate; Steve Powell for his help on the early years of Manchester Karate; Dan Smith 9th Dan for his help on Okinawan Seibukan; Lee Masters Menkyo Kaiden for his help on Tenjin Shinyo Ryu and Koryu Jujutsu; and last but not least my students.

Forewords

By Jim Mather
B.A. M.A (Stanford University)
Karate Hanshi, 9th Dan
Chairman of the United States National Karate Association
Coach: US National Karate team

'Well researched, well documented and enlightening'

In 1955, I met a Japanese college student who was attending nearby San Jose State College. Hiro turned out to be a black belt in Karate, which only a handful of people in the entire United States at the time had even heard of. The only martial art we could name was Judo. Fortunately, one of the few who were familiar with Karate was an ex-Navy sailor who worked for my father. He had lived in Japan for a couple of years and spoke of Karate with such awe that I begged Hiro to let me train with him, which he did.

Besides practising every chance I got, I wanted to learn everything I could about what seemed a mysterious fighting art. I had always loved books so one of my favourite places was the big main library in downtown San Jose. On my next trip, I searched the racks for anything I could find on Karate but came up empty. All I knew about its history was the small amount Hiro had shared with me. And all he knew was what philosopher Karl Popper called Subjective Knowledge, that passed down orally from teacher to student – never the most reliable medium.

It was a couple of years before the librarian called me over and said that they had finally gotten a Karate book in. The book was Mas Oyama's *What is Karate?* Not only did it have lots of photos and explanations on the kihon or fundamentals of Karate but it also had a fascinating series of photos of Master Oyama fighting a bull with his bare hands! Being small for my age and living in the roughest part of town, I was hooked.

Three or four other books followed not long after: George Mattson's *The Way of Karate*; Nishiyama and Brown's *Karate: the Art of Empty Hand Fighting*; and Ed Parker's *Kenpo Karate: Law of the Fist and the Empty Hand* were ones I can recall sixty years later. I bought all of them and read and reread them to glean every scrap of technical or historical information I could harvest.

The first book on Japanese/Okinawan Karate history that attempted to meet a more exacting academic standard was Bruce Haines' *Karate's History and Tradition*. Published in 1968, it was Haines' master's thesis and had earned him a degree in History at University of Hawaii.

Some of the information Haines presented had been passed directly to him by people with firsthand knowledge of the art or style in question. Usually senior in years and experience, they were the developers of a style or kata or had studied directly under the master who had. But there still remained a substantial portion that was based solely on stories passed down verbally from generation to generation. This was far less reliable.

Knowing the lineage of the various Japanese/Okinawan arts and styles and of the kata we perform is more than merely an area of interest. It can reveal keys to the inner meaning of a form or how it was meant to be performed. It can also help us gain greater understanding of the writings left to us by famous masters.

One of my Stanford philosophy professors once lectured about a branch of philosophy known as Hermeneutics. To truly understand a people, he insisted, we had to look at everything they did, not just at what they said or wrote. Within each act was a small, perhaps tiny key to understanding them better. How did they dress? What did they eat? How was it prepared? How did they entertain themselves? What were their religious beliefs? The language they spoke could reveal how they thought as some languages are more expressive in certain areas than others. For example, Eskimos reportedly have fifty words for snow. Those who wrote in pictograms – who communicated via images of the subject as in original kanji – could express themselves in a way that affected the listener differently than those who wrote via phonetic symbols as we do.

In spite of the many intervening years since I began my study of Karate and the massive increase in the number of books available on the subject, many of the original questions about origins and lineage remained unanswered. This is why I was excited when I learned that Simon Keegan had written a book on Karate history.

I had been introduced to Sensei Keegan a few years earlier by a friend, who was one of Britain's most senior and respected martial artists, the late Hanshi Ronnie Colwell. I was immediately impressed with the quality of Sensei Keegan's articles. So I knew his book would be a well-researched, well-documented, and enlightening text. And I wasn't disappointed. In his *Karate Jutsu: History and Evolution of the Okinawan Martial Art*, he ties down many of the loose ends and nagging questions that have existed for many years about lineage and kata origins. As an added bonus, he also included one of the most comprehensive histories of karate in Great Britain I've encountered. I highly recommend his new text to all serious students of Japanese/Okinawan karate.

Jim Mather is the chairman of the United States National Karate Association and head of one of America's oldest Karate schools, the California Karate Academy. He is known for his Guinness World Record for catching arrows with his bare hands (as well as cutting them from the air with katana and nunchaku). His primary instructor was the legendary Tak Kubota. Mather Hanshi has studied Karate since 1955. He served in Korea working in intelligence and reconnaissance. Returning home he opened a Karate Dojo. In 1965 he hosted the US Winter Nationals Karate Championships at the San Jose Civic Auditorium where Chuck Norris won his first grand championship title and Bruce Lee performed one of the demonstrations. Mather also hosted the Pacific Coast Karate Championships at Foothill College as Ron Marchini of Stockton defeated the legendary Joe Lewis. In the 1980s, he joined the USAKF, the official national governing body for Karate under the US Olympic Committee (USOC), and was soon named one of five martial arts instructors comprising the National Coaching Staff for the official US Karate Team, which led the US team into international competition. He was one of a group of coaches who worked with the USA Karate Team at its first training session at the US Olympic Training Center at Colorado Springs.

By Shihan Fumio Demura
Karate 9th Dan
Director of Shito Ryu Karate Genbu Kai

'Visit the old to understand the new'

I was honoured to receive Simon's request for a foreword to his book on the history of Karate. Exploring and sharing the history of Karate, and all martial arts, is a very worthy and beneficial effort. Learning more about history helps masters and students, alike, develop their true Karate capabilities.

The average person who hears about Karate generally thinks first, and quite often only, of the physical elements of Karate. Their imagination is fired with images of powerful, eye-popping fighting techniques, delivered against the foe with decisive and unopposable ability. They think of massive bricks being crumbled and boards being split in two by expertly delivered strikes. Yes, these things are part of the world of Karate, and part of the capabilities developed by many students. However, they are actually only a very small part of Karate training.

Karate is first and foremost about defence. In physical ways students are taught techniques that are designed to help them prevent harm from coming to themselves and their loved ones.

Even more importantly, students are taught how to prevent harm from coming to their characters, their spirits, and all the parts of their inner selves. They are taught what a good character is, and helped to learn to defend themselves against negative forces and experiences that will be part of their lives.

Author Simon Keegan with master Fumio Demura

Karate is about developing yourself as a human being, to be the best person you can be. This is where the benefits of history come into the picture.

"On ko Chi Shin" – this means "visit the old to understand the new" and it is one of the many ideas I teach to my students. To attain a true understanding of what they are learning today, students need to know how Karate began, and why and how it has developed since those early times. Students need to understand what forces and influences shaped Karate in the past, to help them see the directions it is going in the future. Western culture has a somewhat similar saying, with a slightly different message – "Those who do not learn from history are doomed to repeat it." My point is that, knowing what has come before helps people understand what they are learning today, and helps them on their road to developing their Karate capabilities, and their human capabilities, to the greatest extent possible.

The author with Bo standing behind master Fumio Demura on a Kobudo seminar

I am glad to be part of Simon's effort to share knowledge of the history of Karate with this book. I hope that it helps many people increase their understanding of the world of Karate, and their appreciation for all of the many benefits it brings to individuals and societies all over the world.

Fumio Demura was born in 1938 and began studying Karate at the age of 12 with Shito Ryu master Ryushu Sakagami and is now ranked 9th Dan. In 1959 he began studying Kobudo under the legendary Taira Shinken. He is also a master of Batto Jutsu. He wrote some of the west's first books about Kobudo, introducing many to weapons like the sai, nunchako, bo and tonfa for the first time. He famously taught Bruce Lee to use the Nunchaku and was the inspiration for the character of Mr Miyagi in Karate Kid, as well as the stunt double for Pat Morita. His books include Shito-Ryu Karate (1971), Advanced nunchaku (1976) Tonfa: Karate weapon of self-defense (1982), Nunchaku: Karate weapon of self-defense (1986), Bo: Karate weapon of self-defense (1987) and Sai: Karate weapon of self-defense (1987).

By Sifu Steve Rowe
Karate 9th Dan
Founder of Shikon

'A must for any Karateka'

I have known Simon Keegan for many years and watched his development in the martial arts throughout that period. Simon has a long family lineage in the arts and has dedicated his life to them along with his journalistic search for accuracy and the truth. He hasn't been tempted by the money men and business gurus to turn his passion into a business and has always earned his money independently from journalism. This has enabled him to research properly, accurately and thoroughly for both his books on the legendary King Arthur and now to record all his research on Karate.

This book contains a lot of unpublished information and brings together a lot of research that has lain hidden in dark corners of people's libraries and memories. Considering I have been at the centre of the Karate universe for four decades there is much in this book that I have never seen or heard.

We have spent many a late hour on social media messaging, discussing what makes a good martial art and artist, and I'm pleased to see that Simon has managed to collate so much information into one book. It's a must for any Karateka to read time and time again to understand the origins of Karatedo and its structure, and essential for the bookshelf of any serious martial artist.

Steve Rowe has studied Karate since 1973. A direct student of Toru Takamizawa, he was the Chairman of the Takamizawa Institute Of

13

Karate and and published two books with Takamizawa entitled 'Concepts Of Karate' 1 & 2. He was also Secretary and subsequently Chairman of the English Karate Council, the Sport England Governing Body for Karate, and represented Karate on the Martial Arts Commission. He also holds Dan grades in Iaido, training under Okimitsu Fuji and studied Yang Style Taijiquan under the grandmaster Ma Lee Yang in Hong Kong. Blending his Quan Fa, Karate, and other studies together he devised the Shikon Kung Fu system. A world respected instructor, author and researcher, he teaches all over the world.

By Terry Wingrove
Karate Hanshi, 9th Dan
Jujutsu Hanshi, 9th Dan
Technical Director: Karate Jutsu International

'A modern day Sherlock Holmes'

When I was asked by Simon Keegan to write a foreword for this new book I did not hesitate because Simon has earned his place as a modern day Sherlock Holmes determining the true origins of Karate Jutsu and Jujutsu and separating the fact from the fiction which abounds the world of Martial Arts.

Simon's journalistic background stands him in good stead as he seeks to check facts in every corner of the world and the contradictions only seem to make him more objective. I thought with 67 years in Martial Arts that I had a good knowledge of my chosen subject but Simon has opened up so many new sources. I believe that like other projects he is involved in this book will become the foundation of his life study that he will add to and update over the coming years.

I sincerely wish this book the success it deserves and expect to see it quickly become a "standard" all over the world.

Terry Wingrove has studied martial arts since 1952, beginning with Judo and then becoming a founding member of the British Karate Federation in 1957. He led the very first British Karate team in competition. He moved to Japan where he trained in Shito Ryu under Tani and Fujiwara. Terry became the only westerner on the board of FAJKO/WUKO and helped organise the first Karate world championships alongside mentor Tsuchiya Hideo. He was awarded his 5th Dan in 1972 and began to pursue the few masters who taught pre-war Karate Jutsu and Yawara in their purest form. Training with the likes of Fujimoto Hiroshi and Sato Kimbei, he spent 21 years in Japan and was awarded his Kyoshi title in Goju Ryu by Suzuki Masafumi of the Nippon Seibukan. He was awarded both his 8th Dan and 9th Dan and Shihan licence by Okinawan Karate master Hiroshi Kinjo (pictured above). In 2007 he was instrumental in the reforming of the British Karate Federation and English Karate Federation and in 2017 he was one of the first masters to teach at the new Okinawan Karate Kaikan, alongside Okinawan Goju Ryu and Motobu Ryu masters.

Author's Introduction

Like many martial arts Karate was once designed to main, disable or kill but has since become adapted into a way of life and a sport that is seen in both the UFC and the upcoming Olympics. The origins of Karate are shrouded in mythology and a book that tells the art's complete history is both necessary and timely. Karate is a unique martial art historically and technically.

The art we know as Karate was developed in the tiny Ryukyu kingdom we know today as Okinawa, Japan in between the 1600s and 1900s. Before this, its origins could be in adjacent countries, perhaps China, perhaps Thailand, perhaps India. By the 1900s, Karate was monopolised and romanticised by mainland Japan as it joined the model of Budo as established by the venerable Dai Nippon Butokukai. Karate's worldwide popularity came in the 1970s-1980s and then began a partial decline as new martial arts, ranging from the sublime to the ridiculous, came into vogue. In the 2000s Karate was once again appreciated as one of the arts utilised in Mixed Martial Arts (MMA) and is slated to appear at the Olympics in 2020. Its history came full circle in 2017 with the announcing of a new historic Karate Kaikan in Okinawa.

This book identifies Karate's very earliest origins, not only the earliest references to Ryukyu combat but also examples of equivalent Te schools in mainland Japan that are often grouped in under the umbrella of Jujutsu. We also look at some of the early relationships between Karate and Chinese internal martial arts like Hsing-I and the Quan Fa of the Chen family as well as pioneers like General Qi. There is insight into styles like the Fujian Tiger Boxing introduced to Okinawa by Tang Daiji which influenced styles like Goju Ryu and Shito Ryu; for this I was able to speak to, crosstrain with and teach alongside a descendant of the Tang family of tiger boxers, my good friend John Dang.

There is also previously unpublished information on a shadowy period of Karate Jutsu history in Kansai after the war when Uechi, Motobu and Mabuni were establishing their systems and little known masters, such as Hiroshi Fujimoto and Katsumi Fujiwara, were influential in keeping the flame alive. This information comes from first hand sources. There is also new information on the very early years of British Karate from 1956-1966 that has never been published anywhere else. This comes from personal correspondence and letters from those who were there at the time. In both cases Hanshi Terry Wingrove, who has trained since 1952, including 21 years in Japan and Okinawa, was an invaluable resource and his generosity with his time and teachings cannot be overstated.

As well as Wingrove Hanshi I would particularly like to thank Sifu Steve Rowe whose mastery of Karate and Taijiquan and friendship is appreciated; Mather Hanshi one of the pioneers of United States Karate; and Shihan Fumio Demura one of the truly great Karate and Kobudo masters.

In this book we look at the roots of Karate, we look at the branches, but the focus is very much on the trunk – and that is Karate Jutsu.

Simon Keegan (Renshi, 5th Dan)

Special Introduction by Laoshi John Dang

I have an early memory of my father demonstrating a low horse stance. He explained that all good Kung Fu came from good stance-work and while punches, kicks and acrobatics represented the branches of the tree, the stance was the root. He taught me that without a good foundation we could never have good Kung Fu.

Simon Keegan champions this philosophy and has dedicated his life to exploring and uncovering the roots of Karate. He may have been raised in the West but his knowledge of the Eastern martial arts and of Karate in particular is extraordinary. In a world where so many are seduced by accolades and driven by the hype of social media, Simon has worked relentlessly to cut through the noise. For ten years Simon taught Karate, Jujutsu and Taiji Quan at my father's Dojo/Kwoon. We spent a lot of time together talking, teaching sharing ideas and techniques from our respective styles. Simon was always meticulous about his research, approaching subjects without ego, happy to test theories and techniques against their historical significance and in their practical application to get to the heart of the truth.

In Simon we have a rare gem: a martial artist, a scholar, a teacher and a writer. Here is someone that knows what he is doing, why he is doing it and can articulate it all to others, beautifully.

I am confident this book will become essential reading for many a martial artist.

John Dang is the great grandson of the Canton Tiger Boxer Tang Tao Chong and was taught the style from an early age. John grew up surrounded by the martial arts. For over 20 years his father ran the famous Van Dang Martial Arts academy in Manchester. As well as his family system, John also studied under resident instructor Master Chu Siu Woon, a descendant of the legendary Chu Hung Mol Muay Thai under Grandmaster Sken and later Jeet Kune Do with Steve Powell. Today he continues his family tradition running a club in Manchester and furthers his knowledge by studying Brazilian Jiu Jitsu under the guidance of professor Marcos Da Matta Meira (a 5th degree black belt under Carlson Gracie.) John is the owner of Hakutora (White Tiger) Fightwear manufacturers of premium martial arts equipment.

John Dang at his Kwoon in Manchester

Part One: Pre 1700

Karate and Yawara: Two trees intertwined

Today Okinawa is part of Japan, but in the past the Ryukyu kingdom was independent, sometimes dominated by China, sometimes Japan. The boxing art of the Ryukyu is now called Karate. But what is Karate, and what defines it as opposed to other martial arts like Jujutsu, the so called wrestling of Japan?

When we talk of Karate, what we mean is any martial art developed in Okinawa (or derived from Okinawa) that is predominantly empty handed and predominantly using strikes. We might call the Okinawan weapons arts 'Kobudo', and we might call Okinawan wrestling 'Tegumi' or 'Okinawan Sumo'. The word 'Karate' can refer to styles developed in Japan like Wado Ryu, or styles developed in Okinawa like Matsubayashi Ryu - or even Western freestyle systems.

We think of past Karate masters as being any Okinawan master of combat who engaged in predominantly empty handed fighting. However, Karate is in some ways a retrospective term. For example Kanga Sakugawa, who flourished in the late 18th century, is considered a great Karate master, but he may have never uttered the word 'Karate.' Almost every Karateka since 1900 uses the term 'Karate' to describe their art, but before that it may have been called Te, Ti, Tode, Toshu, Uchinadi or another variant. Much like in the West, we might talk of 'boxing', 'fighting', 'pugilism' or 'the sweet science' or talk of 'wrestling', 'grappling', 'catch-as-catch-can' or even 'the science of defence' – they are just terms for similar things.

The point is there was no single approach to Karate, nor did everyone even call it Karate. Some, like the masters of Uechi Ryu, were essentially practising Fujian Kung Fu or Quan Fa, whereas others had a style that was very uniquely Okinawan.

I would define Karate as:

Any predominantly empty handed fighting system of Okinawan origin or descent that is more based around strikes than it is grappling. It is typically defined by one or more formal solo exercises commonly called kata.

Jujutsu is to mainland Japan what Karate is to Okinawa. There have been many famous schools of Jujutsu, from classical ones like Kito Ryu and Takenouchi Ryu, to modern ones like Gracie Jiu Jitsu and Small Circle Jujutsu. Again, not every Japanese fighting man of the past would have even used the term 'Jujutsu'.

They may have used any number of terms like Yawara, Hakuda, Kumiuchi, Kogusoku or even Judo.

Jujutsu literally translated means:

Ju or Yawara: Soft (as in yielding/supple/pliant)
Jutsu: Art (means/method)

In a martial arts sense it has connotations of overcoming an attacker by means of yielding and redirecting rather than meeting strength with strength. Jujutsu is a term that emerged in the Edo

(Tokugawa) era, in around the 1700s as the samurai of the time were interested in applying old Chinese and Confucian ideals to their martial arts.

Jujutsu is used somewhat retrospectively for any unarmed or lightly armed Japanese fighting tradition from before the 1900s. Very few of the old Japanese schools actually referred to their methods as 'Jujutsu' and, depending on the emphasis, instead used phrases like Hakuda, Yawara, Taijutsu, Torite, Kosshi Jutsu, Kogusoku and Kumiuchi.

A good definition therefore of Jujutsu is:

A retrospective term given to any Japanese fighting art prior to the Meiji restoration that is predominantly unarmed or lightly armed.

There was nothing that prescribed 'Jujutsu' to be empty handed. 'Jujutsu' was simply an art used when the primary weapons of longbow, sword and spear were not available. This does not mean the samurai were not armed with daggers, knives, knuckle dusters, gauntlets, spikes and maces. Many Jujutsu schools also taught the Tanjo (something like an Escrima stick) which could also be applied to a Tessen (folded fan). The samurai were adept with rope tying restraints, threw shuriken as a distraction and had several blades and spikes hidden within their armour fixings.

The wider point is that nowadays we see a huge difference between Karate and Jujutsu, but three hundred years ago there were perhaps just Bushi of Japan performing the fighting arts of their school, and Bushi of Ryukyu performing the fighting arts of their school. Neither may have heard the terms Karate or Jujutsu, but now those terms are retrospectively applied to them. There is no evidence Miyamoto Musashi ever used the phrase "Jujutsu" but if he threw someone it would now be described as a "Jujutsu throw."

Even in Japan now, Jujutsu is divided into different types 1) Koryu Jujutsu 2) Gendai Jujutsu (old and modern) and 3) Goshin (self defence), used for eclectic styles.

Some typical differences between Karate and Jujutsu:

1) Karate is Okinawan; Jujutsu is Japanese.

2) Karate tends to use prescribed stances (ie Zenkutsu Dachi); Jujutsu tends to use prescribed hand positions (ie Jodan kamae). There

are exceptions.

3) Karate tends to use solo forms, Jujutsu tends to use paired kata. There are exceptions.

4) Okinawan Bushi (Karateka) were primarily empty-handed; Japanese Bushi (Samurai) were primarily armed.

5) Karate kata often hides its applications within the form (for example an apparent 'block' can be a throw); Jujutsu applications are seen and are self evident.

6) Karate uses many hand shapes (knife hand, single knuckle punch etc); Jujutsu generally does not.

7) Karate was practiced by bodyguards, officials and civilians alike; Jujutsu was mostly practiced by samurai.

8) Karate was developed by a handful of pioneers (maybe a few dozen) across a few hundred years; Jujutsu was developed by thousands of warriors over a thousand years. Karate was taught by individuals on an informal basis; Jujutsu was taught by professional instructors within each warrior clan and taught in a formal arranged fashion.

9) Jujutsu was developed almost solely in Japan. Perhaps around 90% of Jujutsu schools were developed purely by Japanese teachers in an isolated fashion within their Ryu, whereas Karate was developed with direct influences from Okinawa, Japan, China, Thailand, Vietnam and Taiwan. Japan was a nationalistic cultural art; Karate was a mixing pot of influences. There are some exceptions.

10) Jujutsu was designed to be practised in restrictive clothing from full armour to sandals, riding hakama, kimono, while wearing weapons; Karate may be freely executed in a minimal attire, not much different from today's gi.

Terms used to describe Japanese grappling schools

- Yawara (alternative reading of the character Ju in Jujutsu) – Muso Jikiden Ryu, Yagyu Shingan Ryu,
- Ryoi Shinto Ryu, Katori Shinto Ryu
- Wajutsu (alternative contraction of Yawara) – Oguri Ryu
- Taijutsu (body art) – Asayama Ichiden Ryu
- Tori Te (catching hand) – Araki Ryu
- Judo (gentle way) – Jikishin Ryu. Later adopted by Jigoro Kano for the sport of Judo
- Aikijujutsu (harmonious energy supple art) – Daito Ryu
- Hade (white hand) – Takenouchi Ryu
- Kempo (fist law) – Gyoko Ryu
- Hakuda (white hand) – Akiyama Yoshin Ryu
- Koppo Jutsu (bone breaking art) – Koto Ryu
- Kosshi Jutsu (flesh seizing art) – Gikan Ryu
- Yoroi Kumiuchi (grappling in armour) – Takenouchi   Ryu
- Jujutsu (soft art) – Tenjin Shinyo Ryu

As we will discover in the following chapters, Karate and Jujutsu have always been closely linked. The unarmed combat of mainland Japan and the unarmed combat of the Ryukyu islands are as closely related as, say, Cumberland wrestling and Cornish wrestling. They have different regional foibles but really they are the same thing.

A man in 1812 punched somebody in the face, body slammed him and then put him in a chokehold – if that happened in Tokyo we would call him a Jujutsu exponent, but if it happened in Naha we would call him a Karate exponent. The same technique on two different islands is defined by regional identity. We could extend this to say, if it happened in Beijing he was a Kung Fu exponent, or in Bangkok a Muay Boran exponent.

So are terms like Karate, Jujutsu, Kung Fu, Muay Boran, Silat and so on really just regional flavours of the same thing? In some respects, yes. In others, no.

The regions brought distinct laws, climates, technology, customs and training methods that defined their martial arts. For example in mainland Japan those most likely to learn Jujutsu were members of the samurai class. In Okinawa likewise it was the Bushi class most likely to learn Karate. The difference was that in Japan the samurai was armed to the teeth with helmet, spear, sword and bow, whereas in Okinawa the Bushi wore only robes and may have had only a hairpin as a weapon. Therefore the Japanese samurai would have been wasting his time trying to punch an opponent in the stomach. Therefore Jujutsu developed a strategy that we see today in Judo of "throw the man onto his back so he is vulnerable" whereas Karate developed a strategy of "strike fast and strike hard."

There are of course exceptions. Many Karateka were noted weapons masters, many Jujutsu styles (suhada Jujutsu) barely took into account armour or weapons, and many Karateka could grapple as well as the Japanese. This is the paradox.

What defines the art is its kata and the techniques particular to its school. For example one can hardly be described as a Tenjin Shinyo Ryu practitioner without knowing the two main sets of that style, neither can one be a Goju Ryu practitioner without study of Sanchin.

Where Karate differs from Jujutsu is in its kata. The Shuri/Tomari styles are renowned for forms like Kushanku, Gojushiho and Bassai and the Naha styles are renowned for forms like Sanchin and Suparimpei. While the roots of the Naha forms are fairly well established in Fujian/Shaolin styles, the origins of the Shuri Te forms are less easy to identify. Karate also has fairly unique training methods like the Makiwara and Chi Ishi.

At the core however, the two arts, Karate and Jujutsu, are linked. They both contain strikes, throws and locks, but also include pressure points, flesh tears, chokes and rips. Jujutsu is in the shadow of uniquely Japanese weapons like the katana, while Karate goes hand in hand with uniquely Okinawan weapons like the sai, nunchaku and tonfa.

There are some schools that show a far closer kinship than others and we will examine some of these schools.

The first is the Yoshin Ryu, because like the Okinawan Bushi, its founder Akiyama learned his art (which he called *Hakuda* not Jujutsu) from the Quan Fa masters of China.

Yoshin Ryu and Fudo Chishin Ryu – The Hakuda schools

Akiyama Yoshitoka (circa 1600-1670) is thought of as a Jujutsu patriarch, but he actually studied Quan Fa in China and returned to his native Nagasaki with his newfound art. Akiyama called his art Hakuda (white hand). The character Da is the same as Te - meaning hand. So in some respects Akiyama was a practitioner of "Te" before the art was recorded in Okinawa.

Even the famous founder of Judo, Kano Jigoro, described Akiyama's study of Hakuda, saying: *"There once lived in Nagasaki a physician named Akiyama, who went to China to study medicine. There he learned an art called Hakuda which consisted of kicking and striking, differing, we may note, from Jujutsu, which is mainly seizing and throwing."*

The founder of Goju Ryu Karate, Chojun Miyagi spoke about the Chinese origins of this method, stating: *"In China, in the old days, people called Hakuda or Baida for Chinese Kungfu, Kenpo or Chuanfa"*.

A Chinese punching and kicking art called Te was adopted by a Bushi. This is hardly any different to the Okinawan masters of the 1800s. It also raises the possibility that when he was travelling from Japan to China, and vice versa, Akiyama stopped off at Ryukyu. What if he learned – or taught – his Te in Okinawa? Could 'China' actually have been Chinese occupied Ryukyu? In other words could Akiyama have learned Hakuda in Okinawa?

Yoshin Ryu Hakuda was not the only Jujutsu system derived from Chinese Kempo; the most notable was Kito Ryu, famed as one of the styles from which Judo was derived.

According to Mol, Fudo Chishin Ryu also used the term Hakuda for its Jujutsu. He writes: *"I have seen only one copy of a kudensho that included this term, from the Fudo Chishin Ryu, a Hakuda system whose roots are believed to be in what is now Yamaguchi Prefecture."*

The Haku in Hakuda means white and Da means hand. White hand has been translated as 'to strike without impurity' but this seems like a needlessly flowery translation, especially when names like white crane and black tiger are so common in China.

The other consideration is that reversing the characters gives us Shu Baku. Here Da/Te uses the alternative pronunciation. Shu is used for hand in the knife hand strike (shuto) for example. *Haku* becomes *baku* in the same way that Harai (as in Harai Goshi) becomes Barai (as in Gedan Barai). It is worth exploring whether Baku could therefore have a linguistic link to Bagua. Although Bagua (Pakua) Zhang is considered to have been created in the 1800s, it is believed that an older style of Bagua Chuan existed prior to this date. Could there be a link between Bagua and Hakuda?

Kito Ryu

Karate master Anko Itosu thought Karate could be traced back to Chinese master Chen Gempin (*A Stroll Along Ryukyu Martial Arts History* by Andreas Quast). It is possible this is because of the Channan forms sharing a similar sounding name to Chen, or possibly Chang Chuan.

Chen Gempin, who lived around 1587-1671, was said to have brought Chinese fighting arts to Japan in 1638 and his students Fukuno and Terada became the founders of the Kito Ryu tradition. Kito Ryu, sometimes called Ryoi Shinto Ryu, has special significance in Japan because it is one of the main influences on Dr Kano's Judo. Fukuno and Terada were from Satsuma, the part of Japan that had the most influence on Okinawa. Therefore it is perfectly reasonable that Okinawans who studied in Satsuma could have indeed been influenced by the Kito Ryu.

Kito means "rise and fall"; the character "to" can also mean to "beat down". It therefore suggests opposites – give and take, to rise and fall or maybe to pick up and put down.

It is interesting to note that around the same time Chen Gempin lived the Chinese master Chen Wangting was also around. Chen Wangting was the famous patriarch of Chen style Taijiquan.

Of course Chen is a common surname in China – rather like Smith or Jones in Britain, but this link is indeed one of study and one that has not gone unnoticed by Taijiquan researchers.

Taijiquan expert Dan Docherty (*Decoding the Classics for the Modern Martial Artist*) writes: *"Jujutsu, Karate Jutsu and other Jutsu are supposedly only concerned with combat efficacy and are not martial arts, but purely for fighting. Most Jujutsu practised today comes from the art taught by the Chinese master Chen Yuan Bin to three Samurai in Nagasaki in 1638. Jujutsu (techniques of softness) is exactly the Taijiquan concept of Yin defeating Yang by using the opponent's own force against him; even Jutsu is not immune to Taoist philosophy."*

Docherty further adds (*Complete Tai Chi Chuan*): *"Japanese Jujutsu – literally soft technique/art – traced its origins from a Chinese named Chen Yuan Pin (1587-1674). The similarity of the theory and techniques handed down by Chen to those of the Taijiquan/Neijiaquan, and the fact that he was a contemporary of Wang Zheng Nan all suggest that Neijiaquan once exercised a profound influence on martial arts in China and Japan, in the same way Taijiquan does today."*

There is some indication therefore that mainland Japanese Jujutsu (Kito Ryu) and some Okinawan forms (perhaps the Channan forms) share a common origin with the Quanfa practised by the Chen family, the famous exponents of the art now called Taijiquan (Tai Chi Chuan) which in turn may have been derived from the Quanfa of General Qi.

It is difficult to know what the original Hakuda and Kito Ryu would have looked like, but one Japanese style that retains its Chinese look and feel is Yagyu Shingan Ryu.

Yagyu Shingan Ryu Yawara

A good example of a school that is the exception to the Japanese "Jujutsu equals grappling" rule is Yagyu Shingan Ryu. This art uses such beautiful strikes, solo forms and drills that it would be easily mistaken for Karate or Kung Fu. Its circular, flowing strikes are reminiscent of the Chinese art of Hsing-I Chuan and the art eschews the usual hip throws and pins that dominate Judo and modern Jujutsu.

A prominent teacher of Yagyu Shingan Ryu in the mid 20th century was Dr Sato Kimbei, known for teaching Chinese internal martial arts in Japan. According to Sato's daughter, *"Yagyu Shingan-ryu is different from other forms of Jujutsu in terms of its practicality on the field of battle and its unrivalled fierceness and ability to kill the enemy. It is said that the experienced practitioner can shatter an enemy arm with one blow."*

But Yagyu Shingan Ryu's similarities with Karate are not limited to both having a possible derivation from Chinese Quanfa. Another interesting factor is that within the art was a method called *Totte no Jutsu* (compare to the Okinawan *Tode Jutsu* – Karate) and the art also taught improvised agricultural implements (much like Okinawan Kobudo).

Again it is possible that a Chinese influence could have led to "Totte no Jutsu" being taught in Yagyu Shingan Ryu before the art arose in Okinawa. Could there then be a link between the two?

Originally called simply Shingan Ryu, it was later renamed Yagyu Shingan Ryu, due to the influence of Yagyu Tajima No Kami Munenori's Yagyu Shinkage Ryu.

Yagyu Shingan Ryu was created to be a battlefield art with a large comprehensive curriculum of weapons, and grappling techniques for use both while armoured and unarmoured, training several arts, including Yawara (Jujutsu), quarterstaff fighting (Bojutsu), glaive fighting (Naginatajutsu), sword drawing techniques (Battojutsu) and sword fighting (Kenjutsu).

Technical characteristics of Yagyu Shingan Ryu:

- Suburi (Suhada Jujutsu, atemi)
- Torite no Jutsu – Torikata no Yawara (restraints)
- Totte no Jutsu (escapes)
- Kogusoku Totte (grappling with armour and short swords)
- Gyoi dori (defence against Iai Jutsu)
- Kobudo agricultural style weapons – Hananejibo (a Jutte originally used to control horses), Bashin (a double edge knife used to bleed horses), Jingama (Kama sickle)

Araki Mataemon (1594–1634) is credited as the spiritual father of the Edo-line of Yagyu Shingan Ryu later to become known as Yagyu Shingan Ryu Taijutsu. Therefore Yagyu Shingan Ryu is considered to have been founded in around 1600. If Tori-Te and To-Te were an original component of its system, then this Te would predate any reference to Te in Okinawa.

Asayama Ichiden Ryu

In 2015 the Motobu Ryu (one of Okinawa's oldest Karate traditions) social media site posted that Okinawan Tuite may have been related to Japanese styles such as Ichiden Ryu – due to similarities in their small joint manipulation techniques.

The Motobu Ryu posted: *"Although Yubi Kansetsu Waza (finger joint locking techniques) are not general in Japanese Jujutsu, they are often used in Motobu Udundi. However, it seems that they were used as basic techniques in some old schools like Asayama Ichiden-ryu old Jujutsu school. The school was trained as the name of Asayama-ryu in Satsuma (current Kagoshima prefecture). Asayama Ichiden-ryu is almost lost in Japan today. It seems that a few lineages of it barely exist. The fact is important in consideration of the origin of tuiti*

28

in Okinawa."

Asayama Ichiden Ryu was another school, along with Yagyu Shingan Ryu, that was mastered by the Yawara expert Sato Kimbei.

Asayama Ichiden Ryu was founded by Asayama Ichidensai Shigetatsu as solely an atemi (striking) and gyakute (reversal) art. Aside from Jujutsu, the art also contains gyaku tejutsu, a rare reversal art utilising a short wooden pole around a foot long.

The art is learned first bare-handed, but its techniques may also be used with a steel fan. The art was initially taught in the Aizu domain, which is the same area that Daito Ryu originated, hence a possible reason for some experts noting similarities in the various waza that are shared. Eventually the art was promoted throughout the region by the Tanaka House, who were elders on the council to the lord of that area. During the Meiji period (1868 to 1912), the head of the art was named Tamatso Tanaka, the 12th generation head of the art.

Its current popularity was due to Tanaka's appointment of Okura Hisajiro Naoyuki as style head. Okura had a Dojo in the Koiskikawa area of Tokyo. He had two senior students, Adachi Yushio, who continued the tradition, and also Naganuma Tsuneyuki, who married his daughter.

As a result, Naganuma was given the responsibility of heading the art. He subsequently appointed his second son, Yoshiyuki, as the head of the art, who left the position and turned it over to a senior student named Ueno Takashi. When Tsuneyuki died a previous head began teaching again, leading to two branches claiming the headmastership.

One branch claims Sato Kinbei as the successor in 1955, while another claims Kaminaga Shigemi was appointed. Kinbei taught many people the art of Asayama Ichiden Ryu.

Sato's daughter wrote: *"Sato Kinbei learned Asayama Ichiden-ryu from the 16th generation lineage holder Ueno Takashi, and in December of 1955 became the 17th generation lineage holder of the line. Sato Kinbei learned also Tenshin-ryu and Bokuden-ryu from Ueno, and taught him as well different arts which he knew in a fruitful exchange."*

Takenouchi Ryu

Considered by many to be the world's oldest Jujutsu school, the Takenouchi Ryu uses the term "Ha-de" which may be a contraction of

Hakuda, and also Torite.

Serge Mol writes: *"The exact meaning of the term Hade is a little obscure, but technically speaking it was one system for attacking the vital points of the body. This term can be found in transmission scrolls of the Takenouchi Ryu... Hade is sometimes also called Kempo Taijutsu."*

He adds: *"From the Koshi no mawari a new system was developed in which the use of short swords was not required. Instead one would attack the anatomically weak points of the body with atemi, in order to weaken the enemy before using nagewaza. Knowledge of these vulnerable points, called Kyusho or also tsubo was passed on by word of mouth."*

Ha-de is another example, here in Japan's oldest grappling school, of the character Te being used.

Tenjin Shinyo Ryu

Along with Kito Ryu, Tenjin Shinyo Ryu is one of the main styles that influenced Judo. But it would be a mistake to think of Tenjin as a purely grappling art or a sporting form like Judo. It contains numerous strikes, and makes reference to Buddhist Temple symbolism, in the same way that Shaolin and modern Karate is known to.

Shike Paul Masters, one of the original students of British Karate founder Vernon Bell, went on to become the only Westerner to earn a Menkyo Kaiden in Tenjin Shinyo Ryu Jujutsu. His son Lee also now holds that title. In a Jujutsu feature I commissioned for a magazine, I asked Masters Sensei to explain the 'Hiden' of Tenjin Shinyo Ryu. This secret teaching reveals esoteric and Buddhist influenced striking rituals:

"When the monjin of TSR reaches the Menkyo level he is regarded as being a correct person to start to teach the esoteric, cosmological concepts of TSR. Within these concepts are the Sanmitsu or three secrets or three mysteries. The Sanmitsu has its origins both in Ko Shinto and Shingon Buddhism. The Sanmitsu comprises of three principles: 1) Mandara – visualization, 2) Inkei – hand seal 3) Dharani – special word sounds. "These three principles are usually practised simultaneously for the purpose of unifying the mind, body and speech in order to eliminate the mind of all distractions and be able to focus with absolute clarity. Mandara uses the principle of

visualizing sacred symbols, mystical illustrations and deity forms, inkei or ketsu-in uses various hand and finger formations, and dharani uses vocal intonations, known as kotodama in Shinto or mantras in Shingon Buddhism."

Conclusions

In 1532 we see Takenouchi Ryu founded which used the term Ha-De for its striking system. Thirty years later in the 1560s we see the founding of Asayama Ichiden Ryu, cited by the Motobu Ryu as a possible relation to Okinawan Te.

Thirty five years later in around 1600 we see the founding of Yagyu Shingan Ryu, a percussive Yawara style somewhat resembling Hsing-I and utilising agricultural implements as Kobudo weapons. Around 15 years later the Chinese master Chen Gempin, cited by Anko Itosu himself as an ancestor of Karate, introduced what would become Kito Ryu Jujutsu to Japan. In 1650 Akiyama Yoshitoka studied a percussive Quan Fa system in China. He returned to Japan with 'Hakuda' (Haku Te), a term meaning 'white hand.'

The story of some of the Yawara schools parallels that of Okinawan Karate. They borrowed from Quan Fa, they utilised agricultural weapons, and they called their boxing 'Te'.

Koryu Bujutsu performed by the author's father

Early Records of Karate

There are very few records of the art of Karate prior to the 1800s but numerous records give us an idea of what warfare and martial arts were like in Okinawa in this period.

For example there is a record dating back to 1434 that lists various Ryukyu swords being sent to China. One example of a Ryukyu weapon from the period is the Choganemaru – a sort of one handed katana that may also be said to resemble a Chinese broadsword or scimitar. While the original katana was a kind of cross between the Jian (Ken) and Dao (To), Okinawa had more direct Chinese influences.

In 1477 a Korean record of Okinawa (see *A Stroll Along Ryukyu Martial Arts History* by Andreas Quast) describes *"bows and arrows, axes, large irons, cut and thrust weapons, flat adzes, war sickles and war hammers, armour and helmets, for the production of which they used iron as well as leather."* This conjures up images of well armed and armoured Okinawans, dressed something like samurai. Another 15th century sword of Japanese design is the Chatan Nakiri, a Tanto with very Japanese mountings including Kozuka utility knives and sharkskin hilt. Likewise the Jiganemaru is a katana style sword, with resemblance to both the Choganemaru and the Chatan Nakiri in its hilt designs.

But it was clearly not just Japanese style swords possessed in the Ryukyu – they must have also had some mighty Bushi armour. The imperial envoy Xiao Chongye describes how the Okinawan Bushi had *"their faces covered with copper demon face masks and wearing armour as well as swords."*

Therefore again Ryukyu shares its Bushi heritage with Japan.

However nowhere in these early records are there particular references to empty handed combat or Karate but there is to Kobudo. In the book *Kyuyo*, there is an account of an event in 1614 of a young man practising Bojutsu in Okinawa, which states: *"Jiryo picked up a staff and jumped down to the yard, and began nimbly handling the stick, which whirled and twisted like a dragon, and his method of handling the staff was true to the techniques."*

Uni-Ufugusuku was a martial arts master and Ryukyuan general who served the Ryukyu Kingdom. "Uni" is an Okinawan cognate of the Japanese "oni," which means ogre. He received this nickname because he was about 6 feet tall, something of a giant at the time. He was the personal attendant of King Sho Taikyu's daughter, and lived in Katsuren Castle when she married the Aji Amawari. During the Aji's grab for power in 1458, Ufugusuku took the King's daughter back to Shuri Castle. He led the Ryukyuan army to depose Amawari, and personally executed him. He was a master of sword, bo and empty handed fighting. A number of Karateka including Mabuni Kenwa, Oyata Seiyu and Hokama Tetsuhiro are said to be descended from the Ufugusuku clan.

One of the earliest records of 'Te' was by the scholar Tei Junsoku (1663-1734). He wrote: *"No matter how you may excel in the art of Te, and in your scholastic endeavours, nothing is more important than your behaviour and your humanity as observed in daily life."*

But of course Te just means hand, so it is entirely possible he didn't quite have "hand to hand combat" in mind when he described Te. If he was describing the fighting art, it suggests Te was prized as something for the well educated. Tei is particularly famous for his contributions to scholarship and education in Okinawa and Japan.

Holding 'uekata' rank in the Ryukyuan government, he served at times in his career as magistrate of both Nago and Kumemura, and as a member of the Sanshikan, the elite council of three chief advisors to the king. He is sometimes known as the "Sage of Nago."

Tei Junsoku (1663-1734) an early advocate of studying Te.

Tei was actually born in Kumemura, the Okinawan centre of classical Chinese learning, so it may even be that the Te he referred to was the product of Chinese influence. He first journeyed to China in 1683 (exactly contemporary with Wang Ji and Hama Higa who we will meet later) and stayed there for four years, studying the Confucian classics, among other subjects, just as many others raised and educated in the scholar-bureaucrat system in Kumemura did over the course of the kingdom's history.

He would return to China several times during his career, serving as interpreter and in other roles as a member of official missions from the kingdom. It seems unlikely that he never encountered Chinese martial arts.

Junsoku was, in a sense, the Okinawan education minister. He was a learned man who had travelled to both China and Japan. But we should note he referred to the art as Te, rather than Kara Te, To Shu or To Te (simply as Hand rather than Chinese Hand).

It is also interesting that in a story of "Gima from Hija village" in 1709 he is said to have encountered a wild boar which he defeated using his bare hands. Unfortunately the phrase "bare hands" in Chinese calligraphy is "empty hands" which is the same as the current characters for Karate. It is unlikely that Gima subdued a boar using Karate, and more likely that he simply used his bare hands. But, all the same, this is an example of an Okinawan using "Kara Te" to subdue an attack, even if it was from a disgruntled animal.

Another early reference to Okinawan fist fighting was in the *Oyamise Nikki*. One record, dated to the first year of the reign of the Qianlong Emperor (which would be 1736) told of a scuffle that started when one Chikudun Pechin (an Okinawan samurai rank) planted flowers at the roadside. Kinjo Pechin told him to remove them because they hindered pedestrians, and it states: *"When Kinjo Ucchi Pechin's second son removed the flowers, since Takamine knocked down (Kinjo's second son) with Tetsukumi, his father and older brother appeared and struck Takamine in the face with a stone."*

It is interesting that Tetsukumi, which may translate as "iron fist", is referenced here. The syllable Kumi could also be the same as in Kumiuchi, Kumite or Tegumi. The Kumi here is literally translated as "set" (as in group or grouped). So Kumite means "grouping hands" or "hands brought together". It is reminiscent of the American slang "throwing hands with each other" for boxing.

Tetsu is literally iron (compounded of the characters 'black' and 'metal'). So perhaps "iron sets" were considered a form of hand conditioning.

This was also cited in a Japanese article of the 1800s that referred to Okinawa's Kenjutsu and Yawara as "lukewarm" and saying they are most skilled at thrusting with the clenched fist. One example given was a man who could break seven roof tiles.

According to a translation by Quast, a student of Choki Motobu referred to Tijikun (a variation of Tetsukumi) as being an old name for Karate. Could it be that Tijikun or Tetsukumi was an old Okinawan term for their "iron hand" boxing that was used even prior to terms like Karate and Te?

It is interesting that in around the 1930s Gichin Funakoshi changed the name of the Okinawan kata Naihanchi to "Tekki" which means "iron horseman" and modern day Karate includes as one of its fundamental techniques the Tettsui Uchi (hammer fist, but literally perhaps iron hammer fist).

According to Charles C Goodin (Seinenkai), a Tijikun Bushi or Tekobushi (knuckle fighter) was a fighter who prided himself on looking like a brutal fighter, with calloused knuckles and scars. A Japanese Kendo teacher stationed in Okinawa in the early 20th century described: *"drinking, courtesans, roughs with acts of nameless cruelty if their blood was stirred... The Luchuans [Ryukyuans] had developed through centuries of practice the peculiar art of self defence and aggression known as tekobushi which consists in making incredibly deft and powerful thrusts of the fists after the fashion of Jujutsu or even boxing... A Luchuan expert in the deadly art could smash every bone in his victim's body with the thrusts of the arms, as if he had been struck with a giant hammer... Near Tsuji [the red light area where Choki Motobu would apparently pick fights] at night there were always gangs of roughs supposed to be skilled at tekobushi who were ready to pick quarrels with unwary strangers."*

The Japanese view of the Ryukyuans was that they were uncultured thugs fond of punching things, and their 'Yawara' was unsophisticated.

Again it's interesting that Teko (a tekko is a knuckle duster as well) is similar sounding to Tekki.

Goju Kai master Gogen Yamaguchi referred to old Karate as *Toshu kuken* (Chinese hand empty fist). He wrote: *"Karate-do was born combining kakutojutsu which had been studied in Okinawa 500 years ago, and kempo, which was introduced from China. As you can see in* many countries, fighting martial arts have been handed down in each country.

"In Okinawa, for a long time, using any kinds of weapons was prohibited because of a policy of prohibiting weapons. For that reason, they had to invent Toshukuken, the way to fight without a weapon. This was especially true in the beginning of the 17th century since it was thought that fighting martial arts, referring to Chinese kempo, was invented among Ryukyu samurai because their weapons were banned. In Okinawa, before it was called Karate, it had two names, one was Naha-te and the other was Shuri-te."

The invasion of the Ryukyu Kingdom by the Shimazu clan of Satsuma Domain took place in April 1609. Three thousand men sailed from Kagoshima, Kyushu. The Ryukyuans were defeated in the Amami Islands, then at Nakijin Castle on Okinawa Island. After this the Satsuma apparently banned the Okinawans from carrying weapons, although this is now disputed. As we have seen there were clearly weapons in Okinawa.

All of the very earliest references to combat in Okinawa suggest a samurai-like society with battle armour and weapons, but then we clearly see an era where "iron fists" and powerful thrusts are the hallmarks of the civilian warrior. The image of an Okinawan Karateka pounding his fists on a wooden board to gain calloused and conditioned iron knuckles is clearly not a modern idea.

From Tang Shou Tao to Toshu Jutsu

Among the greatest Chinese (or to be precise Taiwanese) martial arts masters of the 20th century were Hung I-Hsiang and his brothers Hung I-Wen and Hung I-Mien. The brothers famously came to Japan (see later chapter) to teach their art to the Karate community in order that the origins of Karate be better understood. The Hungs were featured on the classic TV series and book *Way of the Warrior* (which many British martial artists may remember for the episode about Higaonna Morio of Goju Ryu and Otake of Katori Shinto Ryu).

The Hung brothers were masters of Tang Shou Tao which is essentially the Chinese way of pronouncing Toshu Do or Karate Do. Tang/To is of course 'Chinese', Shou/Shu is hand (also Te) and Tao/Do is the way. According to the Hung brothers, this is the correct way of describing Chinese martial arts. Hung said Shaolin as we know it today is not the most ancient of Chinese martial arts. He believed that prior to the seventeenth century even Shaolin resembled Hsing-I. Hung I-Hsiang said: *"During the Tang Dynasty, foreigners called the Chinese 'men of Tang'. Therefore Tang Shou means 'hands of Tang'. Foreigners came to refer to Chinese martial arts as Tang Shou Tao, the way of the hands of Tang. Since ancient times, the term Tang Shao Tao has been used to designate Chinese martial arts."*

Buddhist Myths

"Karate which is the Japanese form of a method of combat known here under the name of Chinese boxing means 'hand empty'. Empty of any weapon, empty of any evil intentions. In accordance with the Chinese Buddhist class who invented it a little more than 2,000 years ago to protect the monks for whom it was impossible to carry weapons."
- Henri Plee, founder of European Karate.

This is a perfect example of the kind of myth that has been doing the rounds in Karate circles for more than 100 years, and such storytelling is common in Japanese martial arts.

In Japan and Okinawa there is a concept called Tatemae (built in front) and Honne (true sound), which loosely translated means "official truth" and "actual truth". Another way of looking at it would be "propaganda" and "truth." Sometimes Tatemae is used for political or marketing purposes and other times to enhance a legend. To use a Western comparison, it is rather like the Trump administration's "alternative facts".

Each martial art has a Tatemae and a Honne. Later when we encounter stories of Gogen Yamaguchi killing a tiger with his bare hands and taking down an entire platoon of armed Chinese soldiers, we should assess whether such stories are tatemae or honne!

The equivalent of Tatemae in Chinese martial arts is that of 'face'. Kennedy and Guo (*Chinese Martial Arts Training Manuals*) point out: *"Most purported histories of Chinese martial arts systems do not have 'the truth' as their goal, be it an absolute truth in the metaphysical sense or even the historical truth. Rather, the goal of most martial arts systems' histories is to give that system prestige – what the Chinese refer to as 'face'."*

For example, the Tatemae/face of Shotokan Karate is something like: *"Karate is an ancient Okinawan martial arts developed by peasants who were not allowed weapons. They were able to use their bare hands and farmyard implements to defend against the ruling Samurai. The three ancient schools were Shuri Te, Naha Te and Tomari Te. From Shuri Te and Tomari Te the Shorin Ryu school developed and from Naha Te the Shorei Ryu school developed. Gichin Funakoshi mastered the Shorin and Shorei schools and combined them to form Shotokan."*

Remember this is Tatemae. This is the kind of thing Funakoshi's assistant instructors would pass on as "history". But if we examine it, Karate as such was not ancient, it was not developed by peasants, Shuri Te, Naha Te and Tomari Te were not ancient either, Funakoshi never mastered Shorin and Shorei and he never created Shotokan! And Okinawans didn't knock samurai off horseback using rakes. In reality Karate evolved over a few hundred years largely as the result of a small number of middle and upper class Okinawans studying a hotchpotch of Chinese martial arts. The Goju Ryu form Sanchin (also used in Uechi Ryu etc) is often said to be the most ancient Karate kata, although this isn't strictly the case. Rather it may be the oldest Quan (still in existence in China) that has been transmitted - comparatively recently - to Okinawa. Sanchin may be an old form, but there is no evidence to suggest it was always a part of Karate.

Shotokan family forms (also Wado, Shorin etc) such as Bassai, Kanku and Empi are not known at all in China. They almost certainly derived from Chinese martial arts, but there is no Kung Fu school practising anything like Kanku Dai. However the southern Chinese schools of Quan Fa such as White Crane do still practise what is clearly the ancestor of the Sanchin kata - even if Sanchin was only introduced to Okinawa relatively recently (say 1820s). There is a hint of honne therefore in the tatemae that Karate is ancient, in the sense that it borrows from other schools that do have ancient origins.

Forms like Sanchin are not only a throwback to Karate's Chinese origins, but also to their Indian pre-origin where they are thought to derive from a style called Kalaripayat. Pervez B Mistry (*Understanding Sanchin Kata*) states: *"Mudras in martial arts of Kung Fu and Karate-do are hand, arm and body positions meant to stimulate different areas of the body in conjunction with breathing and to affect the flow of vital force in the body... In India this symbolisation is called Mudra."* Sanchin is Karate's living link to the Indo-Chinese Buddhist schools.

Kalaripayat was developed in Kerala, which is towards the southern tip of India. Its shores were the part of India that drew the most foreigners, whether that be Greeks and Romans or Chinese. Kalaripayat's mythical founder was Parasurama, said to be an incarnation of Vishnu. According to Patrick Denaud (*Kalaripayat: The Martial Arts Tradition of India*) the art was then passed to Drona who is recorded elsewhere in Indian folklore. Another master named Agastya Maharshi passed on Kalaripayat to 18 students and recorded his curriculum in a 13th century work called Agastya Samhita.

As far back as the 1500s, a French writer recorded the martial arts of the region, saying they *"go around half naked, armed with a dagger and a sword that never leaves their side... They fight on foot and are skilled in archery and the use of the spear."*

If Kalaripayat was the art introduced to the Shaolin Temple by Bodhidharma, then on some level and in some lineages it may be considered a very distant ancestor of Karate. Kris Wilder (*The Way of Sanchin Kata*) recalls the story of Indian prince Bodhidharma coming to the Shaolin Temple and showing the monks Yoga exercises to improve their Kung Fu. Kalari and Karate have very little in common stylistically. But Kalari is perhaps a time capsule glimpse at an ancestral form of the art, before its transmission to Okinawa via China.

Karate forms like Sanchin may very well trace their origins to Shaolin and beyond that to India, but this is a relatively new aspect of

Karate. Before 1800 there is little to suggest these Buddhist schools influenced Karate.

Wutang Myths

According to Canadian Karate teacher and researcher Patrick McCarthy (*Bubishi*, 1995) and Wilder, Karate's ancient origins are also to be found in the mythology of the indigenous Chinese 'Wutang' styles. McCarthy points out that the pressure points alluded to in the Bubishi have their origin in the Wutang styles. The Wutang styles are considered indigenous Chinese martial arts connected to indigenous Chinese gods and folk traditions. They nowadays famously include Tai Chi (Taijiquan), Hsing-I and Pakua.

We may point out that external Kung Fu schools (such as Wing Chun) are happy to trace their origin back to a Buddhist (and therefore Indian) origin such as the Shaolin Temple, whereas the Wutang styles are citing a purely Chinese, nationalist and Taoist origin.

The history of Shaolin (Buddhist) and Wutang (Taoist) martial arts are forever intertwined. The Shaolin traces its skills back to Boddhidarma who showed Indian martial arts to the Shaolin monks. If Shaolin had a founder as divine as Boddhidarma, then Wutang had to go one better and have an immortal!

Therefore the founder of Wutang Kung Fu is Zhang San Feng, an Immortal who, if he had really lived, would have done so from about 1300 (and being immortal I suppose he must still be alive).

According to McCarthy, Zhang San Feng, said to be an expert in Chang Quan (Long Fist Boxing), developed what we call today vital point combat. He developed a series of techniques based on his (Shaolin) Long Fist Boxing skills and developed 36 vital point strikes. These were later developed by a Taoist called Feng Yiquan. His student Zhang Zhuan Yi in turn developed 72 postures and eventually 108 postures were taught.

Docherty (*Complete Tai Chi Chuan*) states: *"I believe on the available evidence that there was one Chang San Feng who in the mid fourteenth century became famous as a Taoist. Earlier dates are likely to be due to carelessness, or to confusing him with others or to give him greater antiquity as befits a sage."*

Wilder thinks Sanchin itself can be traced to the legendary Taoist. He states: *"As Chinese tradition has it, part of the Sanchin kata history can be traced to a 13th century priest. Zhang San Feng began his martial arts instruction with the Shaolin monks... The story has it that the next destination was on the Wutang mountain at a temple called the Purple Summit Temple.... The next leap we make in time is from the 13th century to the 20th century and some 600 years where according to the history of the Goju Ryu lineage, Kanryo Higashionna (1853-1915) brought Sanchin kata back to Okinawa."*

Another legendary, but probably historic Taoist who lived at around the same time as Zhang San Feng was General Yue Fei, a great war leader, archer and spearman. Over time Zhang San Feng came to be regarded as the legendary founder of Taiji Quan and Yue Fei as the legendary founder of Hsing-I Quan.

General Qi: The Kata Innovator

Even if we can accept that Karate was influenced by these Shaolin and Wutang schools, it is not much help treating Buddha, General Yue and Zhang San Feng as ancestral figures, since they are far too mythological to be of any practical interest in our studies. However there was a historic general, much closer in time than General Yue, and that was General Qi.

In around 1580 Chinese martial arts developed a new trend which was of solo Quan/Hsing. The notable Chinese general Qi Jiguang (November 12, 1528 – January 17, 1588) resurrected many lost practices of this kind and from his influence lots of Kung Fu styles developed which taught what we recognise today as kata.

Qi included a description of Quan Fa in his book, *Ji Xiao Xin Shu* which can translate as *New Book Recording Effective Techniques*. This book spread to East Asia and was in some ways the first widely read kata syllabus.

General Qi was a historically attested general, martial artist and author and may have had a greater influence on the martial arts of Kung Fu and Karate than anybody else in history! He took various family forms and presented them in words and pictures so they could be preserved and studied for the masses.

General Qi described 32 hand to hand combat positions and said they were *"not so much used as a means of fighting but rather as a skill to gain additional physical strength."*

41

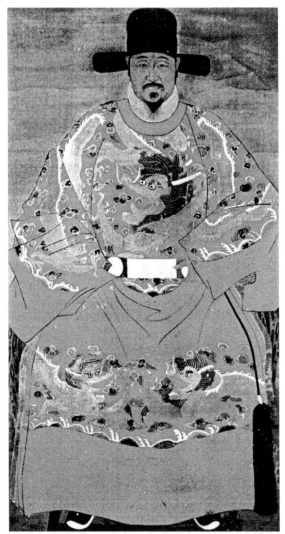

Qi Jiguang: The pioneer of Quan based training

Qi points out quite rightly that in the era of swords, armour and horsemanship, *"Quan Fa didn't count as an individual branch of the armed service"* but he says, *"the habit to regularly exercise the whole body are the foundation for all learning.*

"This is the reason why a preparation in this one school of unarmed combat is necessary for continued training in the armed combat arts."

He talks about strength, speed and agility. Clearly Qi felt Quan Fa starts internally, making the body hard and the mind alert. Interestingly he used the same character for staff (Gun) that the

42

Okinawan Kon (an alternative to the Japanese 'Bo') uses, for example in kata such as Sakugawa no Kon sho. General Qi's thoughts on solo practice being for body conditioning would have been welcomed by the 'iron fisted' Okinawan warriors. It is doubtful that in this era, intricate throws, locks or trips were very popular in Okinawa. All the evidence points towards early Okinawan Karate as training the body to be hard, and the strikes to be deadly. Hard body, hard mind.

The Rise of Karate in the Ryukyu

Every country in the world has some kind of hand to hand combat tradition; however, few of these traditions could be said to be Karate-like. Similarly in Okinawa, there may well have been punching and kicking going back to primitive times, but at what point can we classify this as Karate? In order for it to be classed as Karate or Te, it must be a uniquely Okinawan method, perhaps influenced by the earlier arts of Japan or China. Therefore we should look to the Okinawan families best equipped to practise these arts.

We must cast aside any ideas of Karate as a peasant art. Peasants or plebeians did not practise Karate. They had some fighting based games that perhaps resembled Sumo or arm wrestling, but these did not much resemble Karate.

Motobu Ryu inheritor Matsuo Kanenori Sakon (*The Secret Martial Arts of Ryukyu,* translated by Joe Swift) wrote: *"The martial artists (bushi) on Ryuykyu can be divided into five distinct groups. First of all are the Shuri bushi, who were in charge of protecting Shuri Castle. Next the Tomari bushi who were in charge of domestic law enforcement. Third the Naha bushi who were in charge of protecting the Chinese envoys (Sappushi) as well as the tribute ships sent from Ryukyu to China. Next were the Udun bushi who were involved in the politics of the Ryukyu kingdom. Finally the bushi of Naha's Kume village who were in the service of Chinese immigrants."*

For the origins of Karate as we know it we should look at two main sources: privileged classes among Chinese communities (Yukatchu) and Okinawan privileged classes (Pechin).

Chinese Communities

The Chinese communities, known as the 36 families, were largely based in Kumemura (Kume village). Imagine Manchester, Liverpool or London's China Towns and how they are anglicised communities of second and third generation Chinese; how they have some modern English customs, some old Chinese customs and some Chinese novelties to sell to tourists. There are restaurants, shops, and behind closed doors martial arts are taught. This is exactly what Kume was in Okinawa – a China Town. One of these Chinese families living in Okinawa was the Cai family, known locally as the Kojo. Within Kume, the resident families studied and taught Chinese Quan Fa, which the local Okinawans may have called Tang Shou or Toshu Jutsu. It seems likely they would have had at least some Chinese martial traditions but we do not know if they were Quan-based. The people of Kumemura, traditionally believed to all be descendants of the Chinese immigrants who first settled there in 1393, came to form an important and aristocratic class of scholar-bureaucrats, the yukatchu, who dominated the royal bureaucracy, and served as government officials at home, and as diplomats in relations with China, Japan, and others. By the middle of the fifteenth century, the community was enclosed within earthen walls, and consisted of over one hundred homes.

A painting of Kumemura where Okinawa's Chinese community emerged

Children in Kumemura began their formal studies at the age of five, and would travel to the palace at Shuri for a formal audience at the age of 15. At this point they would be formally added to the register of yukatchu scholar-bureaucrats and could begin their government careers. One of the defining features of the scholar community at Kumemura, and its relationship with China, was the system by which students and scholars of Kumemura spent periods in Fuzhou, both as students and as members of tributary missions. Most if not all students and scholar-bureaucrats spent at least a few years of their lives studying in Fuzhou; a few travelled to Beijing, and beginning in the 17th century, some studied in Kagoshima.

Only a few hundred Ryukyuans were ever resident in Fuzhou at a time, and only eight at the imperial university in Beijing, where they were allowed to stay for three years, or up to eight in exceptional circumstances.

Sai Choko (Kugusuku, Kojo) Uekata (1656 – 1737) may be an example of a Fujian-born Chinese national who settled in Kume and whose family became renowned for its Karate. The Kojo family are considered one of the 36 families; however, it is not known how long the family practised hand to hand combat traditions. It is entirely possible that their martial arts only arose in the mid 19th century and the idea of the 'Kojo Ryu' being an ancient style is tatemae.

Okinawan privileged classes

Okinawa, the central Ryukyu kingdom, is part of a chain of islands that has affinity with both China and Japan, in the way Jersey and Guernsey are halfway between England and France. The nobility in Okinawa regularly visited both on diplomatic exchanges. An example of this would be a family such as the Motobu. Other early examples of this are the Chinese envoy Wang Ji visiting Okinawa in the late 1600s and the Ryukyu native Hama Higa visiting Japan around the same time. In around 1800, young men from Shuri began to be sent abroad to study in Fuzhou and Beijing, breaking the monopoly on Chinese scholarship held by Kumemura for roughly four centuries. This was the start of the original "Shuri Te". According to Sakon, an expert on the martial traditions of one such noble family, the Motobu, the requirements for Ryukyuan officials were as follows: Academic studies, Medicine, Chinese Music, Mathematics, Cooking,

Calligraphy, Handwriting, Cosmetics, Tea Ceremony, Noh Chanting, Horse Riding, Flower Arrangement.

We have seen evidence of Japanese style swords and armour in Okinawa between the 1400s and 1600s, and we have seen examples of sources like General Qi that could have inspired Karate, but we have not yet met a tangible Karate master to whom we can link back our schools.

Wang Ji

Not only is Wang Ji a historically recorded Chinese diplomat who visited Okinawa and *may* have taught some Quan Fa, he is also the first figure we meet who has been connected to a specific Okinawan kata.

While we have encountered very early Okinawan bushi involved in warfare, and examples of Okinawan 'knuckle fighters', and we have also suggested a Chinese cultural influence, Wang Ji could be the start of a stylistic approach to Karate.

Wang Ji, who came to Okinawa in 1683, was a graduate of China's Hanlin Academy. Incredibly we have a record from Wang Ji, who recalls seeing Okinawans with staff and spears. He wrote: *"There were a dozen or more persons, two of which carried long poles similar to lances at the tips of which were short scabbards protecting the iron blades."* Even more fascinatingly, Wang Ji it seems visited an early Okinawan "Dojo".

He states: *"Lying in the harbour in between Qingzhi-shan and Linhai-si temple is a flat ridge with a large space which serves as a place to drill arms and for the practice of combat arts. This place was used by the officers and men of the Tenshikan for arms drill and combat arts practice."*

This was located in Kume. Therefore the Chinese Wang Ji went to Kume, where the Chinese families of Okinawa lived and observed their drilling of combat arts. It is not impossible therefore that Wang passed on a little of what he knew to the men there.

Sakagami Ryusho (1978) and Kinjo (1999) suggested that the kata Wansu or Wanshu (known in Shotokan as Empi) was named after Wang Ji - and it may have even been taught by him.

The author demonstrates Chin na wrist and neck control

Another tantalising detail about this kata is that its name is said to denote a swallow – Gichin Funakoshi changed its name to Empi and said the meaning was "flying swallow". The most notable Chinese art at the time to use a swallow form was Hsing-I Chuan, and the founder of that art Ji Ji Ke lived in the previous generation to Wang Ji.

It is possible - but there is no evidence - that Ji Ji Ke was related to Wang Ji. It would certainly be a tidy narrative that Ji Ji Ke taught Wang Ji the swallow form of Hsing-I and then when Wang Ji came to Okinawa he called his art the Swallow Form, and when he visited the Kume school those he taught came away with a kata named after Wang Ji and one that meant Swallow – Wansu and Empi. Whether Wang Ji taught 'swallow boxing' to Okinawans or not, at least we now know that Okinawans who interacted with Chinese dignitaries were drilling combat in a training hall in 1683. This is a perfectly descriptive idea of early Karate. We now have an idea of two possible Chinese Hand (Kara Te) influences on the Okinawan fighting systems – that of General Qi and that of Wang Ji.

It is also interesting that the name Empi was also used by the very Japanese sword school most associated with Karate. Several notable Okinawan Karate masters also trained in Satsuma's Jigen Ryu which features a form called Empi. The characteristic move of Empi (in Shotokan) resembles the principle (not the physical manifestation of the technique) behind the Hsing-I swallow form – float high and then swoop low. The opening move of Empi is textbook "swordsmanship" as it uses a diagonal sweep with the right hand from a kneeling position. Jigen Ryu is a very unusual sword style in that it uses a makiwara. Jigen Ryu practitioners literally strike a hard wooden post with their bokken. If the concept of Wansu/Empi/Swallow did not come from Wang Ji then maybe it came from Jigen Ryu.

The author performing Shotokan 'Empi' (Wansu)

Jigen Ryu: Sword Art of Karate

Multiple founding fathers of Karate also studied the style of Japanese swordsmanship called Jigen Ryu. This is interesting because Jigen Ryu trained its students in the use of farming implements as weapons and also used a makiwara as a training system.

Jigen Ryu is a highly unusual art to watch. Its exponents bash bundles of bamboo with their makeshift bokken emitting a shrill kiai. It may look odd to those who are used to seeing more sedate styles of Iaido, but it also has a very familiar sense to Karateka, Karateka who are used to bashing their knuckles on wooden makiwara.

Shotokan Karate master Taiji Kase (interview by Pasquale Petrella) explained the relationship between Karate and Jigen Ryu. Kase said: *"Sensei Funakoshi always said he trained mainly with Sensei Azato and not with Sensei Itosu. So his first teacher is Azato and not Itosu. Azato and Funakoshi were the same generation. Azato had a very high social position in Okinawa at that time, he was something like a mayor of a town. Azato taught Funakoshi and afterwards Funakoshi had to teach Azato´s son.*

"That's why Shotokan kata and Shito Ryu kata are different. In Shotokan we do a lot of o-waza, big techniques. In Okinawa and in Shito-Ryu they all do ko-waza, small techniques. Matsumura Sokon was the bodyguard of the king of Okinawa. With him he traveled to Kyushu, Japan and there he got to see Kendo. He was very impressed of the style Jigenji-Ryu therefore he studied this martial art in Kyushu. In Jigenji-Ryu they do big techniques as well and this influenced Matsumura's Karate. He taught it to Azato Sensei, and Azato Sensei taught it to Funakoshi Sensei.

"And another example is the Kata Sochin, only in Shotokan we do Sochin. A few years back Sensei Shirai went to Okinawa to study some Goju Ryu. The instructors asked him to show one of his favourite kata, and Shirai showed Sochin. The Okinawan instructors were very surprised, because they said this must be Samurai Sochin, they thought the kata was lost."

Here Kase theorises that the reason Shotokan uses large movements is not because Gichin Funakoshi went to Japan, but because his teacher's teacher did. To Kase, the elegant moves of Shotokan are the elegant moves of Jigen Ryu.

It is probably tatemae to think that Shotokan forms like Sochin were directly influenced by Jigen Ryu, but we cannot ignore the fact that its founding fathers like Matsumura and Azato were strongly influenced by the Japanese art.

One account of Jigen Ryu states that it came originally from the Hakugen Ryu. From the ancient samurai school of Kashima no Tachi Shinmyoken, a master named Jigensai Kazutou Jiichibou created his own school called Hakugen Ryu in 931AD. The name would seem to refer to the white crest of the Minamoto. According to records of the style, Hakugen Ryu was passed to the Minamoto clan (Genji) which held its secrets in a set of two scrolls, Ryuko Nikan no Hidensho (the two secret scrolls of Dragon and Tiger).

The art was apparently passed to Minamoto no Yoshiie (1039 – 1106) who decoded the secrets and created a system which he called "Ten Chi Jin In Yo Godan no Houkei" (the form of the Five Techniques of Heaven, Earth, Human, Darkness and Light). Yoshiie's younger brother Minamoto Yoshimitsu (1045 – 1127) created a branch of the tradition later known as Daito Ryu, famed for its Aikijujutsu, the art which later gave birth to Aikido. Minamoto Yoshiie apparently passed Hakugen Ryu to Kiichi Hougan and he to Minamoto Yoshitsune (1159 – 1189) who was the brother of the shogun Minamoto Yoritomo. Yoshitsune passed the art on to Shunjobu Jugen who taught it to Yaobettoh Kenko. Yaobettoh passed the art to Tose Nagamune who also mastered Tenshin Shoden Katori Shinto Ryu and called his teachings Tenshinsho Jigen Ryu. Nagamune moved to Satsuma and changed the name Jiken to 'Jigen' and changed his own name to Setoguchi Masamoto.

According to present branches of Jigen Ryu (see www.jigenryuflorida.com), Masamoto is recorded as saying: *"The origin of my style traces back its roots to Jouko Ryu Kashima no Tachi Hakugen Ryu. The style has incorporated many other different styles by the past successors. 'Gen' also contains several meanings like; the source of everything in the world, the war strategy (Heiho) of the Minamoto (Genji) clan. I hereby name my style as Tenshinsho Jigen Ryu Hyoho with absolute certainty and confidence."* Setoguchi died in 1519 but left behind hidden in Satsuma all the secrets of his art, which was passed down to only one disciple of each generation and royal guards of the Shimazu clan for about 500 years. Within Satsuma the art of Jigen Ryu was further developed by Togo Chui (1561-1643) in Satsuma Province, now Kagoshima prefecture, Kyushu, Japan. This branch of the art was passed through to Togo family and then a branch of it, called Kojigen Ryu, was taught to Karate masters from Okinawa. Kojigen Ryu was unique in that it taught exponents to use makeshift farming implements as weapons. Was this a practice the Okinawans gained from Kojigen Ryu or vice versa? In the Ryukyu no Bugi, 1914 it stated: *"Since he introduced Jigen Ryu to Okinawa, Haebaru Uekata from Onaka was considered a master of the martial arts..."*

In his foreword to the 2016 McCarthy *Bubishi*, Joe Swift makes a valid point on the stylistic differences of Shuri Te contrasted with Naha Te and he seems to suggest that Jigen Ryu is the explanation for why Shuri kata are more linear to the Kung Fu style kata of Naha Te: *"The Chinese boxing forms that were introduced during the time of the Ryukyu Kingdom would have been seen through the eyes of Japanese swordsmanship and subsequently reinterpreted through such principles. This would explain part of the reason that the Karate kata passed down mainly in and around the old castle district of Shuri such as Naihanchi and Kushanku do not look much like Kung Fu."*

In other words Shuri forms like Kushanku and Naihanchi (and I would suggest Wanshu) were not only influenced by Quanfa (in the way that Goju Ryu and Uechi Ryu are almost solely Quanfa based) but by the Koryu Bujutsu of Japan. Again we find Karate and Jujutsu – or Ryukyu and Japan, intertwined historically and technically.

Jigen Ryu timeline

1540　Higashi Shinnoji is born in Satsuma Japan, he will become a master of Taisha Ryu.

1561　Togo Hizen no Kami Shigetada is born in Satsuma.

1569　Shigetada studies under Higashi.

1578　Shigetada fights his first battle.

1581　Shigetada is awarded Menkyo Kaiden certificate of mastery.

1588　Shigetada studies in Kyoto in the art of Tenshinsho Jigen Ryu with Zenkitsu.

1604　Shigetada defeats his former teacher Higashi and his son Shigemasa is born.

1604　Shigetada becomes founder of Jigen Ryu.

1620　Shigemasa implements a "makeshift weapons" in Jigen Ryu including the staff, oar, sickle, spade and axe.

1623　Shigetada's grandson (Shigemasa's son) Togo Shigetoshi is born.

1624　Shigetada writes Enpi no Shidai.

1632　Ijuin Mondo Hisaaki is born.

1645　Hisaaki studies Jigen Ryu under Shigemasa and Shigetoshi.

1650　Hisaaki introduces the art to the Ijuin clan. The branch is called Ko-Jigen Ryu.

1672　Shigetoshi's son Shigeharu is born.

1680　Shigetoshi suffers a fit, so Hisaaki becomes caretaker headmaster.

1680　Haebaru Ueikata is born in around 1680 in Onaka, Okinawa.

1695　Haebaru Ueikata begins to study Jigen Ryu and later takes it to Okinawans.

Hama Higa and Takahara Pechin

Wang Ji visited Okinawan in 1683, one year after Hama Higa (1663 – 1738) travelled to Japan where he performed a form with the Sai. Hama Higa clearly learned his martial arts prior to Wang's arrival. This detail that Wang Ji and Hama Higa were contemporaries gives us two perspectives on the martial arts of the time and illustrates a Japan-Okinawa-China three way relationship.

If the kata Empi/Wansu can be linked to Wang Ji's 1683 visit then the kata 'Hama Higa no Sai' can be linked to the visit the previous year of Higa to Japan. As we have seen, Okinawans had swords, staff, halberds and many other weapons. It is not known whether the Sai is how we have it today or even what form his kata took.

However not everyone accepts the Sai's role as an ancient Okinawan weapon. In recent posts on social media Okinawan history expert Mark Bishop (*Okinawan Karate*) says he doubts the Sai was ever the bona fide weapon (or arrest tool) that the Jitte was in Japan. In Bishop's opinion, the Sai was a conditioning tool (rather like Indian clubs or chi-ishi) and its only martial role was in battle re-enactments.

The story of Hama Higa in Japan was told by Taira Shinken, and can be found in the 1998 re-publication of his 1964 *Ryukyu Kobudo Taikan*. Higa was supposedly a famous Go (a board game) player and also accompanied Nago Oji Chogen on his visit to Shogun Tokugawa Tsunayoshi in 1682. With the permission of Shimazu Hidehisa of Satsuma, Hama Higa performed Karate and Saijutsu in front of the Shogun.

Those who subscribe to the theory that Wang Ji introduced Chinese martial arts to Okinawa might suggest Hama Higa could be a likely student - and the dates certainly fit, but this is no more than speculation.

In a similar manner, Higa is sometimes cited as a potential teacher of Takahara Pechin (1688-1755) who lived in Shuri's Akata, and became known as a talented mathematician and cartographer. Maps of the Ryukyu islands made by him were sent in 1797 via Satsuma to the imperial court of Japan. We know very little about Hama Higa and Takahara. Richard Kim (*Weaponless Warriors*) suggests that Takahara was the teacher of Tode Sakugawa. In his work about the 20th century Kobudo master Taira Shinken, Patrick McCarthy (*Koryu Uchinadi*) states that some of the Kobudo techniques passed on date back to Takahara's teachings. It is only oral tradition and speculation, but it is certainly possible that Wang Ji taught Hama Higa and he taught Takahara. After all we have very few names at all from this period in Karate history so we may well be trying to piece together a jigsaw with the majority of the pieces missing.

One family however that does have fairly solid records is the Motobu clan – one of those families of privileged class - who were of Japanese rather than Chinese origin. It may even be that Hama Higa, who we know flourished in around 1680, studied under Motobu Chohei or could have been a Motobu himself. According to Matsuo Kanenori Sakon, it was Choken who perfected the Sai in 1668, a generation before Higa.

Part Two: 1700s-1800s

The Motobu Family

The Motobu family in Okinawa is a riddle wrapped in an enigma. The martial art which traces back to Motobu Choyu, commonly called Motobu Udundi, today resembles something like Aikido or Daito Ryu Aikijujutsu (or as suggested in the previous chapter Asayama Ichiden Ryu). It is often claimed that the similarities between the two arts are due to a mutual descent from the arts of the Minamoto. The Motobu were descended from Minamoto Tametomo (1139-1170) and the Takeda (Aikido founder Ueshiba Morihei studied under Takeda Sokaku) were descended from Minamoto Yoshimitsu (1045-1127). It seems more likely that both arts have a more recent common ancestor or were mutually influenced by a more recent Chinese martial art such as Pakua.

Ironically the most famous Motobu of all never practised the Motobu family system. While his brother Choyu apparently taught this flowing Aiki-like form that included no kata but resembled Okinawan dance, Motobu Choki was a streetfighter known for his brutal applications of the kata Naihanchi.

When Choki listed the martial arts pioneers of Okinawa he did not list any of his own immediate family. For the 1700s he listed Nishinda Uekata, Soryu Tsushin and Gushikawa as being pioneers in the early part of the century. In the mid to late 1700s, Motobu listed Tode Sakugawa, Ginowan Dunchi, Makabe Chan, Ukuda, Matsumoto, Bo Miyazato, Sadoyama and Tokashiki Pechin. However there may be another reason why Choki did not list any of the Motobu family – perhaps because he was not permitted to learn the family martial arts system, or perhaps he was just being humble about his family.

The Motobu clan was an aristocratic family in the Ryukyu Kingdom of Okinawa. Its progenitor was Motobu Aji Chohei (also known as Sho Koshin, 1655-1687), sixth son of the tenth monarch of the Second Sho Dynasty (1469-1879), Sho Shitsu (1629-1668). According to Sakon, the Motobu martial arts "udundi" were secret but influenced mainstream Karate. While suggesting the Motobu art was an old system, he also seems to suggest it was eclectic and evolving. Sakon writes: *"Their martial arts remained secret and passed on to only the eldest son, until the art was passed on from Motobu Choyu to*

Uehara Seikichi.

"Udundi combines the soft elements of Northern Chinese boxing with the hard elements of Southern Chinese boxing as well as Japanese swordsmanship. Techniques of impact, throws and grappling were also formulated, and both Chinese and indigenous weapons, such as the cane, the cudgel, long swords, machetes, double edged swords, boat oars, nunchaku and tuifa [tonfa] were also studied. This secret royal art also greatly influenced the arts of the Shuri bushi, Tomari bushi and the Naha bushi."

Of the soft techniques, which Sakon hints derived from Taiji, Hsing-I or Pakua ("the soft elements of northern Chinese boxing") he says: *"Ju ken is described as flowing with the opponent's energy and can be broken down into throws, finger thrusts to vital points, fighting hand, entangled hand and praying hand."*

According to Sakon, the Okinawan weapons of Nunchaku and Tonfa were a traditional part of the curriculum – but we do not know when this tradition began. Could it be that the privileged Motobu were the first to introduce both Tuite (Qin na) and Kobudo weapons to Okinawan practice?

From the 17th century to the Meiji Resoration of the late 19th century, successive heads of the family held the rank of Aji – below only the king – and served as vassals to the Shuri monarchy. The family claim that they excelled in both cultural and military fields, producing important politicians as well as performing and martial artists.

The family patriarch was Chohei, born on May 4, 1655, the sixth son of King Sho Shitsu and his wife Honko. His wife was Urasaki Oshu (princess), daughter of Adaniya Uekata Seibo.

In 1666, at the age of 11, Chohei received the domain of Motobu Magiri (now the village of Motobu in the northern part of the main island of Okinawa) and assumed the title of Motobu Aji. From then on, successive heads of the house used the name Motobu.

The Te of the Motobu family (Motobu udundi) is believed to originate with Chohei, but information about his activities and achievements was lost with the family genealogical record in the Pacific War, and the details of his personal history are not well known.

According to lineages, Chohei was succeeded by his eldest son, Chokan, while his second son, Chotaku, was adopted into the Urazoe Aji family, becoming its heir.

Bishop (*Okinawan Karate*) describes the internal, relaxed nature of the Motobu Ryu: *"One could say that* [Motobu Ryu] *combines the finer points of the three most acclaimed internal Chinese boxing styles and more, having within its various guises the swift, straight lined attack of Hsing-I, the softness of Tai Chi and the everchanging circular defence of Pa Kua."*

Bishop has since clarified that he did not mean to suggest an actual link between Te and Chinese internal martial arts – he has often stated he believes the origin of Te to be Japanese. But in my opinion the similarities are self evident.

Motobu Ryu had a now-lost kata called Anji kata no Mekata (kata dance of the Lords) which was similar to ladies dancing. According to Bishop it was 'slow balanced postures performed to music while in a trance like state.' So again, the image is of a Tai Chi-like form.

While Motobu Choki was feared and respected for his 'iron fists', the Motobu Ryu of the senior members of his family were often scoffed at. Sokon Matsumura contrasted them unfavourably to 'true' Karate.

Sokon Matsumura said of Court styles such as Motobu Ryu: *"The court instructors' styles are practised in a very unusual way; movements are never the same, formless and light becoming (like women) more and more dance-like as the proponents mature."*

The Te of Motobu Ryu was also referred to as Tuishu Jutsu or Tuite Jutsu, recalling somewhat Sifu Hung's description of Tang Shou. Tuite, often equated with the Japanese Torite, is considered an Okinawan equivalent to the Chinese Chin Na.

The official website of the Motobu family describes their skills as follows:

"Meant to be applied against real attacks, tuiti was originally not learned through Japanese aikijutsu-like kata training, or pre-arranged kumite drills, but through means of training akin to jiyu kumite, or free sparring. The Meiji Period master Itosu Anko sensei stated in his Itosu jyukkun (Ten Precepts of Karate) of 1908 that Okinawan tuiti was not contained in karate kata. By this, he meant that it was not learned through bunkai of karate kata or kumite drills developed from bunkai."

Here the Motobu are suggesting that Tuiti (Chin na) was very much a part of Te – or at least Motobu Te, but they do not think it was encrypted into kata such as the Pinan forms.

The Motobu site continues to say that there are in fact differences between their style and Aikido in the way that techniques are received:

"A number of characteristics differentiate Okinawan tuiti from aiki jujutsu. First, the waza of tuiti are generally applied from the palm side of the hand rather than the back of the hand. Second, tuiti waza employ linear movement whereas aiki jujutsu emphasizes circular motion. There is also no za-waza – aiki-style seated defense – in tuiti."

Author's note: Aikido's circular nature may be somewhat over-emphasised. I enjoyed many long conversations with Alan Ruddock who trained directly with the founder of Aikido Ueshiba Morihei and he told me: *"O Sensei's Aikido was linear not circular."* He demonstrated this with a 'Nikkyo' wristlock. Instead of the usual circular movement commonly demonstrated for this technique, Alan applied a linear application cutting into my centreline. The movement resembled the Yang style Taijiquan technique 'needle at sea bottom' and was far more painful than the circular method. He explained that if the hand slipped off during the technique, his spear hand would aim directly at my throat.

The Motobu continue: *"The te-waza in tuiti are believed to arise from applied variations on three hand positions that correspond to those used in the classical Ryukyuan court dances: oshi-te (forward push hands), ogami-te (supplication hands), and koneri-te (kneading hands). The names of these hand positions appear in the earliest collection of Ryukyuan poetry, Omorosaushi (1531-1623), and they seem to have been gestures used in rituals and ceremony in ancient Okinawa. These gestures are said to have been incorporated into the court dances by Tamagusuku Chokun (born 1684), who was connected to the Motobu Udun.*

"These dances were originally entertainment for only the aristocracy, so were almost never seen or learned by commoners or even lower-ranking members of the military class responsible for teaching Karate. This would explain why tuiti cannot be found in Okinawan Karate."

Of its study of weapons the Motobu family state: *"Weapons used include bo (staff), jo, eku (modified oar), and paired tanbo (short bo), nichiku (nunchaku), tonfa, sai, and kama (sickle). In addition, Motobu udundi used bladed weapons that lower-ranking members of the military class did not possess, such as the sword, spear, and naginata."*

This is a significant characteristic of the royal Motobu Udun's Ti. Even after Ryukyu fell to the Satsuma forces in the invasion of 1609, members of the aristocratic udun and tunchi ranks were allowed to possess bladed weapons.

In Motobu udundi a style of Kenjutsu particular to Ryukyu called tachi no te (sword hands) is taught. The sheathed sword is not worn at the hip as in Japanese Kenjutsu, but held directly in the hand. It is drawn with the cutting edge facing downwards; this manner is closer to the Chinese use of the Dao broadsword.

The Motobu family also used twin Chinese short swords similar to the Dip Dao (Butterfly swords) of Wing Chun and other Cantonese Kung Fu forms.

The Motobu state: *"In Motobu udundi, Kenjutsu is also practised using a special kind of short sword, typically in nito-ryu fashion.*

"According to Uehara sensei, Choyu sensei's weapons were different than the Japanese short sword known as wakizashi. Apparently, they were a type particular to Ryukyu and the ends of the grips were decorated with tassels [like Wushu swords are today].

"Because they were similar in length and shape to the blade used in Ryukyu for cutting brush and tree branches, Uehara sensei used the term for that implement, yamanaji. However, Choyu sensei's swords were most likely closer in form to weapons that originally came from China or their replicas made in Ryukyu.

"Also according to Uehara sensei, Choyu sensei would carry these swords along with other ornament on the occasion of the Bon festival, so they seem also to have had ceremonial significance."

Of the apparent weapons ban, Sakon writes: *"the arts of sword and spear fighting all but disappeared from the Okinawan martial arts scene, being transmitted only in the royal palace. After that, even under the watchful eye of the Satsuma, the arts of the Nunchaku, Tonfa, Ueko [oar], Tsue [cane], Kama, Tanbo, Dabo as well as empty hand techniques were developed and passed on in secret in the royal family."*

Contrary to the claim that the Motobu's Aiki-like skills were derived directly from the Minamoto, the presence of Chinese style tassel-clad broadswords would seem to suggest a later Chinese influence. The Motobu Ryu were renowned for the use of Tuite, a kind of Chin Na. Javier Martinez, a student of Fusei Kise who trained under Hohan Soken, writes (*Okinawan Karate: The Secret Art of Tuite*): *"We can, with certain amount of accuracy, determine that the the origin of Tuite is closely related to an identical art, although much older, Chin Na."* In China, "chin na" (qinna) is not a martial art as such, it's the central core of all the martial arts. It means grasping and pressing. It is precise joint manipulation and targeting of weak points. Chin Na can generally be categorised as:

- "Fen jin" or "zhua jin" (dividing the muscle/tendon, grabbing the muscle/tendon). Fen means "to divide", zhua is "to grab" and jin means "tendon, muscle, sinew". They refer to techniques which tear apart an opponent's muscles or tendons. Note in Japan this is sometimes called Kosshijutsu.
- "Cuo gu" (misplacing the bone). Cuo means "wrong, disorder" and gu means "bone". Cuo gu therefore refer to techniques which put bones in wrong positions and is usually applied specifically to joints.
- "Bi qi" (sealing the breath). Bi means "to close, seal or shut" and qi, or more specifically kong qi, meaning "air". "Bi qi" is the technique of preventing the opponent from inhaling. This differs from mere strangulation in that it may be applied not only to the windpipe directly but also to muscles surrounding the lungs, supposedly to shock the system into a contraction which impairs breathing.
- "Dian mai" or "dian xue" (sealing the vein/artery or acupressure cavity). Similar to the Cantonese dim mak, these are the technique of sealing or striking blood vessels and chi points.

Motobu Ryu lineage

Motobu Chohei (1655-1687)
Motobu Chokan (C1670)   Contemporary with Hama Higa
Motobu Choryu (C1700)
Motobu Choko (C1720)
Motobu Chokyu (1741-1814)
/   \
Motobu Choei   Motonaga Chogi
Motobu Chotoku   Motonaga Choyo
Motobu Chosho   Kyan Chofu
Motobu Choshin   Kyan Chotoku (1870-1945)
/   \
Motobu Choyu   Motobu Choki (1870-1944)
                    Motobu Chosei

Matsuo Kanenori Sakon further describes the Karate Jutsu of the Motobu: *"The vital points (kyusho) were studied vigorously, as were methods of attacking these points based on their size and structure. Such methods of attack include nukite (finger thrust), ippon ken (one knuckle thrust), uraken (back fist), seiken (normal fist), keri (kicking) etc."*

He points out some of the elements of Karate Jutsu that are now missing in modern sports Karate: *"The methods of Kyushojutsu in which one can drop an opponent with very little physical strength, as well as nage waza (throwing techniques) in which the opponent's movement and body weight is used against him is also very seldom researched or practised."*

At this point we will access what we know of Okinawan Te. We know that from the 1400s to 1600s the Okinawan military had Japanese style armour, swords and spears. We know that when Wang Ji arrived in Kume in the late 17th century he witnessed martial arts demonstrations. We have seen references to Te and to Tetsukumi.

We have an idea that the Okinawan were renowned for their powerful strikes and thrusts.

We have looked at the Motobu Te, an Aikijujutsu-like style that uses no kata, but is related to delicate courtly dances. This method of Te also resembles Taiji, Hsing-I and Pakua.

We have seen that Japanese schools like the Jigen Ryu used Kobudo style weapons and Makiwara style sword training.

We have seen Japanese Yawara schools like Yagyu Shingan Ryu, Kito Ryu and Yoshin Ryu variously incorporating Chinese concepts, solo forms, strikes and makeshift weapons into their curricula. We have seen the combat manual of General Qi bring solo Quan/kata to the wider public, referencing unarmed combat drills as a way of building strong, fit soldiers.

It is very possible that Wang Ji introduced a method of Quan Fa, possibly Hsing-I, to Okinawa, and it is very possible that Hama Higa and Takahara Peichin were Kobudo masters. It seems likely that the Motobu family maintained a Japanese-style Bujutsu in Okinawa, and that the Chinese families of Kume practised unarmed combat drills that we might know as kata today.

The Five Fists of Hsing-I

Hsing-I Chuan (Xing Yi Quan) may be one of the Northern Chinese boxing arts that influenced practitioners like Wang Ji, Hama Higa, Takahara and Sakugawa. But how does the art itself relate to Karate?

San-Ti
Karate has Sanchin, Hsing-I has Santi. Both are 'trinity' stances. The Santi stance is something like a cross between Sanchin Dachi and Kokutsu Dachi. When both hands raise for standing meditation, the result is something like the start of Pinan Yondan.

Splitting Fist (Pi Quan): Metal Element
The Pi Quan is most similar to Karate's Shuto Uke. To execute the technique first a kind of drilling punch is used (something like the Ura Tzuki in Naihanchi) and then the Pi Quan chops over like an axe, hence its metal element.

Smashing Fist (Beng Quan): Wood Element
The Beng Quan is something like a Tate Tzuki or Gyaku Tzuki. It shoots forward like an arrow, hence its wood element.

Drilling Fist (Zuan Quan): Water Element
The Zuan Quan uses the drilling fist mentioned in the Pi Quan description. It is almost an uppercut in the sense that it has an upward trajectory and the palm is up, but it has a sense of drilling forwards. The finishing position is something like Soto Ude Uke. The water element is of waves crashing.

Pounding Fist (Pao Quan): Fire Element
The Pao Quan is something like a Jodan Age Uke with Gyaku Tzuki. It is something like covering and then firing a cannonball, hence the fire element.

Crossing Fist (Heng Quan): Earth Element
The Heng Quan is executing with a side step and strike something like when executing an Uchi Ude Uke with a wedging forward action. It crosses a stable attack and counters.

Tode Sakugawa

Satunuku 'Tode' Sakugawa, born Teruya Kanga (1733-1815)

While so far we have been piecing together a jigsaw on early Karate practitioners, with Teruya Kanga, later Sakugawa, we have finally reached a man whose name is synonymous with both Karate and Kobudo.

Kanga was so synonymous with the history of Karate that his nickname was Tode Sakugawa – Tode being another way to pronounce Karate or Toshu.

Choki Motobu, who was not easily impressed by anyone, was indeed impressed by the reputation of Kanga/Sakugawa. Motobu says of him: *"Sakugawa is a person who drew a line in terms of Budo when comparing it with the Bugei of the previous era of Ryukyu. After him there was no-one like him. As a man admired among martial artists still in posterity, there was no man superior to him in terms of ability and other things."*

Teruya was born in Shuri in 1733 and at the age of 17 began his martial arts training with a man who folklore remembers as Takahara Pechin.

Teruya's father had been beaten to death by bandits, so the young Teruya was determined to master the martial arts. It is not known exactly what martial arts Teruya learned from Takahara but it seems likely he would have been taught powerful striking techniques of Tetsukumi and Bojutsu techniques. Pictures of Okinawan processions of the period show officials armed with poles, bo and spears and a kata survives called Sakugawa no kon sho. Unlike the sai, nunchaku and tonfa, there is ample evidence that the bo was a weapon used throughout Okinawan history.

Oral tradition holds that Teruya went to Fujian and Beijing to study Kung Fu. Some sources link him to Yue Fei Chuan, which would again identify Sakugawa as a Hsing-I practitioner.

Taira Shinken said of him: *"Master Sakugawa who was from Shuri's Akata district, studied martial arts in China more than 100 years ago. He was responsible for influencing the growth and direction of Bojutsu in Okinawa. He developed powerful ways of using the staff."*

A typical hypothetical lineage may be as follows:

Wang Ji	Possibly taught a Wansu form. A Chinese official.
Hama Higa	Sai and Te master. An Okinawan official.
Takahara	Map maker and astronomer at Shuri castle.
Sakugawa	Employed by Shuri castle.
Matsumura	Employed by Shuri castle.

Sakugawa Meets Kushanku

Like Wang-Ji before him, Kushanku was in Okinawa on official business. The story goes that Sakugawa met Kushanku by trying to push him into the water as a prank. Kushanku was able to evade the attack, and take him down with Kumiaijutsu in the form of a leg scissors manoeuvre.

Sakugawa's elderly teacher Takahara told the young man to learn what he could from Kushanku.

In the *Karatedo Kyohan* Funakoshi records: *"There is no doubt that the many experts who travelled between Okinawan and China contributed heavily to the bringing of Karate to its present level. For example, it has come down by word of mouth that about two hundred years ago* [Funakoshi was writing in the 1950s, therefore referring to around 1750] *a certain Sakugawa of Akata, in Shuri travelled to China and then returned to Okinawa after mastering Karate to become known as Karate Sakugawa in his time.*

"Again, according to Shiodaira of Shuri one hundred and fifty years ago (as noted in the Oshima Note by Tobe of Tosa, Japan), a Chinese expert, by name of Ku Shanku arrived in Okinawa with a few of his students and introduced a type of Kempo."

The founder of Goju Ryu Karate, Chojun Miyagi, similarly recalled the arrival of Kushanku: *"In 1762, the merchant ship of the Ryukyu Kingdom was caught in a heavy storm on the way to Satsuma (Kagoshima prefecture now), and cast ashore on the coast of Oshima, Tosa (Kochi prefecture now). Shiohira Pechin, a high rank official of the ship, was an intelligent person. He was helped by Choki Tobe, an intellectual who lived in Oshima. Tobe wrote down Shiohira's interesting stories about the Ryukyu Kingdom. His notes were called 'Oshima Notes'. The 3rd volume of 'Oshima Notes' says: 'Koshankun, a kung fu warrior, came from China to Ryukyu (Okinawa) bringing his disciples with him.' According to the Notes, at that time people called the martial arts 'Kumiaijutsu' instead of karate. These notes are the most reliable literature on karate."*

Richard Kim (*Weaponless Warriors*) tells us that Kushanku was living in Kume-Mura and was already teaching a young man called Kitani Yara.

According to Kim, Sakugawa trained for six years with Kushanku but at the age of 29 he received a message that Takahara had been taken ill. Two days later Takahara died and asked Sakugawa to carry on his teachings.

Kim also tells a separate story that Chatan Yara was taken away aged 12 to become a student of Wong Chung-Yoh, thought to be identical with Wang Zong Yue, who taught Quan Fa to the Yang family of Tai Chi fame. Kim tells us that the main lesson Wong taught him was that of the "value of balance and the principle of harmony" and that "all things find their inception in unity."

From Kim's account the young Okinawan Sakugawa trained with the Chinese master Kushanku, and the young Okinawan Chatan Yara trained with the Chinese master Wang Zong Yue. But the two cross over. There is a kata called Chatan Yara Kushanku, and Kushanku had a student called Yara.

Kim tells us the arts that Wong passed to Yara stating *"Yara initiated the concept of inner strength to Okinawan Karate... Yara studied Hsing-I and Chi Kung."* He says: *"Thus began Yara's time as deshi (apprentice) of Wong Chung-Yoh, during which he received the spiritual discipline his brute force so badly required. Under Wong's tutelage he became a martial artist. During his stay in China, Yara spent most of his physical energies on the art of the Bo and the twin swords."* Kim does not say what kind of swords they were but I would suggest medium size Chinese broadswords would be likely.

Fujiwara Ryozu also says that Sakugawa studied Beijing martial arts, including Yue Fei Quan; this is again a reference to Hsing-I which was famously developed by General Yue. It seems a strange coincidence that Fujiwara would link Sakugawa to Hsing-I, and Kim would link Wang to Hsing-I, were there not a connection. Combining this with the idea that the Motobu Udon resembled Hsing-I, and that Wang Ji may have taught the 'swallow' form of Hsing-I it does seem likely that this art was in some way an influence on pre-1800 Karate.

Given that Kushanku taught Sakugawa and someone called Yara, and that Chatan Yara taught a version of the kata Kushanku, it would suggest that the two Chinese figures that Richard Kim calls Kushanku and Wong Chung-Yue are in fact references to the same event. What if a Chinese master brought over a book called *Kushanku* by Wang Zong Yue, and this is where the teachings came from that shaped Sakugawa and Chatan Yara's *Kushanku* kata? This seems nothing more than speculation until we consider that we do know that one of Wang Zong's Yue's poems did indeed contain the words "Kung Hsin Chieh" in the title.

Wang is always associated with the forerunner to Taiji Quan (sometimes called Cotton Boxing) so it is interesting that Kim associates him with Hsing-I. The possibility is that Wang Zong Yue's poem has included in its title the phrase "kung hsin-chieh." Could Kung Hsin Chieh be the origin of the name Kushanku?

"*Shih-san shih hsing-**kung hsin-chieh**"* means "mental elucidation of the practice of thirteen postures" and the alternative "*Shih-san shih hsing-kung ke-chieh"* means "song of the practice of the thirteen postures." Thirteen postures are also referenced in the Okinawan form Seisan (known as Hangetsu in Shotokan).

We have seen that General Qi's combat manual may have made its way to Okinawa, and now there's the possibility that Wang's Evergreen Classic was also passed on. Could these books have been contained in the martial arts anthology of Shuri that Gichin Funakoshi, according to Gima Shikin, received from Sokon Matsumura? Funakoshi's Bubishi was different to Miyagi's and Mabuni's; perhaps the 'lost book of Kushanku' was actually in Funakoshi's Bubishi that was burnt in a fire. According to Otsuka Tadahiko the Bubishi had similar content to General Qi's book. In Funakoshi's 1922 book he reproduced content consistent with the Bubishi, but nowhere did he refer to it as the Bubishi.

Bubishi expert Patrick McCarthy writes: *"The Funakoshi manuscript itself was destroyed by fire together with the Shotokan*

Dojo. It is only through Gima Shinkin (1896-1989) that we hear that 'although I was only able to throw a fleeting glimpse at the Bubishi manuscripts of both Funakoshi Gichin and Miyagi Chojun, there seems to be a considerable difference between the two as regards their contents'."

McCarthy also suggests that it may have been Kenwa Mabuni who coined the name Bubishi. If therefore Chojun Miyagi had an anthology handed down the Naha line and Gichin Funakoshi had an anthology handed down the Shuri line, and they both differed in content, could they both be described as the Bubishi? Perhaps Mabuni and Miyagi had a copy of the Bubishi and Funakoshi's manuscript was something different.

Miyagi Tokumasa says: *"I became aware of on the last page of Shimabukuro Eizo's Records of Okinawa Karatedo and the Royal Dynasty, one single sheet of illustrations appeared as a fragment of the Bubishi or otherwise martial arts related materials... Illustrations that were presented from Tode Sakugawa to Matsumura Sokon (destroyed by fire during the Battle of Okinawa)."*

Who was Wang?

Wang Zong Yue is a forefather of the art of Taijiquan, that is to say a master of a Northern Chinese boxing system that eventually came to be called Taijiquan.

Crompton in his concise book *The Elements of Tai Chi* writes: *"A third claim* [as to the origins of Tai Chi] *gives the credit for founding Tai Chi to the Wang Tsung Yueh of Shansi mentioned earlier. Like a wandering adventurer of the Wild West he was passing one day through a Chen family village in the Honan province between 1736 and 1795.... This provoked a number of challenges from the Chen villagers. Wang accepted them all and trounced them all. His method of fighting was soft or internal... This impressed the Chen fraternity and the leaders of the village asked Wang to stay on and teach them.... Attempts have been made to push Wang Tsung Yueh out of the picture but an interesting story is told about Yang Lu Chan, the founder of the Yang style Tai Chi, which helps retain Wang's image. Yang said he was a pupil of Chen Chang Hsing (1771-1853) of Chen Chia Gou village. Chen had learned from Chiang Fa who in turn learnt from Wang.... In most of the genealogies produced outside China by*

66

Chinese writers who hail from pre-revolutionary China, Chen is shown as a pupil of Chiang Fa who was in turn taught by Wang Tsung Yueh."

Wong Kiew Kit (*The Complete Book of Tai Chi Chuan*) however adds to the mix: *"The Chen family, the originators of Chen style Tai Chi Chuan, maintain that Tai Chi Chuan was developed in the 17th century by their 9th generation ancestor, Cheng Wang Ting, a general of the Ming Dynasty and that Wang Zong Yue actually learnt it from the Chen family."* Kit adds that Chen may have learned his art in the army of General Qi, the pioneer of solo forms.

Yang style quan fa, which traces its origins to the teachings of Wang Zong Yue, emerged as Yang Lu Chan (1799–1872) studied under Chen Chang Xin. Yang Lu-ch'an was a poor farmer from Hebei Province, Guangping Prefecture, Yongnian County and he also did odd jobs at the Tai He Tang Chinese pharmacy located in the west part of Yongnian City.

The significance of this is that it was run by Chen De Hu of the Chen Village in Henan Province, Huaiqing Prefecture, Wenxian County, who agreed to teach Yang some Kung Fu. Chen later referred Yang to the Chen Village to seek out his own teacher—the 14th generation (according to the family) of the Chen Family, Ch'en Chang-hsing.

One story has Yang saving face for the Chen family by fighting off a thug and being made an honorary member of the family so he was not an outsider. Yang was then given permission by his teacher to go to Beijing and teach his own students, including Wu Yu-hsiang and his brothers, who were officials in the Imperial Qing dynasty bureaucracy. In 1850, Yang was hired by the Imperial family to teach his boxing art to them and several of their elite Manchu Imperial Guards Brigade units in Beijing's Forbidden City.

Yang style Quan Fa and Shuri Te 'Kushanku' lineage:

Wang Zong Yue	Kushanku
Chiang Fa	Tode Sakugawa
Chen Chang Hsing	
Yang Lu Chan	Sokon Matsumura
Yang Jian Hou	Gichin Funakoshi

Wang Zong Yue's Evergreen Classic: Kung-hsin-chieh
('The Lost Book of Kushanku')

Tai Chi comes from Wu Chi and is the mother of yin and yang.
In motion, Tai Chi separates; in stillness yin and yang fuse and return to Wu Chi.
It is not excessive or deficient; it follows a bending, adheres to an extension.
When the opponent is hard and I am soft, it is called tsou
When I follow the opponent and he becomes backed up, it is called nian .
If the opponent's movement is quick, then quickly respond; if his movement is slow, then follow slowly.
Although there are innumerable variations, the principles that pervade them remain the same. From familiarity with the correct touch, one gradually comprehends chin [intrinsic strength]; from the comprehension of chin, one can reach wisdom.
Without long practice, one cannot suddenly understand Tai Chi.
Effortlessly the chin reaches the head top.
Let the chi sink to the tan-tien.
Don't lean in any direction; suddenly appear, suddenly disappear.
Empty the left wherever a pressure appears, and similarly the right.
If the opponent raises up, I seem taller; if he sinks down, then I seem lower; advancing, he finds the distance seems incredibly long; retreating, the distance seems exasperatingly short.
A feather cannot be placed, and a fly cannot alight on any part of the body.
The opponent does not know me; I alone know him.
To become a peerless boxer results from this.
There are many boxing arts.
Although they use different forms, for the most part they don't go beyond the strong dominating the weak, and the slow resigning to the swift. The strong defeating the weak and the slow hands ceding to the swift hands are all the results of natural abilities and not of well-trained techniques.
From the sentence 'A force of four ounces deflects a thousand pounds', we know that the technique is not accomplished with strength.
The spectacle of an old person defeating a group of young people,

68

how can it be due to swiftness?
Stand like a perfectly balanced scale and move like a turning wheel.
Sinking to one side allows movement to flow; being double-weighted
is sluggish.
Anyone who has spent years of practice and still cannot neutralise,
and
is always controlled by his opponent,
has not apprehended the fault of double-weightedness.
To avoid this fault one must distinguish yin from yang.
To adhere means to yield.
To yield means to adhere.
Within yin there is yang.
Within yang there is yin.
Yin and yang mutually aid and change each other.
Understanding this you can say you understand chin.
After you understand chin, the more you practice, the more skill.
Silently treasure knowledge and turn it over in the mind.
Gradually you can do as you like.
Fundamentally, it is giving up yourself to follow others.
Most people mistakenly give up the near to seek the far.
It is said, 'Missing it by a little will lead many miles astray.'
The practitioner must carefully study.
This is the Treatise

Kushanku and Channan

As we have seen Kushanku/Wang Zongyue are a tantalising link between Shuri Te and the art which became Yang style Taiji Quan. There is another strand to this as there is also an assumed link between the Channan forms and Chen style Taiji Quan.

Kushanku is often linked to the five kata called Pinan, Heian or Channan. Some suggest that the Pinan forms were developed by breaking up the Kushanku into little pieces, but actually the evidence points towards the Channan having their own heritage.

Now we return again to General Qi. Before we only had an inkling of Qi's influence on Karate kata; now we start to see something more clear. The series of five basic kata called Pinan (Heian in Japan) were developed by Anko (or Yasutsune) Itosu (1832-1915) in around 1907 for inclusion in the Karate curriculum of the Okinawan school system.

However, one theory is that Itosu was re-working a longer Chinese form called Channan. Choki Motobu, a descendant of the previously mentioned Motobu Ryu masters and a student of both Matsumura and Itosu, referred to the Channan forms in 1934, saying: *"I visited [Itosu] one day at his home near the school, where we sat talking about the martial arts and current affairs. While I was there, two or three students also dropped by and sat talking with us. Itosu Sensei turned to the students and said 'show us a kata.'*

The kata that they performed was very similar to the Channan kata that I knew, but there were some differences also. Upon asking the student what the kata was, he replied 'It is Pinan no Kata.' The students left shortly after that, upon which I turned to Itosu Sensei and said 'I learned a kata called Channan, but the kata that those students just performed now was different. What is going on?' Itosu Sensei replied 'Yes, the kata is slightly different, but the kata that you just saw is the kata that I have decided upon. The students all told me that the name Pinan is better, so I went along with the opinions of the young people.' These kata, which were developed by Itosu Sensei, underwent change even during his own lifetime."

Shito Ryu founder Mabuni Kenwa also mentioned the Channan forms in 1938 and his successor Sakagami Ryusho (1915-1993) wrote that Itosu developed the five Heian katas by extracting the principal techniques of Kushanku and adding his own interpretations. He continues: *"In the beginning these kata were known under the old name Channan. Subsequently the tenor changed somewhat and they were called Pinan."*

Sakagami also indicates that the original version of the Channan kata can be found in the old Chinese book *Chi Hsiao Hsin Shu* (or *Ji Xiao Xin Shu* known in Japan as *Kiko Shinsho*) written by General Qi.

General Qi, who we met earlier, was known for his military might, but he also documented Chinese boxing. There was even a temple built for him in Fuzhou (Fukien Province) in 1567.

Extracts of his writings were including in the 1617 publication *Wu Pei Chi* (not to be confused with the later Okinawan 'Bubishi').

General Qi divided the Chinese boxing into three themes – boxing, wrestling and grappling. He also included the 32 positions of Chang Quan of T'ai Tzu, a longfist boxing style thought to have been studied by mythical Taiji Quan founder Zhan San Feng. It is possible that the name Channan is derived from this style – Chang Chuan (Chan nan).

Are Pinan forms the legacy of General Qi? [Picture: Jamie Tozer]

As noted by researcher Henning Witttwer, some of the postures shown by General Qi resemble Channan/Pinan techniques. These include:

– The flag and drum position (similar to Morote Uke - used in Pinan Sandan)
– The winding arm position (similar to Nukite - used in Pinan Shodan)
– Carrying a cannon at the head (similar to start of Pinan Yondan)
– The riding a tiger position (similar to Manji Gamae - used in Pinan Godan)

Qi's 32 self defence positions are similar to some of the 48 postures shown in the Okinawan Bubishi.

But Karate and the Channan forms are not the only style linked to General Qi's Quanfa. Chen style Taijiquan also has this link.

Douglas Wyle (*Lost Tai Chi Classics from the Late Ching Dynasty*) wrote: *"If traced as a distinctive form with specific postures and names, then Tai Chi's history may be said to begin with Ming General Ch'i Chi Kuang's [General Qi] Chuan Ching (Classic of Pugilism), twenty nine of whose postures are borrowed for the Chen village age of Henan, possibly as early as Chen Wang Ting in the seventeenth century..."*

Therefore if Wittwer and Wyle are both correct, both the Channan/Pinan/Heian forms and Chen style Taijiquan are both derived from the works of General Qi and as we have seen, the kata Kushanku and Yang style Taijiquan also seem to have a common origin.

Docherty also points out the similarity between the postures presented by General Qi and in Chen style. These include 'lazily binding the clothes' (sometimes called 'grasp sparrow's tail'), 'golden cockerel stands on one leg', 'pat the horse', 'bent single whip', and 'seven stars fist'.

Could it be that there is a linguistic link and Channan comes not from Chang Chuan but from Chen?

Conclusions:

- General Qi wrote about Chang Chuan
- Wang Zong Yue influenced Yang style and Chen style
- Chen style was influenced by Chang Chuan
- Wang Zong Yue's manuscript 'Kushanku' influenced the kata Kushanku
- The kata Kushanku was linked to the Channan kata
- The Channan kata resembled the Chang Chuan forms of General Qi
- Channan could be a Ryukyu pronunciation of 'Chang Chuan' or Chen.
- Kushanku is a Ryukyu pronunciation of 'Kung-hsin-chieh'
- Funakoshi's manuscript that belonged to Matsumura and Sakugawa contained both the 'Lost book of Kushanku' and General Qi's fighting illustrations
- The original Shuri Te lines of Wang Ji-Hama Higa-Takahara-Sakugawa and Kushanku-Sakugawa-Matsumura were influenced by the boxing of General Qi, the boxing of Wang Zong Yue and the boxing of Hsing-I rather than the Southern Chinese Shaolin styles

Students of Tode Sakugawa:

Bushi Satunuku Okuda:	The one punch specialist
Bushi Chokun Satunku Makabe	The 'bird man'
Bushi Matsumoto	Sakugawa's favourite student.
Bushi Kojo	From the Kumemura family
Bushi Sakumoto	'Yamaguchi of the East'
Bushi Unsume Yamagusuku	The 'old man of Andaya'
Bushi Sokon Matsumura	The legendary Karate master
Bushi Tachimura Senior	The Jujutsu master

According to Motobu Choki, Bushi Matsumoto was the ancestor of Kentsu Yabu. According to Gichin Funakoshi, master Tode Sakugawa was indeed the significant starting point of Karate in Okinawa. But according to Funakoshi, the son of one of his students also introduced Judo/Jujutsu.

Funakoshi wrote: *"Everyone should know that the term Karate originated from 'Tode Sakugawa' from Akata Village. Judo in Okinawa commenced with Tachimura from Tōbaru Village (today a manor of Shinzato-gwā), who trained in Kagoshima at state expense. His father, it is said, was a student of Tode Sakugawa'. And here we can clearly see that Karate was already developed when Jūdō was not yet introduced in Okinawa."*

If Tode Sakugawa lived 1733-1815, then his students such as Bushi Tachimura Senior would most likely have been born circa 1780-1810 (about the age of Matsumura). So then their students, such as Bushi Tachimura Jr would have been born circa 1830-1860 (about the age of Itosu and Azato). So it is possible that Tachimura actually did study Judo, rather than Jujutsu, since Jigoro Kano developed Judo in 1882. But on balance it is more likely that Funakoshi was simply using Judo as a synonym of Jujutsu. Tode Sakugawa, master of Karate and Bojutsu, was a true master of Karate, the likely innovator of the Kushanku and Channan forms and teacher of some of the greatest Karateka ever including Bushi Matsumura. Bushi Matsumura was of a generation of Karateka who began to travel to Fujian and who were taught by visiting masters from Fujian. Whereas Matsumura's forefathers seemingly looked towards the Northern Quan Fa of General Qi and General Yue Fei, it seems his generation looked towards Southern Quan Fa from the southern Shaolin tradition.

Part Three: Shuri Te, Tomari Te and Naha Te

Bushi Matsumura

Sokon Matsumura is the Karate master who more than any other bridged the gap between Sakugawa's era and Funakoshi's era. The 1800s were also the approximate lifespan of Sokon Matsumura. There are four different theories on his date of birth and date of death, and they are all within a few years of him being born in 1800 and dying in 1900. The dates are: 1809-1901 or 1798–1890 or 1809–1896 or 1800–1892. So whichever theory you subscribe to Matsumura saw pretty much all of the 1800s (the second theory is the best fit in my opinion as it allows for his training under Sakugawa). He is the archetypal 19th century Karateka.

According to oral tradition, just when Sakugawa thought his legacy had ended (aged 78 he had already retired and passed his school onto Bushi Matsumoto) he began to teach his most notable ever student, Sokon "Bushi" Matsumura.

Sokon Matsumura: Shuri Te pioneer

There is however another Okinawan teacher attributed to Matsumura, and that is Lord Yabiku. Andreas Quast translated an article from the Ryukyu Shinpo newspaper from 1915 dedicated to Master Itosu and other teachers. Among them there is a passage about a man referred to as 'Yabiku no Shu' (Lord Yabiku), under whom

74

Matsumura Sokon had studied.

It states: *"Besides these there was a hiding person of real courage. This was a person from Shuri. Lord Yabiku is the person who moved down [from Shuri] to his territory (shima), the Yabiku fief. He was by far senior to the venerable old Matsumura. Since he handed down an old style of martial/military arts, and since he moved down [from Shuri] to his territory (shima), he appeared a bit like what is referred to as hermit, hiding from the world in recluse. Even [a great master] such as the venerable old Matsumura, until the prime of his life had almost exclusively made practical experiences only. Because venerable old Matsumura was not familiar with the old-style of karate, he visited Lord Yabiku and finally received instruction."*

As a young man Matsumura entered service at Shuri castle, a bodyguarding role that saw him make trips to Satsuma (Japan) and Fujian (China). In 1828, aged about 30, Bushi Matsumura and his colleague Bushi Kojo made their first trip to China. Taking a Kojo to China was perhaps the key to the door. The Kojo family of Kume were already Chinese boxing experts and may have already had relationships with the Ryukyukan, the dormitory in Fujian where Okinawans would stay. And with Matsumura's diplomatic role and knowledge of old style Okinawan Karate from Lord Yabiku or Tode Sakugawa it seems they were well qualified to learn.

This date is significant because it meant breathing new life into both Shuri Te and Naha Te. Whereas the old Shuri forms were largely based around Kushanku, and the old Naha Te (the forms practised in Kume) may have been old style Chinese boxing dating back to the original 36 families, this 1828 visit led to the introduction of the so-called "Shaolin" forms.

This visit debunks another myth. Most will say that Goju Ryu came from Naha Te which was only developed when Higaonna Kanryu went to China in around 1870, but Goju Ryu founder Chojun Miyagi himself denied this and cited the 1828 visit as the true origin of Naha Te.

Miyagi wrote: *"In 1828, our ancestors inherited a Quan Fa style of Fujian province in China. They continued their studies and formed Goju-Ryu Karate. Even today, there still exists an orthodox group which inherited genuine and authentic Goju-Ryu karate."*

The "orthodox" Goju Ryu that Miyagi referred to could be the similar sounding "Kojo Ryu" or he could perhaps view any style that blended the hard and the soft as being authentic Goju. Regardless,

Miyagi knew his art could be traced to an 1828 visit a generation before his teacher was born.

If 1756 was the date when Kushanku was introduced to Okinawa, therefore establishing our oldest Shuri Te form, then it would seem the Kojo visit to China in 1828 was the next stage of Karate's development, opening the door to Shaolin forms like Sanchin, Seisan and Suparimpei and leading to the creation of Naha Te. It is here that perhaps we could view the Channan and Kushanku as being Shorin (possibly derived from the Northern Shaolin of General Qi) and the Southern forms as being Shorei.

The life story of Matsumura

Matsumura was born in around 1797, and died in 1889. Some push his birthdate to as late as 1809. According to some sources, Matsumura's family name was Kayo and they were of Chinese descent. Matsumura grew up in Yamagawa village of the city of Shuri, Okinawa. Sakugawa began training Matsumura at Akata when he was 14 years old, in 1810. According to tradition, it was at Matsumura's father's request that Sakugawa teach him. Legend says that to train Matsumura to block, Sakugawa tied to him to a tree so he could not move. Then he threw punches at him.

Sakugawa trained him up until his death, and then Sokon may have trained under Yabiku. According to oral history, he studied under Sakugawa for 4 years, so only until he was 18 (by the 1797 birthdate).

Matsumura was recruited into the service of the Sho family. At that time, Sho Ko, the king of Okinawa, desired to have him change his last name, as was the custom, and suggested the name Muramatsu (Muramachi), or "village pine." After discussing the matter with some friends and relatives, he decided that Matsumura (Machimura), or "pine village", would be more appropriate. Sokon asked the king to let him change the name to that, and the request was granted. Some say this happened at age 17, which would probably put it around 1813.

Many sources say that Bushi Matsumura trained in China, and it is certainly a strong tradition. Hohan Soken said that Bushi trained at "Fukien Shaolin" for 26 years. This seems like an unreasonable exaggeration.

According to Hohan Soken's *Matsumura Seito* style, in keeping with samurai tradition, a close family member was selected as

Matsumura's successor in his personal system. His grandson Nabi Matsumura was apparently chosen, although contemporary accounts such as Funakoshi and Motobu do not mention Nabe.

Sources which quote Matsumura as teaching a variety of kata (typically including Bassai, Kushanku, Chinto, Rohai, Jutte, Gojushiho etc) are possibly making one of two errors: confusing Matsumura with Matsumora (even the Karatedo Kyohan makes this translation error) and assuming that because Itosu taught certain kata, and Matsumura was his teacher, he must have taught them too. But this theory does not take into consideration the possibility that Itosu learned them from someone else.

In his 1932 book, *Watashi no Tode Jutsu*, Motobu is quoted as saying: *"Sensei Itosu was a pupil of Sensei Matsumura, but he was disliked by his teacher for he was very slow (speed of movement). There (in the dojo) for although Itosu sensei was diligent in his practice his teacher did not care about him so he (Itsou) left and went to sensei Nagahama."*

Nagahama may be the same man who Funakoshi cited as a Naha Te teacher and fellow student (along with Aragaki) of Wai Shinzan.

Funakoshi also seems to say that while Azato was a primary student of Matsumura, Itosu, while a student of Matsumura, was mainly a student of Gusukuma of Tomari.

In his book *To-te Jutsu* Funakoshi states, *"It is confirmed through written documents and collections that ... Azato followed Matsumura and Itosu followed Gusukuma, according to what has been told through generations."*

In his later text, *Karate-do Kyohan*, Funakoshi says again that *"It is stated that masters Azato and Itosu were Students of Matsumura and Gusukuma respectively. Masters Azato and Itosu were the teachers who instructed this writer and to whom the writer is greatly indebted."*

So if Itosu learned - let's say - Jutte, Chinto, Chinte and Rohai from Gusukuma, it is still a reasonable bet that he learned Kushanku and Bassai from Matsumura. We should note that styles which claim descent from Matsumura seem to include the kata Seisan but it would appear this was not an Itosu form.

Choki Motobu, who at least knew of Matsumura and trained with Matsumora, listed kata too but did not attribute them to any particular masters. He did however allocate Wansu and Rohai (Empi and Meikyo) to the Tomari schools and lists Sanchin, Seishan, Gojushiho,

Seiunchin, Naihanchi, Bassai, Chinto, Chinte, Wansu, Rohai and Kushanku as being "from ancient days." He identifies Sanchin, Gojushiho, Seisan and Seiunchin as being old Chinese forms. Motobu identifies Naihanchi, Chinto, Bassai and Rohai as being forms no longer found in China.

In the Karate-do Kyohan Funakoshi lists Matsumura's teacher as Iwah. He writes: *"Matsumura of Shuri and Maesato and Kogusoku* [Kojo] *of Kume,* [trained] *with the military attache Iwah."*

Funakoshi is a good source because he personally trained with Matsumura but trained at greater length with Matsumura's students Itosu and Azato.

In *Karatedo My Way of Life*, Funakoshi calls Matsumura *"one of the greatest Karateka."* He tells a story about Matsumura as an old man.

A stone engraver asks "Aren't you Matsumura, the Karate teacher?" and he finds that Matsumura has grown disillusioned with Karate. The reason is because of an incident in which Matsumura was teaching "the head of the clan". Matsumura asked the chieftain to attack him and the chieftain lunged in with a double kick (presumably a double jumping kick as in Kanku Dai) and Matsumura blocked the kick with a shuto and slammed his body into the chieftain. He knocked the chieftain across the room, almost knocked him out cold and was immediately fired. The engraver ended up challenging Matsumura to a fight, which Matsumura won simply by staring at his opponent, who lost his nerve and became paralysed with fear. Matsumura was subsequently re-appointed by the clan chief.

In this book Funakoshi also mentions learning the Pinan kata, Naihanchi, Chinto, Bassai, Seisan, Jutte, Jion and Sanchin from his teachers, but he does not say from which teacher he learned each from.

In *Karatedo My Way of Life* Funakoshi recalls learning kata from Azato. He writes: *"Often in the backyard off the Azato house, as the master looked on, I would practice kata time and again, week after week, sometimes month after month until I had mastered it to my teacher's satisfaction... Practice was strict and I was never permitted to move on to another kata until Azato was convinced that I had satisfactorily understood the one I had been working on."*

So although Funakoshi does not name the kata he learned from Azato, the implication was that he learned at least three (he went through the progress of learning a new kata at least twice). It is not thought Azato taught the Pinan forms so it is likely these first forms were Naihanchi or perhaps Seisan although it is also possible Funakoshi learned Bassai and Kushanku from Azato.

In the *Karatedo Nyumon* Funakoshi says *"as far as I know the only styles that have been handed down from the past are the Goju Ryu of Master Miyagi and the Shito Ryu of Master Mabuni. I have never given a name to the Karate I am studying but some of my students call it Shotokan Ryu."* He later mentions Shorin Ryu and Shorei Ryu but points out these are not styles but "types" of Karate; therefore Shotokan or Goju Ryu could contain both Shorin and Shorei type forms.

Here other styles are conspicuous by their absence. It may be that Funakoshi considers Shito Ryu and Goju Ryu to have both developed from the teachings of Aragaki and Higaonna, and that he alone is the successor of Itosu, Azato and Matsumura. Or perhaps the other Okinawan masters just did not use Ryu names for their styles. Or perhaps Funakoshi was referring only to styles that had been passed over to mainland Japan.

In this book Funakoshi does not name a single kata taught by Azato or Matsumura. He states that he and Azato's son used to go and train with Itosu together. And he states that Itosu taught him the Pinan and Naihanchi forms. However, despite Itosu being a student of Matsumura we need not assume that Itosu learned all his kata from Matsumura.

In this book Funakoshi repeats the story of the stone engraver, but this time he is a metal craftsman called Uehara. In this version of the story the clan chief would appear to be the king himself since it is at the castle that Matsumura loses his job.

Chosin Chibana claimed to teach Karate exactly as it had been taught to him by Itosu. Chibana was of exceptional character and we have no reason to doubt this. The kata taught by Chibana to Higa in Shorin Ryu (also written Kobayashi Ryu) were as follows:

- Pinan Shodan and Nidan (possibly developed from a kata called Channan)
- Pinan Sandan, Yondan, Godan (possibly created by Itosu)
- Naihanchi (Itosu likely learned this from Matsumura)
- Naihanchi Nidan and Sandan (developed by Itosu)
- Bassai Dai (Itosu likely learned this from Matsumura)
- Bassai Sho (possibly derived from Passai Guwa)

- Kushanku (Itosu likely learned this from Matsumura)
- Kushanku Sho (Itosu may have created this)
- Chinto (Itosu probably learned this from Gusukuma)
- Chinte (Itosu probably learned this from Gusukuma)
- Unsu (usually attributed to Aragaki but possibly learned from Nagahama of Naha)
- Jion (possibly based on Jutte, either learned from Matsumora or Gusukuma)
- Gojushiho (almost certainly learned from Matsumura)

An interview with Choki Motobu confirms he was taught by Matsumura (as well as Matsumora) and states that Matsumura taught the kata Naihanchi: *"I was taught by the renowned Matsumura and the renowned Sakuma, both from Shuri. I was also taught by Matsumora from Tomari, Pēchin Kunigami (Kunjan in Okinawan) and Itosu, as well as on occasion by "Yanbaru" Kunishi from Kumoji. Among all these instructors, the two with whom I was closest and shared emotional bonds with were Matsumora from Tomari, and Sakuma from Shuri."*

Richard Kim tells us some information with at least dates, but he does not attribute a source: *"Once under the tutelage of Sakugawa, Bushi Matsumura developed quickly into a proficient martial arts expert. By the winter of 1816* [when he was 19 by my preferred birth date of 1797] *he was deemed valuable enough to be recruited into imperial service as a Chikudin, allowing him to feel secure enough to marry two years later. Her name was Yonamine Chiru."*

Kim tells half a dozen stories about Matsumura. One is Funakoshi's Uehara story, another is a strange incident where Matsumura fights a hooded stranger who turns out to be his own wife. In another he is forced to fight a bull and so secretly broke the spirit of the bull leading up to the fight by stabbing it with a needle. He does however tell one story of actual combat, where Matsumura ducks a Sai and destroys an opponent's wrist by striking it with a Tessen fan. Kim also states that in 1846, Itosu became a student of Matsumura who, it is implied, taught him strictly for eight years.

Founder of Matsumura Seito, Hohan Soken gave an interview, saying: *"My style comes from Kiyo Soken. To mark the occasion when Kiyo was appointed the chief bodyguard to King Sho Ko (and later to Sho Iku and then Sho Tai), he was allowed to change his name. This was a custom back then, especially if something important or notable* happened to you; he changed his name to Matsumura — Matsumura Soken. It was later that King Sho Tai officially gave Matsumura the title of "Bushi," and to this day he is, with affection, referred to as Bushi Matsumura. When Bushi Matsumura died he left the Te of his teachings to my uncle, who was his grandson, Matsumura Nabe. My mother was Nabe-tanmei's sister. Tanmei means 'respected senior or respected old man.' This was and still is a title of much respect in Okinawa. I became a student of my uncle around 1902 or 1903 and learned the original methods of Uchinan Sui-di [Shuri Te], as it was then called."

When asked about kata, Hohan replied that Kushanku (ie Kanku Dai) was the most important form: "The most important Matsumura Seito kata is the Kushanku. Sometimes we would practice the Kushanku with kanzashi (hairpins) held in the hands – this was a common method of fighting. The hairpins were symbols of rank and many Okinawans carried them for decoration and also for protection."

When asked if he taught the white crane kata Hakucho, Hohan replied: "No, hakucho is another kata that, I believe, came from the Chinese tea seller, Go Kenki. He moved to Japan but my kata is much different. I call it hakutsuru. It was about... no, it was after ten years of training my uncle taught me the most secret kata of Matsumura Seito shorin-ryu, the hakutsuru (white crane) kata."

When asked to elaborate on the kata he taught, he replied: "I teach the Matsumura kata. The kata that I teach now are pinan shodan, pinan nidan, naihanchi shodan, naihanchi nidan, patsai-sho and dai, chinto, gojushiho, kusanku, rohai ichi-ni-san, and last, the hakutsuru. The last one is my favourite kata that I demonstrate – because it is easier to do. When I was young, the best kata was the Kushanku. This is the Matsumura Kushanku — the older version that is not done much now."

On May 13, 1882 Sokon Matsumura sent a makimono (handwritten scroll) to his student, Ryosei Kuwae:

"Make a firm resolution to master the secrets of martial arts, otherwise go away. You must have the firm determination to accomplish the resolution. The sword and the pen are but one. Literature consists of poetry, exegetics, and Confucianism. A student of poetry works at words and produces sentences in order to seek fame, peerage and fief. A student of exegetics studies Chinese classics

81

to instruct people. He may make a scholar but ignorant of the world. Poetry and exegetics only make people woo fame, thus they are not the true art. Confucianism, however, makes us understand the nature of things. By the teachings on knowledge, honesty, and righteousness one may not only be able to manage a household but govern a country. Thus peace will reign over the land. These are Confucian ideas, the true art. In the case of martial arts, there are three kinds of pursuers. A scholar pictures many ways of training in his mind so that his moves become like movements of dance; superficial and of no practical use for offence and defence. A normal student of martial arts is a good promiser of victory, but a bad performer. A dispute caused by such a man will harm people as well as himself. It will even bring disgrace upon his parents, brothers and sisters. The true pursuer of martial arts, however, does not idle away his time but accomplishes his task ingeniously. He controls his mind and watches for a chance. His calm arouses a disturbance among enemies. He then grabs this chance and defeats the enemy. Everything ripens and the mystery of nature shows its secret to the master of martial arts, who has no hesitation or disturbance in his mind even in case of emergency. The power of a tiger and the swiftness of an eagle dwell within him. He defeats enemies completely and shows his loyalty and filial piety. There are seven virtues in martial arts: the prohibition of violence, the control of soldiers, the support for people's need, the establishment of distinguished services, the relief of the poor, the settlement of disputes among people and the enrichment of assets. As seen in his teachings, Confucius also praised these virtues. Thus the sword and the pen are but one, whereas the scholar's martial arts and the ostensible martial arts are useless. Therefore study the true literary and martial arts. Be sure to watch for a chance and then strike into the enemy. Keep the above words in mind and practise hard. I wish you understand my unreserved words."

The letter demonstrates that Matsumura's outlook was very much in keeping with Bushido virtues and a Confucian outlook. He does not talk of Karate, rather he discusses 'the pen and the sword'.

A student of Matsumura's who may give a clear idea of his teacher's style was Bushi Ishimine. His style consisted only of a few kata, namely Kumade Sanchin (a unique bear form), Sanchin, Naihanchi and Bassai. Once again there is the suggestion that Matsumura, like Motobu and seemingly Azato, may have only practised a few kata. In Azato's case we have already established though that he taught at least three.

Although Hohan Soken is most famous for his claims to be the descendant of Matsumura, there is another Karate master with that honour.

Tsuyoshi Chitose 10th Dan, founder of Chito Ryu (1898-1984) was the grandson of Matsumura. His style, as well as being it would seem a pun on his name Chitose, used the name Chito because Chi means 1,000 and To (as in Toshu or Tode Jutsu) means Tang Dynasty – he was therefore referring to his style as containing 1,000 year old Chinese Kung Fu. Chitose was a maternal grandson of Matsumura. He began his training under Aragaki Seishō in 1905. He was seven years old and continued to train with Seisho until 1913/1914. While there is some discrepancy as to whether Chitose's first kata was Sanchin or Seisan, his book "Kenpō Karate-dō" states that he learned Sanchin from Aragaki for seven years before being taught another. Chitose's Nijushiho is said to resemble Hakutsuru.

Interestingly a student of Azato (who it seems only ever studied Karate under Matsumura) also practised Nijushiho. Although some sources say that Funakoshi was Azato's only student, Hisataka Masayoshi (Kori) (1907-1988) learned the kata Niseishi (Nijushiho) from him. Hisataka founded his school of Shorinjiryu Kendokan Karatedo in 1945 (Ross).

Taiji Kase, a student of Gigo Funakoshi, seemed to suggest that Sochin (along with Nijushiho usually considered an Aragaki form) also came from the Matsumura-Azato branch. Chito Ryu also includes a unique version of Sochin. Chito Ryu also includes a form called Sanshiryu which by some accounts resembles Gojushiho.

Remember the sources Kyan stated for the sources of his kata: Seisan, Naihanchi and Gojushiho (from Matsumura), Kushanku (from Chatan Yara), Passai (from Oyadomari) and Wansu (via Kosaku Matsumora). Let's marry up some of these forms with the ones mentioned by Motobu:

"Among those styles or katas which have been used in Ryu Kyu from ancient days are: Sanchin, Gojushiho, Seisan, Seiunchin, Ippaku Re Hachi, Naihanchi, Passai, Chinto, Chinte (bamboo yari style), Wanshu, Rohai and Kushanku.

Once again the Shuri forms he mentions are the ones Kyan cited (Seisan, Naihanchi, Gojushiho, Kushanku, Passai, Wansu), whereas Motobu does not mention Unsu, Nijushiho, Wankan, Sochin,

Jutte, Ji'in, Jion, Kanku Sho, and Bassai Sho. This seems to support the theory that Unsu, Nijushiho, Wankan and Sochin were Aragaki innovations and that Jutte, Ji'in, Jion, Kanku Sho and Bassai Sho came via Itosu's studies with Gusukuma; whereas Motobu is more likely to have knowledge of Tomari forms that came via Kosaku Matsumora, so it looks like these are Chinto (Gankaku), Chinte and Rohai (Meikyo). I have already suggested that Sanchin was studied before the conventional Naha Te stylists (Goju, Uechi, Ryuei Ryu) by the likes of the Kojo family.

Iwah: Quanfa Teacher of Bushi Matsumura

It is likely that Iwah was therefore the root of Matsumura's Seisan kata, the one form that is in almost all Karate styles and one most can agree Matsumura taught.

Seisan has been called the 'universal kata' appearing in everything from Shotokan (where it is called Hangetsu), to Goju Ryu, to Uechi Ryu, to Shorin Ryu.

According to Chotoku Kyan, Seisan was the preferred kata of Matsumura. Funakoshi's Seisan (before it became Hangetsu) and Kyan's Seisan were very similar, suggesting a Matsumura origin. Seisan is also seen in a very different form in Goju Ryu and Uechi Ryu but pre-dates both as we know Aragaki demonstrated it in 1867. Therefore it seems likely that Matsumura and Kojo introduced it to Okinawa via the Iwah Dojo and then somehow the Goju Ryu version split off from Aragaki and the Kojo line.

From examining the various versions of the Seisan kata it appears to contain movements consistent with southern Chinese Tiger Boxing systems.

Funakoshi writes: "*Okinawan experts such as Sakiyama, Gushi and Tomoyori of Naha studied some time with the Chinese military attache Ason* [other translations say Buken]; *Matsumura of Shuri and Maesato and Kogusoku* [Kojo] *of Kume, with the military attache Iwah; and Shimabuku of Uemonden, and Higa, Seneha, Gushi, Nagahama, Aragaki, Hijaunna* [Higaonna Kanryo] *and Kuwae all of Kunenboya, with the military attache Waishinzan. It is said that a teacher of Gusukuma, Kanagusuku, Matsumura* [he means Kosaku Matsumora], *Oyatomari, Yamada, Nakazato and Toguchi, all of Tomari, was a southern Chinese who drifted ashore at Okinawa.*"

So Funakoshi alone gives us the following masters:

- Kushanku who we already know taught Karate Sakugawa
- Ason who taught students from Naha
- Iwah who taught Matsumura of Shuri and students from Kume
- Waishinzan who taught students such as Aragaki
- A Southern Chinese who taught students such as Gusukuma, Matsumora and Oyatomari.

Which masters taught which forms, and from what styles did they come? Before we visit these Chinese pioneers, we must first look to a few key Okinawans:

- Higaonna Kanryo, founder of Naha Te or Shorei Ryu and teacher of Goju Ryu founder Chojun Miyagi and To-On Ryu founder Juhatsu Kyoda. Higaonna visited China in 1870 where he became the student of RyuRyu Ko.
- Nakaima Norisato founder of Ryuei Ryu who was in China around the same time.

The tatemae of Goju Ryu is that Chojun Miyagi was taught Sanchin, Seisan, Sanseiryu, Seiunchin and Suparimpei by Higaonna, and he had introduced them to Okinawa after training with Ryuru Ko. But this cannot be the case – as a number of these kata were already in Okinawa. We will disregard Wang Ji (Wansu) and Wang Zong Yue (Kushanku) as potential originators/bringers of these forms, and we return to what Funakoshi told us:

Matsumura of Shuri and Maesato and Kogusoku of Kume, with the military attache Iwah; Shimabuku of Uemonden, and Higa, Seneha, Gushi, Nagahama, Aragaki, Hijaunna [Kanryo Higoanna] *and Kuwae all of Kunenboya, with the military attache Waishinzan.*

One thing we know is that Aragaki knew some of the above Naha Te forms before Higaonna ever went to China: in 1867, some 20 years before the Naha Te pioneers went to China, Aragaki led a public demonstration of Karate and Kobudo. This was the first public demo of Karate in the world, in which kata, Kumite and Kobudo were demonstrated as an art form and a way of life.

The running order of the event was:

- Tinbei and Rochin (shield and straight sword) by Maesato Peichin
- Tesshaku (iron ruler or Sai) and Bo by Maesato and Aragaki
- Seisan by Aragaki
- Bojutsu and Tode Jutsu by Maesato and Aragaki (unarmed vs staff)
- Chishaukiun (Shisochin) Kata by Aragaki
- Tinbei and Bojutsu (shield vs staff) by Tomimura Pechin and Aragaki
- Tesshaku (Sai) by Maesato
- Kou Shu by Maesato and Aragaki (two man sets)
- Shabo (wheel staff – perhaps Nunchaku) by Shusai Ikemi Yagusuku
- Suparinmpei by Tomimura
- Kogusuku Peichin reading poetry and playing the Biwa lute

So we can conclude that Seisan, Suparimpei and possibly Shisochin predated Higaonna, Uechi, Norisato and Kyoda in Okinawa.

Miyagi's quote on the 'original Goju Ryu' in full is: *"Most styles of Chinese kung fu were created by mimicking fights of animals or birds. You can see it from the styles' names such as Tiger Style, Lion Style, Monkey Style, Dog Style, Crane Style and so on. In the age a little later, Chinese kung fu split into Southern school and Northern school. Moreover, each school split into Neijia and Waijia.*

"According to popular opinion, we can categorize karate into two styles: Shorin-Ryu and Shorei-Ryu. They (traditional view) insist that the former is fit for a stout person, while the latter for a slim person. However, such an opinion proved to be false by many studies. In the mean time, there is only one opinion we can trust.

"It is as follows: **In 1828, our ancestors inherited a kung fu style of Fujian province in China. They continued their studies and formed Goju-Ryu karate.** *Even today, there still exists an orthodox group which inherited genuine and authentic Goju-Ryu karate."*

So 1828 was remembered as the year "our ancestors inherited a Kung Fu style of Fujian province in China." So who were the ancestors who went to China? It seems likely they were Bushi Matsumura and Bushi Kojo.

Since we know Seisan was in Okinawa as early as 1867 and since Miyagi referred to Goju Ryu (and Seisan is a core kata of Goju) as having been brought to Okinawa in 1828, it stands to reason that these could be forms brought back. Seisan and Gojushiho were both kata that were taught by Matsumura, and indeed the only kata he taught to some students such as Kyan. Gichin Funakoshi's Seisan resembled Kyan's but Funakoshi does not seem to have learned Gojushiho – or at least not the extent he was comfortable demonstrating it.

If Matsumura studied under Iwah in 1828 and he and Kojo brought back the kata Seisan, then Matsumura could have also brought back Gojushiho, a form which according to McCarthy's Bubishi commentary was practised in Fujian. Gojushiho (which means 54) may also be related to the form "the 54 steps of the Black Tiger" referenced in the Bubishi. Could Seisan and Gojushiho be the living embodiment of the White Crane and Black Tiger referenced in the Bubishi? Seisan and Gojushiho are both suggestive of Tiger boxing.

Author's note: In addition to the information already presented I would now like to refer to quotes by Dan Smith Sensei (9th Dan) of the Seibukan (personal correspondence), who has researched Kyan's Karate at length in which he clarifies Matsumura's teaching of Seisan:

During research for the book on Kyan's Karate we found that Chotoku Kyan's father, Chofu, was a Motanaga at birth and was adopted into the Kyan family to preserve the family name. The importance of this is that when Chotoku (Motanaga) Kyan wrote a self biography for the Ryukyu Shimpo in 1943 he gave the account of his Karate training. His article revealed that he studied from an early age with his grandfather and father. He was taken to Sokon Matsumura at the age of 16 (1886) for further studies. The only kata he learned during a two year period was Gojushiho.

He gave a detailed account of his two year training with Matsumura at the garden Dojo where Matsumura was conducting training. We also found during the research, conducted by the Kyan Research group of Kadena, that [Chotoku] Kyan's father was a student of Matsumura (once we understood that Kyan had been a Motonaga we found the records of his training) and he was 25 years senior to Azato and 16 years senior to Itosu. The research assisted in our understanding that Chotoku Kyan had learned Seisan prior to his training with Matsumura and that this Seisan came from his father through Matsumura.

[Chotoku] Kyan wrote in the previously mentioned article that he appreciated Funakoshi's efforts introducing Karate in Japan under the guise of Okinawan Karate. This clearly demonstrated the awareness of Kyan what Funakoshi was doing in Japan and that he obviously was not teaching the methods of Matsumura. Perhaps of Itosu would be conjecture. I think it is notable that Kyan even mentioned Funakoshi. I have had the hypothesis for some years that Kyan and Funakoshi were at the garden Dojo around the same time. This would account for the similarities in methods of Shotokan and Kyan's Karate as demonstrated by the photos of Yoshitaka Funakoshi in H.D Plee's book and those of Kyan's methods taught by Zenpo Shimabukuro. The photos of Yoshitaka clearly do not resemble Itosu's Karate.

The discovery that Chofu Kyan was a Motonaga changed the dynamics of understanding who Chotoku Kyan really was. There is little recorded information on Chofu Kyan but the researchers found significant aspects of Chofu Motonaga's history with Matsumura. Chofu Motonaga had six brothers. He was the middle brother. As it was a custom on Okinawa that if a family had all daughters and no way to pass on the family name Chofu (the middle son) was allowed to be adopted into the Kyan family. The Motonaga were of royal blood. The Kyans were aristocrats but not royal blood. Choftu Motonaga was adopted and married into the Kyan family. He also had six sons and Chotoku was the middle son. Chotoku Kyan had moved to Japan and was living on the Imperial grounds and attended Todai University (the Emperor's University), he lived in Japan for eight years.

There is record of he and his father training outside in the royal gardens in the snow with his father. Chotoku adopted the western style dress and cut his hair while living in Japan. In 1896 he was dispatched back to Okinawa by his father to be adopted back into the Motonaga family, Kyan gave an account in the magazine article of his return to Okinawa and subsequent training. Many of the stories about Kyan concerning the other Okinawan teachers and Itosu specifically are called into question after reading this article written by Kyan.

Ason: Shorei Ryu Master

Ason was famously the teacher of Sakiyama, Gushi and Tomoyori but what was his background and contribution to Karate? All Funakoshi tells us about Ason is that he was a military attache and the students he taught were based in Naha. We don't know from this when he lived or what kind of martial arts he practised. So let's instead try to track down his students.

Sakiyama Kitosu lived from 1830 to 1914. He was a peer/training brother of Nakaima Norisato who was the founder of Ryuei Ryu. Norisato was a student of a Chinese master called RyuRyu Ko. It seems somewhat likely then that Ason and Ryuru Ko taught a similar or the same style. Patrick McCarthy identifies Ryuru with a master of Whooping Crane, while others have claimed he taught Hsing-I. It is also possible he taught a type of Tiger Boxing related to Pangai Noon since the kata believed to have been passed from RyuRyu to Higaonna Kanryo are the same as those passed to Kanbun Uechi from the Pangai Noon style. RyuRyu may have taught a style called Kingai Noon.

Mark Bishop tells a story of Sakiyama that also relates him to RyuRyu Ko: *"Kuniyoshi had been a student of Kitoku Sakiyama who had travelled to Fuchou with Norisato Nakaima and trained with him at Ru Ru Ko's Dojo... When one of Ru Ru Ko's disciples came to Okinawa on official duty, he was grieved to learn that his former brother disciple Sakiyama was almost dead from some unknown illness..."*

Kata shared by Goju Ryu and Ryuei Ryu (and therefore possibly taught by Ryuru Ko):
Sanchin
Sesan
Sanseru
Seiunchin

Therefore the kata Ason taught to Sakiyama and co would most likely resemble these types of movements. Or the kata may have been Suparimpei, which we know was in Okinawa in 1867.

If Ason taught Sakiyama, he would have arrived in Okinawa in around 1845 (when Sakiyama was 15 to 20), so he post-dates the 1828 introduction of Naha Te staple Seisan. He also post-dates the Shuri Te staple form Kushanku. But he pre-dates people like Aragaki, Itosu and

Azato. Funakoshi tells us that Ason taught Shorei Ryu and we can determine from the previous evidence that it was likely to have been a form somewhat akin to the Goju Ryu forms it was related to. The forms Funakoshi calls Shorei Ryu are Naihanchi, Jion, Jutte, Chinto, Sochin, Nijushiho and Seisan.

We have already identified Seisan as being from the Iwah transmission. We will also eliminate Nijushiho and Sochin as these were Aragaki kata and Chinto and Jutte/Jion, as these are Tomari kata. So this leaves one form for Ason – Naihanchi, which is indeed one of the most "Goju" looking of the Shuri repertoire. Of course it is possible that the forms taught by Ason were some lost White Crane form that has not survived in Okinawa. But of the Shorei group it seems most likely that Naihanchi was the kata introduced by Ason.

Alternatively the Kishimoto Di school, which traces its lineage back to a master parallel to Matsumura, suggests that Matsumura received Naihanchi, Bassai and Kushanku from Tode Sakugawa. If this is the case, then Ason cannot be the origin of Naihanchi. In which case perhaps he taught Suparimpei.

Regardless of whether Ason introduced Naihanchi to Okinawa, it seems certain that Ason had a certain amount of White Crane influence in his repertoire whether that be from Whooping Crane or Kingainoon.

The author teaching Te Oyo for Naihanchi

Naihanchi

Naihanchi was and is a crucial part of training everywhere in Okinawa outside of Naha. In fact Shoto founder Gichin Funakoshi spent the first nine years of his training with Master Azato learning only Naihanchi. Naihanchi was in Shuri what Sanchin was in Naha – the fundamental form designed to strengthen the core and basic postural movement. Both Itosu and Azato taught Naihanchi and therefore both probably learned it from Sokon Matsumura.

I would now like to explore the origins of the form and how it was transmitted to Okinawa. I will do this with a number of theories. Firstly we should point out that although the origins of this form are said to be Chinese, there is no current Chinese style that practises it. We cannot therefore say "Naihanchi is a Preying Mantis form" for example with any certainty. I have already suggested Matsumura could have learned it from either Ason or Sakugawa. But there are other theories.

Karate forms are typically divided into two groups, Shorin Ryu and Shorei Ryu. On the surface this seems like a straightforward classification. Itosu's style was Shorin Ryu, Higaonna's style was Shorei Ryu. Therefore Shorin equals Shuri and Shorei equals Naha. But unfortunately it is not that simple, because masters like Funakoshi and Mabuni applied that classification to all katas regardless of style. For example the Pinans are Shorin, Tekki is Shorei, Hangetsu is Shorei, Kanku Dai is Shorin and so on, despite all deriving from Shorin Ryu. It is unlikely that if Shorin Ryu means "Shaolin Ryu", then the Shorei refers to some other temple somewhere. It is even more confusing since some of the forms classified as Shorei (Jutte and Hangetsu for example) are the ones with the closest affinity to Shaolin. Funakoshi also contradicts himself. In one volume he will refer to Empi as Shorin, and in another as Shorei. I suspect that Funakoshi may have intended to list all the traditional Shuri forms (Kanku Dai, Bassai Dai, Pinan) as Shorin and the Chinese forms imported to Naha and Tomari (Hangetsu, Sanchin) as Shorei but then he became confused when he reached forms where he did not know the origin and so oversimplified as "slow powerful forms are Shorei, fast light forms are Shorin." Some of Funakoshi's writings imply he thought the two Okinawan schools (Shorin and Shorei) equated to the two Chinese schools Shaolin and Wutang but we know this is not the case. The speed of Shotokan and Shaolin may be comparable, as may the speed of Sanchin and Tai Chi, but that's where the similarities end. But if Funakoshi believed the Naha and Tomari forms to be Shorei, and the Shuri forms to be Shorin, why did he class Naihanchi, the cornerstone of Shuri Te and Tomari Te, as Shorei?

Could it be that somewhere along the lines Funakoshi heard that Naihanchi was derived from Shaio Jao (Chinese wrestling) and translated this as Shorei-Ji? A simpler explanation may just be that Funakoshi knew this form had been introduced in recent memory by a Chinese master from Fujian. It was, therefore, Shorei. But the Chinese master was not from the famous Kojo Dojo where people like Aragaki and Higaonna learned the white crane based forms (Sanchin, Seishan, Jutte, Niseishi, Useishi). It was introduced by a master named Ason.

As well as Naihanchi, it was also written as Naifanchin, which may be translated as "inner claws." This may suggest that it is was derived from one of the animal boxing forms such as lion boxing or tiger boxing. I have theorised elsewhere than one of the styles many of our forms derived from was lion boxing. The name lion can be written in the Fujian dialect as Sai, and in Japanese as Shizhi. Could Naihanchi be some version of this? Perhaps Naihanshi?

Another theory which seems to deserve serious consideration was presented in the 1960s after a Kung Fu practitioner, Daichi Kaneko, studied a form of Taiwanese White Crane Boxing, known as Dan Qiu Ban Bai He Quan (Half Hillock, Half White Crane Boxing). Kaneko, an acupuncturist who lived in Yonabaru, Okinawa, taught a form called Neixi (inside knee) in Mandarin. This form includes the same sweeping action found in the nami-gaeshi (returning wave) technique of Naihanchi. Neixi is apparently pronounced Nohanchi in Fuzhou dialect, which could indicate Neixi is the forerunner to Naihanchi.

Shuri Te

Shuri martial arts trace back to Bushi Matsumura. According to Funakoshi, his teacher Azato was a dedicated student of Matsumura. The sense of Shuri Te is that of professional soldiers and court employees. Matsuo Kanenori Sakon writes: *"The Shuri Bushi who worked under the scribes and treasurers and justice officers, and also worked as castle guards, tax collectors, finance officers, or agriculture and forestry officers studied a martial art which was characterised by the horse riding stance and fast, light techniques."*

Bassai

The kata Bassai is often cited as having been developed by Sokon Matsumura and it remains one of the most important kata in the Shoto and Shorin Ryu family. It is almost always a requirement for blackbelt in Shotokan. We do not know for sure whether Matsumura created it, learned it from Sakugawa, Iwah, Yabiku or someone else, but there are clues we can pursue.

Kanazawa states that Bassai was present in other styles passed down by Itosu, Matsumura, Oyadomari and Ishimine. He adds: *"Does this mean that the influence of Bassai Dai leans more towards the Tomari Te style of Master Oyadomari? If not perhaps the Shuri Te style linked to master Itosu? We can state with a considerable degree of confidence that this kata is not related to the Naha Te style."*

When Bassai was introduced to the wider public most translated the name as "Penetrate the Fortress" when actually the Kanji seem to read nothing of the sort. Bassai is comprised of the characters Batsu (also pronounced Nukitsu) which means withdraw (a drawing cut in Iaido is called Nukitsuke); and Sai which means obstruct. Bassai therefore means to withdraw and obstruct. However, Funakoshi uses the character Chai (fortress) rather than Sai and it has been argued that "to blockade a fortress" is a reasonable translation. However it is possible that in the days when few martial artists could read or write, Bassai meant nothing of the sort. In Taijiquan the move Lan Za Yi (lazily tying the coat) was misheard in another region of the country as Lan que wei (grasp sparrow's tail) – thereby completely changing the meaning of the move. Likewise with Dao Jun Hao and Dao Jun Hong – changing the meaning of the move from "repulse the monkey" to "whirl the arms".

There is a style in China called Baji Quan (originally Bazi Quan) which has forms called Baji Da and Baji Xiao. An Okinawan like Matsumura could have easily misheard Bazi Da as Bassai Dai and Bazi Xiao as Bassai Sho.

It may be that Bazi Quan originally meant White Lion Boxing. Okinawan Karate researcher Akio Kinjo pointed out that Bassai shares techniques with Lion Boxing. The Chinese word for white is pai or bai and in the Fujian dialect "lion" is "sai" so Baisai or Paisai would mean White Lion. As we discovered in the earlier chapter, in the 1600s a Japanese physician named Akiyama went to China and studied a fighting art which, depending on how the Kanji is translated, can be called Hakuda, Hakushi, Shubaku or Baida.

So what was this Te that Hakuda founder Akiyama studied? Could it be the elusive White Lion Boxing? The Shi in Hakushi is the same as the Fujian Sai (lion). The syllables "Bai shi da" seen in "baida, hakushi, hakuda" are homonyms of Bassai Dai (white lion hand – rather than blockade the fortress major).

In the Bubishi Patrick McCarthy discusses extant forms of Crane, Lion, Tiger, Monk and Dog boxing and which Quan/kata they use. He reports: *"There are four other styles of Crane Boxing each of which use their own Sanchin Kata, and one also uses Sanseiryu and Niseishi. Dragon Boxing uses Seishan, Suparimpei, Sanchin....Tiger Boxing also uses Sanchin, Sanseiryu and Suparimpei.... Monk Fist uses Sanchin, Seishan, Jutte, Seipai, Useishi and Suparimpei....Lion Boxing uses Sanchin and Seishan among others..."*

According to my calculations Bushi Matsumura of Shuri and Bushi Kojo of Kume went to Fujian in 1828. Matsumura was already a formidable fighter in his prime (aged about 30). He had been taught Te and Bojutsu by Sakugawa and Yabiku.

At the "Kojo Dojo" in Fujian, Matsumura and his friend were exposed to various Chinese forms, which we now think included the following forms: Sanchin, Seishan, Jutte, Useishi (Gojushiho), Peichurin (Suparimpei).

While it is likely Matsumura studied Seisan, Jutte and Gojushiho while staying at the Kojo Dojo it would appear that something else inspired him more. That something was the form we now know as Bassai. When Matsumura returned to Okinawa he was not a professional Karate instructor. There was no Shuri Te, no Naha Te and no Tomari Te. Instead there were civilians, and there were professional fighters. Matsumura was the latter. His job was literally to prevent people storming the fortress and perhaps this is where we get that name for Bassai.

Anko Azato (1827-1906)

Anko Azato was the son of a Tonichi, one of the two highest classes of the Okinawan society, and was born in the town of Azato. He was advisor to the Okinawan king in military subjects and one of the greatest experts of Karate, horse riding, kendo and archery.

His older son's teaching in the martial arts was left in the capable hands of Yasutsune Itosu.

He was very strict in his teaching method. He would have students repeating once and again the same kata; from him the rule of three years per kata arose.

Azato maintained a very complete registry of all the martial artists of the island; in these he would detail their abilities and defects. He used to say "Know yourself and your enemy: this is the secret key of strategy".

One day he was challenged by Yorin Kanna, the most famous sword trainee of Okinawa, and even though Azato was an expert in Jigen Ryu kenjutsu, he confronted his adversary unarmed. Kanna was known for his enormous strength. He attacked Azato again and again and each time Azato would throw him almost without effort. Azato took the sword out of its trajectory and immobilised Kanna.

In a 1934 article, Funakoshi noted that Azato and Itosu had studied Karate together under Sokon Matsumura. He also related how Azato and Itosu once overcame a group of 20-30 attackers, and how Azato set a trap for troublemakers in his home village.

In his 1956 autobiography, Funakoshi recounted several stories about Azato, including Azato's political astuteness in following the government order to cut off the traditional men's topknot.

Funakoshi's rival Choki Motobu was complimentary of Azato saying: *"The venerable Azato had a light body and a fast technique."*

His given name Anko can be pronounced Yasutsune in Japanese but it is doubtful he used this pronunciation. According to Funakoshi, *"he used the pen name Rinkakusai when signing the plethora of literary compositions he authored"* and *"Since his youth Azato has been referred to as the child prodigy because he excelled in both the fighting traditions and in literary studies."*

Azato's father was the local village chieftain, or according to Funakoshi, *"held an honourable rank of Keimochi, not unlike that of a lower Daimyo in Japanese society."* It is likely Azato began his martial arts training in about 1840 aged 13 since this would seem to be the accepted age to begin study. We know of no other teacher of Azato in Karate, other than one Sokon Matsumura and so it would seem this is who taught him.

Funakoshi writes that Azato, *"had diligently studied the martial arts under the strict tutelage of Masumura Soken. An advocate of the Chinese ways. Instruction under that taskmaster was always conducted early in the morning before dawn until the sun came up, without change or observation of holidays. During these times, Azato Sensei was also studying at the National school where he was peerless. Particularly, in the study of the Chinese classics, Azato was an honour student and received financial scholarship amounting to more than his tuition."*

It is believed Matsumura knew the forms Naihanchi and Bassai, more than likely Kushanku and probably a few others. But the kata that history most strongly links him with are Seisan and Useishi (Gojushiho). It seems likely Matsumura learnt these forms from Iwah in around 1828 so when Azato came to study with him in around 1840 he was probably an experienced teacher of them.

Azato was a keen horseman. Gichin Funakoshi writes: *"Excelling in various martial arts, Sensei was particularly fond of horsemanship, which he studied under Megata Sensei, the trainer who groomed the Meiji Emperor himself. Sensei apparently decided to pursue Megata's tutelage because his horsemanship was the trendy style being introduced from the West, which really appealed to a stalwart like Azato. Master Azato first observed Megata giving a lesson to a few students on the grounds next to the Hirakawa Emperor's gate. Mr. Megata could tell that Sensei wanted to give the new saddle a try but was too modest to ask, so the trainer asked him instead. With some coaxing, Sensei finally accepted and was applauded by Megata for his brilliant performance and command over the reins. I think that Azato was a perfect example of the expression, "A person who excels in one thing can excel at everything."*

According to Funakoshi, Azato was also a keen archer. He said: *"Sensei also loved archery and diligently studied under Master Sekiguchi, and like his teacher (Matsumura Sokon) before him, so did Azato study Jigen Ryu swordsmanship directly under the noted Japanese instructor Ishuin Yashichiro. However, among all the combative disciplines, it was the swordsmanship of Jigenryu that Sensei most favoured. I remember that whenever Sensei got excited he used to say to me, "I'm ready to compete anytime if the opponent is serious." In my opinion, Sensei was peerless in Karate but judging by his preoccupation with Jigen Ryu, swordsmanship was his real passion."*

Gichin Funakoshi told us that he and Azato's son Anri would go and train with Itosu together. But what became of Azato's son? If we imagine he was born between Azato's 16th and 40th birthdays, he would have been born between 1843 and 1867. Because Funakoshi was born in 1868, we suggest Azato's son may have been born closer to that date. If Azato's son was born in the 1860s, then his children would have been born in around the 1890s or early 1900s. That grandson, named Yoriyuki, became a Karate teacher and moved to Japan. There the name Azato became Yorisato. He was close to Funakoshi and so probably taught in around the 1930s-1950s. In turn his son in law has taken the mantle of the school, which is known as Shobukan.

Azato liked to train with Hoju Undo equipment. Funakoshi wrote: *"His home virtually looked like one big training facility. Both standing and hanging makiwara (impact training equipment) were located in various rooms of the Azato residence along with other training equipment, which included wooden cudgels (club) and swords of various configurations, a wooden-man, stone weights, iron balls for grip-strength development, shield and machete, flails, iron truncheons, and even a wooden horse for mounting practice and archery spotting. Master Azato had created a living environment where he could train at anytime and anywhere he liked."*

Gichin Funakoshi striking the makiwara

SHURI TE LINEAGE

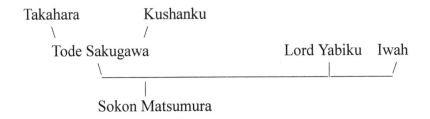

Notable students of Matsumura:

Anko Azato   Anko Itosu
Kentsu Yabu   Chotoku Kyan
Motobu Choyu   Motobu Choki
Gichin Funakoshi Nabe Matsumura
Sakihara Pechin   Kiyuna Pechin
Chomo Hanashiro Ryosei Kuwae
Ishimine Pechin

The author teaching bunkai for Shuri Te's most advanced form Gojushiho to World Kata champion and Danish national team member Kicki Holm who studied under Hirokazu Kanazawa.

Tomari Te and Shorin Ryu

Matsumura was beginning to teach what became known as Shuri Te while teachers like Ki Teruya and Karyu Ure were teaching Tomari Te.

Matsuo Kanenori Sakon writes: *"The Tomari Bushi worked in domestic law enforcement, public welfare, construction as well as guarding the Chinese Sappushi, Satsuma envoys and Satsuma administrative office in Ryukyu, studied an art that stressed the ability to stand on the boats that travelled the two rivers that spanned between Shuri Castle, Naha Port and Tomari Port."*

Throughout the 1840s and 1850s there were further "Naha Te" advances concerning the Kojo family and we will return to them in due course.

But first we have a development in Tomari that will once again change the shape of Karate Jutsu.

In 1854 another Chinese master arrived in Okinawa, this time in Tomari. His name was Anan (also recorded as Chinto or 'the Southern Chinese').

Anan did not teach a powerful bombastic style like Bassai, or a steady, short range, rooted style like Naihanchi. Neither did he teach an internal power form such as Kushanku or Wansu.

Anan of Taiwan taught a dynamic form called White Heron. He stood on the rocks in Tomari like a heron and Okinawa was captivated by him. And ever since, Karate has been synonymous with White Crane Boxing.

Anan was the creator of the form known as Chinto (called Gankaku in Shotokan). According to legend, it is named after a Chinese sailor, sometimes referred to as Anan, whose ship crashed on the Okinawan coast. To survive, Chinto stole from the crops of the local people. Matsumura Sokon, a Karate master and chief bodyguard to the Okinawan king, was sent to defeat Chinto. In the ensuing fight, however, Matsumura found himself equally matched by the stranger, and consequently sought to learn his techniques. Some suggest that it was not Sokon Matsumura that met with Anan, but Kosaku Matsumora.

Anan seemingly taught not only Chinto but also Chinte and Rohai.

Rohai, known in Japan as "Meikyo" (mirror) is often translated as "vision of a heron" but Rohai could easily be a corruption of Lohan. So perhaps Anan taught Eighteen Monk Fist Boxing (Lohan Quan).

Kosaku Matsumora

The most famous Tomari-te masters were the chikundun peikin Kosaku Matsumora (1829-1898), Kokan Oyadomari (1827-1905) and Gikei Yamazato (1835-1905). They were also disciples of Anan/Chinto.

According to Tomari-te tradition, Anan was a castaway from a shipwreck in the Okinawa coast. Being a pirate, he took refuge in the cemetery of the Tomari's mountains, starting to live in a cave. Matsumora and Oyadomari were also disciples from two local masters, Kishin Teruya (1804-1864) and Giko Uku (1800-1850).

From Teruya they would learn Passai, Rohai, and Wanshu, and with Uku the kata Naifanchi. According to Shoshin Nagamine (*Tales of Okinawa's Great Masters*) Teruya was considered by Matsumora as his true master. Matsumora was also an expert in Jo-jutsu (short staff) from Jigen-ryu.

A history repeated in several Okinawan sources teaches that the successor of Anan was Kosaku Matsumora. A little before coming back to China, Anan gave to Matsumora a parchment with a drawing of a woman in a fighting posture holding a willow branch in one of the hands.

The interesting thing here is that in Japan, the school of Hakuda that became known as Yoshin Ryu was also symbolised by the willow.

Could this finally confirm the link between Akiyama's Hakuda and Okinawan Karate?

Anan or Chinto: Southern Chinese Shorin Ryu master of Tomari

Kushanku and Channan were the original Shuri forms, it would seem Seisan was the original Naha form, and then Gojushiho and Naihanchi became core Shorin and Shorei forms, but from where did the Tomari Te forms originate? From, it seems a "Southern Chinese" otherwise identified as Anan or Chinto.

Funakoshi tells us: *"It is said that a teacher of Gusukuma, Kanagusuku, Matsumora, Oyatomari, Yamada, Nakazato and Toguchi, all of Tomari, was a southern Chinese who drifted ashore at Okinawa."*

Hirokazu Kanazawa refers to Wansu (Empi), Jion, Ji'in, Jutte, Chinto (Gankaku), Chinte and Rohai (Meikyo) as Tomari kata and writes: *"Chinto is an old Tomari based kata that has been passed down to the Shotokan and Shito Ryu styles. While details regarding its creator and origins are not well known, historical evidence indicates that it was passed down to the early Tomari Te master Kosaku Matsumora, after which modifications were introduced by Masters Chotoku Kiyatake and Yasutsune Itosu."*

Kanazawa reasons that Jutte and its related forms originate in a Buddhist Temple. He writes: *"Jion, Jutte and Ji'in which belong to the same family of kata are all believed to have come from the Tomari region. Long ago it was commonly thought that these kata had come from China... Further reinforcing this view was a Buddhist temple bearing the name JionJi (literally Jion temple) which was known for its tradition of martial arts. Today however, the correct assumption appears to be that these kata originated at Jionji and from there were conveyed to the Tomari region."*

This allows us to see how the family of katas came together in the mid 1800s:

Matsumura's probable repertoire (early Shuri Te):

Channan	From Sakugawa
Kushanku	From Sakugawa or Yara
Bassai	From Yabiku or Sakugawa
Seisan	From Iwah
Naihanchi	From Ason via Sakiyama
Useishi	From Iwah or Ason

The probable repertoire of Gusukuma and Kosaku Matsumura (early Tomari Te):

Chinto	From Anan
Chinte	From Anan
Jion, Jin, Jutte	From Monk Fist Boxing
Rohai	From Monk Fist Boxing

Rohai seems mostly likely to be a linguistic corruption derived from 'monk' (Lohan) with Lohan becoming Lohai and then becoming Rohai. The Okinawans would often pronounce L as R, hence the Europeans who discovered Ryukyu islands writing "Lew Chew" on their maps.

In a 1914 article Funakoshi recalls Azato telling him who learned which kata from the 'castaway [from] Annan'. He wrote: *"Gusukuma and Kanagusuku (Chinto), Matsumora and Oyadomari (Chinte), Yamasato (Jiin) and Nakasato (Jitte) all of Tomari (Okinawa), who learned the kata separately. The reason being that their teacher was in a hurry to return to his home country."*

Anko Itosu (1831-1915)

Yasutsune Itosu was born in 1831 and died in 1915.

Itosu was small in stature, shy, and introverted as a child. He was raised in a strict home of the keimochi (a family of position), and was educated in the Chinese classics and calligraphy. Itosu began his study under Nagahama Chikudun Pechin. His study of the art led him to Sokon Matsumura. Part of Itosu's training was makiwara practice. He once tied a leather sandal to a stone wall in an effort to build a better makiwara. After several strikes, the wall was demolished. Itosu certainly had that iron fist punching power that the old Okinawans admired. Itosu served as a secretary to the last king of the Ryukyu Islands until Japan abolished the Okinawa-based native monarchy in 1879. In 1901, he was instrumental in getting Karate introduced into Okinawa's schools.

In 1905, Itosu was a part-time teacher of Te at Okinawa's First Junior Prefectural High School. It was here that he developed the systematic method of teaching Karate techniques that are still in practice today. He created and introduced the Pinan forms (Heian in Japanese) as learning steps for students, because he felt the older forms (Kata in Japanese) were too difficult for schoolchildren to learn. In 1908, Itosu wrote the influential "Ten Precepts (Tode Jukun) of Karate," reaching beyond Okinawa to Japan.

Notable students of Itosu include:

Kentsu Yabu	Choki Motobu	Shigeru Nakamura
Hanashiro Chomo	Kenwa Mabuni	Moden Yabiku
Gichin Funakoshi	Kanken Toyama	Anbun Tokuda
Shinpan Shiroma	Choshin Chibana	
Chojo Oshiro	Jiro Shiroma	

Itosu himself set about creating new forms. He increased the number of Pinan forms to five, added Kushanku Sho to go with Kushanku, and perhaps created Chinte to go with Chinto.

The Itosu school of Shuri/Tomari Te included around 20 kata including:

Pinan 1-5 (Heian)
Naihanchi 1-3 (Tekki)
Bassai Dai and Sho
Kanku Dai and Sho
Jutte, Jin, Jion
Wansu (Empi)
Chinto (Gankaku)
Chinte
Gojushiho

TOMARI TE LINEAGE

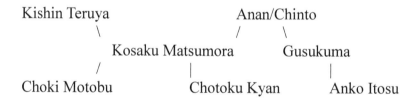

ITOSU'S 10 PRECEPTS OF KARATE

1.   Karate is not merely practised for your own benefit; it can be used to protect one's family or master. It is not intended to be used against a single assailant but instead as a way of avoiding a fight should one be confronted by a villain or ruffian.
2.   The purpose of Karate is to make the muscles and bones hard as rock and to use the hands and legs as spears. If children were to begin training in Tang Te while in elementary school, then they will be well suited for military service. Remember the words attributed to

the Duke of Wellington after he defeated Napoleon: *"The Battle of Waterloo was won on the playing fields of Eton."*

3.   Karate cannot be quickly learned. Like a slow moving bull, it eventually travels a thousand miles. If one trains diligently every day, then in three or four years one will come to understand Karate. Those who train in this fashion will discover Karate.

4.   In Karate, training of the hands and feet are important, so one must be thoroughly trained on the makiwara. In order to do this, drop your shoulders, open your lungs, take hold of your strength, grip the floor with your feet, and sink your energy into your lower abdomen. Practise using each arm one to two hundred times each day.

5.   When one practises the stances of Karate, be sure to keep your back straight, lower your shoulders, put strength in your legs, stand firmly, and drop your energy into your lower abdomen.

6.   Practise each of the techniques of Karate repeatedly, the use of which is passed by word of mouth. Learn the explanations well, and decide when and in what manner to apply them when needed. Enter, counter, release is the rule of releasing hand (*torite*).

7.   You must decide if Karate is for your health or to aid your duty.

8.   When you train, do so as if on the battlefield. Your eyes should glare, shoulders drop, and body harden. You should always train with intensity and spirit, and in this way you will naturally be ready.

9.   One must not overtrain; this will cause you to lose the energy in your lower abdomen and will be harmful to your body. Your face and eyes will turn red. Train wisely.

10.   In the past, masters of Karate have enjoyed long lives. Karate aids in developing the bones and muscles. It helps the digestion as well as the circulation. If Karate should be introduced beginning in the elementary schools, then we will produce many men each capable of defeating ten assailants. I further believe this can be done by having all students at the Okinawa Teachers' College practise Karate. In this way, after graduation, they can teach at the elementary schools at which they have been taught. I believe this will be a great benefit to our nation and our military. It is my hope you will seriously consider my suggestion.

Shorei Ryu and Naha Te

While the Karate of Shuri was taking shape under Matsumura and the Karate of Tomari under Matsumora, a student of Aragaki Seisho named Higaonna Kanryo decided to follow in the footsteps of Aragaki, Matsumura and Kojo and go to train in Fujian. This was an early example of Naha Te.

Matsuo Kanenori Sakon writes: *"Especially those in the trade and foreign relations posts would leave from Naha port once every two years and travel to Fujian. Then, 30 members, including envoys... would then move to Beijing while the rest stayed on at the Ryukyukan dormitory in Fuzhou... One ship was manned by over 150 guards, in order to protect the tribute ship from the threat of pirates. These guards were Naha Bushi, and in order to be able to effectively deliver a powerful technique on a rocking boat, their training stressed such methods as Sanchin stance..."*

Waishinzan

While Iwah, Ason and Anan are ancestral figures in Shuri Te and Tomati Te, Waishinzan seems to have influenced the Karateka of Naha. Funakoshi tells us: *"Shimabuku of Uemonden, and Higa, Seneha, Gushi, Nagahama, Aragaki, Higaonna and Kuwae all of Kunenboya, with the military attache Waishinzan."*

We have already determined that Gushi had studied under Ason in around 1850. And we have determined that Aragaki was teaching in 1867 and that Higaonna was his student. We can therefore work out that between 1853 and 1867 – let's say 1860 - Seisho Aragaki went to China and studied under Waishinzan who was likely an instructor at the Kojo Dojo in Fujian, junior to Iwah but senior to the later Ryuru Ko. Kanazawa refers to Sochin as belonging to the 'Aragaki faction', and says Nijushiho "belongs to the Nigaki family of kata along with Sochin." He says Unsu is "not believed to be very old" and is "thought to belong to the Aragaki family of kata."

Timeline of Chinese martial arts (Tang Shou) introduced to Okinawa before 1870:

17th century
1683   Wang Ji visits Okinawa and witnesses martial arts training

18th century
1756   Kushanku and/or Wang Zong Yue visit Okinawa and teach Sakugawa/Yara

19th century
1828   Bushi Matsumura of Shuri and Bushi Kojo of Kume train under Iwah
1850   Ason comes to Naha and teaches Sakiyama, Gushi and Tomoyori
1855   Anan comes to Tomari and teaches Matsumora of Tomari
1860   Aragaki trains under Waishinzan

Higaonna Naha Te

According to Iken Tokashiki, Higaonna Kanryo was born at Nishimura of Naha City as the the 11th generation junior sibling of the Higaonna family. The name Higaonna is also written Higashionna.

Higaonna visited Fuchou, China, around 1877 for three years. Some make him sound like a humble wood cutter learning some Kung Fu from a man named Ryuru Ko. Others suggest it was a diplomatic mission based on allying Ryukyu to China rather than Japan.

Another man from Naha named Nakaima Norisato (later of Ryuei Ryu) made a similar training trip and he too trained with Ryuru Ko. This gives us two independent sources for Ryuru Ko. By looking at what the two sources share, we can start to understand what they likely learned from their Chinese teacher.

Higaonna Kanryo: Pioneer of Naha Te

After Higaonna's return to Okinawa he eventually began to teach what became known as Naha Te, as contrasted with Shuri Te and Tomari Te.

Koryu Uchinadi pioneer Patrick McCarthy has suggested that Ryuru Ko was none other than Xie Zhongxiang, the founder of Ming He Quan (Whooping Crane Kung Fu). McCarthy Hanshi suggests that Ryuru Ko was just a nickname meaning 'elder brother' and that Whooping Crane is therefore the direct ancestor of Goju Ryu. This view is shared by Hokama Sensei of the Okinawan Karate Museum.

Whooping Crane (also called Calling Crane or Screaming Crane) was based on the Fujian White Crane that Xie Zhongxiang learned from his teacher Pan Yuban whose teacher was Lin Shixian (who was a student of Fāng Qī Niáng, the originator of the first White Crane martial art). This would then give Goju Ryu and Naha Te a very complete, very direct lineage back to the very founder of the White Crane style.

The theory goes that Xie Zongxiang had to conceal his name and aristocratic lineage and took on the name Ryuru Ko, under which he worked, making household goods from bamboo and cane. He had been teaching martial arts at his home to a very small group of students, which included Higaonna who stayed with Ryuru Ko from 1870 to 1881. Ryuru Ko expanded his class to an actual public school

"The Kojo Dojo" in 1883, running it with Wai Shinzan, possibly a student of Iwah. Whether Ryuru Ko was actually Xie or not, it does seem likely that he, Wai Shinzan and Iwah were indeed part of the same Fujian community that welcomed the likes of Kojo, Aragaki, Higaonna and Norisato.

The Bubishi

We cannot tell the story of Karate without referring to Okinawa's Bubishi. This book was an anthology of southern Chinese martial arts and medicine that was regarded as a 'Bible' by many Karate masters throughout the generations.

The Bubishi is one of the most valuable books a Karateka can possess. It is also of tremendous value to practitioners of Wing Chun, Hung Gar and White Crane. The book "The Bubishi" is sometimes called *The Bible of Karate*. It is to Karate what the "Book of Five Rings" is to the samurai. Like the Bible, the Bubishi is an anthology of older stories pieced together and edited on one theme to act as a guide. Most old Karate masters valued it, including masters Funakoshi, Miyagi and Mabuni, the founders of the three biggest schools, Shotokan, Goju Ryu and Shito Ryu. Bubishi comprised some of the traditions of the original styles that influenced Karate including White Crane, Black Tiger and Monk Fist boxing. The Bubishi contains anatomical diagrams, philosophical essays, defensive tactical strategies, and poetry.

The first chapter of Bubishi is entitled "The Origins of White Crane Boxing," and tells us that the White Crane style was founded by a woman, Feng Chi Niang, who seems to be the same character as the woman who created Wing Chun, Fong Chut-Neung (and her successor would seem to be identical with the man who created Hung Gar, a form of Tiger boxing). The Bubishi therefore demonstrates that Karate, White Crane, Wing Chun and Tiger Boxing have a common origin.

The Bubishi has thirty-two chapters dealing with the history of White Crane Boxing; advice and observations from Master Wang Yo Teng; information on vital spots and how to attack them; time strikes; grappling arts; six turning hands; 54 steps of the Black Tiger hand; Sun Tzu's comments on war; and a variety of chapters dealing with herbal medicine and combat techniques. In 1922 Funakoshi published one of the first books on Karate in Japan, *Ryukyu Kenpo Toudi*. Four chapters from the Bubishi were included at the end of the book, but the Bubishi itself was not named. In 1934 when Kenwa Mabuni published *Seipai No Kenkyu* (Study of Seipai) the Bubishi was named. Mabuni included the drawings from five chapters from Anko Itosu's copy of the Bubishi.

The Bubishi was translated into Japanese by the Goju master Tadahiko Ohtsuka and the English translation was by Patrick McCarthy. In Hanshi McCarthy's copy of the Bubishi there are at least ten different theories as to how the Bubishi arrived in Okinawa. Tode Sakugawa, Sokon Matsumura, Yasutsune Itosu and Higaonna Kanryo are all candidates for its introduction. Kenwa Mabuni had a copy given to him by Itosu so this would seem to indicate it had been in Okinawa a long time. Other outside possibilities are that it was introduced to Okinawa in the early 20th century by either White Crane master Gokenki or Tiger Boxing master Tang Daiji (To Daiki). Another possibility is that it came to Okinawa via the Feeding Crane lineage now headquartered in Taiwan.

Kojo Lineage	**Ryuei Ryu lineage**
Kojo Uekata	Ryuru Ko
Kojo Pechin	Norisato Nakaima
Shoi Sai (1816-1906)	Nakaima Kenchu
Kojo Isei (1832-1891)	Nakaima Kenko
Kojo Kaho (1849-1925)	Nakaima Kenji
Kojo Saikyo (1873-1941)	
Kojo Kafu	

Goju Ryu

Chojun Miyagi was born in Naha City, Okinawa on April 25, 1888. He began training in Karate under Higaonna in 1902 and until 1915. Today 13 years hardly seems like a long time to master a martial art, but we must remember there were far fewer other distractions and his study was likely to be far more intensive than the kind of "two hours on a Tuesday night" that can take people to black belt today! But regardless of this, Higaonna was not the only teacher of Miyagi and the year Higaonna died Miyagi journeyed to Fuzhou, China, the city where his teacher had studied the martial arts, to further his own research. On his return to Okinawa, he began to teach the martial arts at his home in Naha.

Later, he also taught at the Okinawan Prefecture Police Training Centre, at the Okinawan Master's Training College, and at the Naha Commercial High School.

In 1921, Miyagi was chosen to represent Naha-te in a presentation to the visiting crown prince Hirohito. In recognition of his leadership in spreading Karate in Japan, his style, eventually called Goju Ryu, became the first style to be officially recognised by the Dai Nippon Butokukai.

Miyagi revised and further developed Sanchin - the hard aspect of Goju, and created Tensho (from the older form Rokusho) - the soft aspect. The highest kata, Suparinpei, is said to contain the full syllabus of Goju-ryu. Shisochin was Miyagi's favourite kata at the end of his years.

And here we come once again to tatemae and honne. The Goju Ryu tatemae is that Miyagi was taught by Higaonna and he by Ryuryu Ko, but actually Aragaki was a main influence on Higaonna, and a man named Gokenki was a major influence on Miyagi.

Wu Xiangi or Wu Hsien Kuei, best known as Gokenki, was a Chinese tea merchant and White Crane practitioner. Gokenki worked for the Eiko Chako Tea Company and taught White Crane in Okinawa between 1912 and his death in 1940.

Gokenki was an enormous influence on many Karateka, and like the Bubishi he was a tangible link to the art of White Crane Quan Fa. Among his students were Chojun Miyagi (later founder of Goju Ryu), Kenwa Mabuni (later founder of Shito Ryu) and Hohan Soken (student of Nabe Matsumura).

Chojun Miyagi

A colleague of Gokenki who also taught in Okinawa was Tang Daiji, an underestimated influence on the history of Goju Ryu.

Tang Daiji or To Daiki (1887-1937) was from Fuzhou. In 1915 he came to Naha and opened a tea shop (Showacha-ten) with his cousin To Daisho (Japanese reading of his name).

The Tang family, whose name was also spelled To, included various Tiger style boxers across Fujian and Guangzhou.

Goju Ryu kata like Suparimpei contain both White Crane and Tiger boxing techniques, a possible homage to both Gokenki and Tang.

The Goju Ryu system flourished in the Kansai area of Japan and

111

Miyagi had an agreeable relationship with Mabuni Kenwa and Motobu Choki.

Miyagi died on October 8, 1953, of either a heart attack or a cerebral haemorrhage at the age of 65. Today the art of Goju Ryu is one of the most popular Karate systems in the world and in almost every Goju Ryu Dojo hangs the portrait of Miyagi Chojun and Higaonna Kanryo.

Feeding Crane and Uechi Ryu

We now return to the Fujian White Crane systems and specifically four masters who established the Feeding Crane branch.

In 1922 four practitioners of White Crane from Fujian arrived in Taiwan. They were Er-Gau, Yi-Gau, A-Fong and Lin De Shun.

Kennedy and Guo emphasise the importance of Taiwan in the preservation of martial arts: *"Taiwan served as a repository of a wide range of systems during a time when the martial arts were being suppressed in China."*

After his arrival in Taiwan, Lin De Shun came to be regarded as the grandmaster of Feeding Crane or Shi He Quan. He started to work for a sugar company and in 1927 Liú Gù (1900-1965) heard about the skills of that master, and immediately invited him to be his teacher, offering some expensive gifts. Liu learnt the full syllabus and became the next grandmaster.

An interesting aspect of Liu family Shi He Quan is that the family had a book called *The Secret Shaolin Bronze Man Book* (Tong Ren Bu) – apparently almost identical to the Bubishi.

In his commentary of the Bubishi, Patrick McCarthy recalls:*"Having met Liu Yinshan's brother, Liu Songshan in Fuzhou, I came to learn of a "secret book" on gongfu that had been in the Liu family for the last seven decades. After meeting him in Fuzhou, hosting him at my home in Japan and visiting him in Taiwan, I have become familiar with that book, entitled The Secret Shaolin Bronze Man Book and can testify that it is, in almost every way, identical to the Bubishi. Master Liu's Bubishi is divided into 17 articles in three sections, whereas the Okinawan Bubishi contains 32 articles. However the same data is covered in both works though it is categorized differently."*

Kennedy and Guo are dismissive of its secrets however, saying,

"Over the years I have had the chance to view a couple of these secret training manuals and I can assure you, at least for the ones I have seen, they contain nothing particularly unique."

We know that the Bubishi – an anthology of Fujian Quan Fa – was considered the Bible of Karate and we see its link with Whooping Crane (through Ryuryu Ko and Higaonna) and with Feeding Crane (through the Liu family) – but could there be more to the crane family than meets the eye?

The Tiger-Crane connection

The founder of White Crane is said to be a woman called Fang Qi Niang and the founder of Wing Chun is said to be a woman called Fong Chut-Neung (alt. Fong Wing Chun or Ng Mui). So could the founder of Wing Chun and the founder of White Crane be the same woman?

In the Hung Gar stories, the Tiger Fist master Hung Hei Gun marries Fong and she teaches him. In White Crane stories, the Tiger Fist master Ceng Si Chu (Zeng Cishu) meets Fang and she teaches him. So could the Tiger master and the Crane lady be the same in both styles?

Could it be that all the three southern Kung Fu styles of Tiger Fist (Hung Gar), Wing Chun and White Crane are all related? On the surface at least it seems that the idea of a man using Tiger Fist and a woman using White Crane Fist are perfect analogies for the hard and the soft or Yin and Yang. If this is the case, perhaps we should regard Hung Gar and Wing Chun as immediate relations of Goju Ryu as well.

Uechi Ryu

Another tiger style that influenced both Karate (Uechi Ryu) and Feeding Crane was taught by Zhou Zi He (in Japanese Shu Shi Wa). Zhou Zi He was one of the teachers of Feeding Crane founder Ye Shaotao as well as Uechi Ryu founder Uechi Kanbun.

Following in the footsteps of Aragaki and Higaonna, Uechi Kanbun arrived in Fujian and like them settled at the Ryukyukan, a Okinawan enclave of buildings including a boarding house, homes and businesses established for those who visited and lived in the area –

including the famous Kojo Dojo.

Uechi didn't like training at the Kojo Dojo because he was bullied, so eventually he went elsewhere and became the student of Shu Shi Wa or Zhou Zhi He. Uechi's teacher, Zhou Zhi He (1874-1926) originated from Minhou, Fujian. He reportedly studied martial arts under Li Zhao Bei and Ke Xi Di and was proficient in a variety of Quan.

The style Zhou Zhi He taught Uechi was called Pangainoon. It was related to another style called Kingainoon. It is clear that the style Uechi learned in China and the style that Higaonna learned in China were related. Is it possible that while Uechi learnt Pangainoon, Higaonna learned Kingainoon?

It has also been speculated that Gokenki and Tang Daiji were students of Zhou. If this is the case, then Zhou Zhi He is perhaps the true forefather of both Goju Ryu and Uechi Ryu.

The only kata Uechi Ryu has in common with Goju Ryu are Sanchin, Seisan and Sanseiru so it could be that these forms are either the ones that both founders learned at the Kojo Dojo or else are the ones that Pangainoon and Kingainoon taught.

The styles were brought together somewhat neatly in the mid 20th century by Goju master Tadanori Nobetsu (10th Dan Kokusai Budoin) who made efforts to study Feeding Crane Quan Fa to return Goju Ryu to its Naha Te origins, calling his school Nisseikai. Nobetsu Hanshi is now chief director of Kokusai Budoin, inheriting the Goju Ryu division from Yamaguchi Gogen.

In an Ikaigaiway.com interview Kimo Wall, a senior Goju Ryu practitioner who trained in Okinawa under the likes of Higa Seiko, told how his Kobudo teacher Matayoshi Shinpo had studied Kingai Ryu.

According to Wall, Kingai Ryu was the style Gokenki taught. He said: *"The Kingai Ryu was taught to* [Matayoshi] *by Gokenki, a Chinese immigrant from Fuchou, Fukien, China.*

"Matayoshi Kin Gai Ryu is a very powerful and complete system. Gokenki taught several people his system, especially Matayoshi Shinko. I know Shinko Sensei was a top student of Gokenki."

Fred Lohse (5th Dan Matayoshi writing in *Meibukan* magazine) offers an alternative account of Kingai Ryu. *"The most common understanding of Kingai-ryu is that it is the unarmed art passed down in the Matayoshi family, stemming from the instruction Shinko Matayoshi received from Roshi Kingai, his teacher in China. However, this initial assumption is incorrect. The Kingai-ryu as taught by Roshi*

114

Kingai is not a solely unarmed style; it includes the use of weaponry, such as the nunti, tinbe, suruchin, and shuriken.

"Shinko Matayoshi traveled to Fuchow on the recommendation of his friend Kenki Go, arriving sometime around 1907-08. In Fuchow, he took up residence with Koki Go, Kenki Go's father. Koki Go soon introduced Shinko to a friend and fellow martial artist, Roshi Kingai. Kingai is said to have been a well known martial artist in the Fuchow area, and is supposed to have been a senior to the same Shu Shi Wa (Zhou Zeihe) that was Kanbun Uechi's teacher in Fuchow. Kingai referred to his system as Kingai-ryu."

In translating Chinese to Japanese dialects, the L and R are often swapped. So the Ryukyu islands became the Lew Chew islands. In this case, perhaps the name of Ryuru Ko was actually Liu Lu Ko. This would suggest that Ryuru was actually of the Liu family who introduced Feeding Crane to Taiwan. Was the man who taught Higaonna actually part of the Liu family?

Higa Seiko, Mabuni Kenwa, Miyagi Chojun, Kyoda Juhatsu, Shinzato Jinang, Tang Daiji and Gokenki [Pic: Patrick McCarthy]

115

Part Four: Karate Jutsu in the 1900s

Gokenki and Tang Daiji

Wú Xiánguì was a Chinese master who arrived in Okinawa in around 1912. Therefore he was too late to really influence the like of Gichin Funakoshi, but he did influence Chojun Miyagi and Mabuni Kenwa. Wu, known in Japan as Go Kenki, was born in 1886 in Fuzhou City, Fuijan Province. He is often said to be a student of Ryuru Ko or alternatively of Zhou Zhihe but these theories are likely designed to tie him in more closely with the established narratives of, respectively, Goju Ryu and Uechi Ryu.

During the Communist revolution in China, many such as the masters of Feeding Crane fled to neighbouring Taiwan which was under Japanese control at the time. Go Kenki instead set his sights on Okinawa. In 1912 he fled there alone and took up work in a tea shop as a clerk. Later he would move to Higashi in Naha district and open his own tea shop. Go Kenki spent his days importing tea from China and his evenings teaching White Crane boxing. He married an Okinawan and took her surname of Yoshikawa.

His friend and colleague, another tea merchant, was Tang Daiji (To Daiki) who lived from 1887-1937 and about whom little is written. According to McCarthy, Tang arrived in Okinawa from China in 1915. Tang was actually born in Yaosha, a few miles west of Fuzhou. He married an Okinawan woman called Ishira Michiko. Like Iwah and Zhou Zhihe, Tang Daiji was a practitioner of Tiger Boxing and this is the missing piece in the Pangainoon-Kingainoon puzzle. According to Tokashiki Iken, Tang Daiji was a master of Sanchin, Shisochin and other forms believed to be identified with Seipai and Suparimpei. However, Fujiwara and Gima believed he taught Five Ancestors Fist, which, as it contains a form called *Chentou*, may have been wishful thinking that he taught 'Chinto'. It is far more likely that Tang was a Tiger boxer. According to Fujiwara and Gima, Tang participated in a public demonstration in 1920, but then returned to China in 1930 where he lived out the rest of his days.

The Tang family (Tang or To is written using the same characters as Tang dynasty or To in Tode) were renowned Tiger boxers originally of the Guangzhou area. This has been confirmed by present day descendants of the Tang/To family of Guangzhou.

116

In the previous generation to Tang Daiji, another Tang/To family tiger boxer of Canton gained fame for his martial arts and famously defended his village from a tiger using a staff. Like Tang Daiji, he emigrated to one of the Japanese islands. It seems likely the two were related.

This warrior's son was Tang Tao Chong (To Dao Chong) who was born in China and whose family moved to Vietnam. Tang Tao Chong maintained the family tiger boxing tradition and used to condition his arms and legs by hitting them with canes. He taught his grandson Ken and today Ken's son John continues the martial arts tradition.

The author is working with Ken and John to research a possible link between their Tang family tiger boxing and the tiger boxing of Tang Daiji.

From Karate Jutsu to Karate Do

In the early years of the 20th century, the old ways of Karate Jutsu began to be replaced by the modern ways of Karate Do. Itosu replaced the old Channan forms with the Pinan forms and Karate began to be taught in schools. Then in the 1920s it became a popular activity in the universities of Japan. Karate Jutsu's grappling, chokes, pressure points, weapons and pins were largely lost with just a few keeping the flame alive.

Matsuo Kanenori Sakon wrote: *"Classical Karate used the methods of atemi waza* [strikes], *nage waza* [throws] *and katame waza* [locks] *as well as various weapons or weapon-useable objects (Ryukyu Kobudo). However, since the 1920s and 1930s and indeed up until the present time the sporting aspect of Karatedo has been the norm...*

"In Karate sport matches, speed is everything and therefore the athletes focus solely upon linear techniques and often ignore angular or circular strikes, finger thrusts, elbow smashes and the like."

He reiterates: *"In sports Karatedo... there is no longer the fear of death and it is in this manner that sports Karatedo differs from Bujutsu Karate. But Karate Jutsu was born from the need for smaller people to overcome larger aggressors in order to survive."*

Karate Jutsu in Kansai 1920-1960

"The Karate that has been introduced to Tokyo is actually just a part of the whole. The fact that those who have learnt Karate there, feel it only consists of kicks and punches, and that throws and locks are only to be found in Judo or Jujutsu, can only be put down to a lack of understanding." – Kenwa Mabuni, 1938

Between 1920 and 1944 there was a huge migration of Okinawans to Kansai, particularly Osaka and Kobe. Among these were Karate masters Choki Motobu, Kenwa Mabuni and Kanbun Uechi. Some of the styles regarded as 'Okinawan Karate' actually had their start in Kansai.

Motobu Ryu in Kansai

Motobu Choki was not permitted to study the family system of Motobu Ryu, and so he learnt Karate from various masters and from his own fights. He famously only practised a handful of kata; some suggest only Naihanchi. But it is likely he would have been familiar with Channan, Kushanku, Bassai and Seisan at the least. He practised older methods pre-dating the modifications of his teacher Anko Itosu. For example Itosu was fond of the cat stance – Motobu was not.

He said: *"In my Karate, there are no stances such as the Nekoashi, Zenkutsu, or Kokutsu, etc. The so-called cat stance is one example of the floating feet, which is most disliked inside martial arts. This because if your body get hit then immediately you're blown away as you lost your balance. Zenkutsu and Kokutsu, are also inferior stances, hindering the free movement work of the legs. In my Karate the same stance work used in both kata and kumite, and is like the stance of Naifanchi. This stance with the knees being gently bent can move freely. During defence or offence the knees are tightened and the hip is dropped. Weight is not applied to either the front or the back foot, instead the weight is put more evenly on both feet."*

Choki Motobu

Motobu was born in 1871 in Akahira village in the Shuri region of Okinawa. He was the third son – which meant he could not train in the family system as he was not a high ranking aji or lord. The Motobu family were skilled at the art of Ti. Motobu did naturally pick up some

119

of the techniques of his family's fighting system, but because of Okinawan tradition, only the first son, Choyu, was educated and chosen to carry on the family's martial tradition. Because of this situation, he went looking for instruction elsewhere.

Choki began training extensively with makiwara and lifted heavy rocks to gain strength. He endeavoured to become as strong as possible and trained with ferocity. He became known as "Motobu saru" or Motobu the monkey because of his agility and speed. Eventually, Motobu became the student of Anko Itosu.

A young Choki spent a lot of time seeking out challenge on the street. He won most of his fights and learned much from these encounters. Itosu Sensei was reportedly not impressed by the young man's attitude and promptly expelled him from the Dojo. Motobu's aggressive behaviour soon earned him a bad reputation and many Sensei would not teach him. One man, however, liked the spirit he showed and accepted him as a student of Karate.

Choki Motobu demonstrating Karate Jutsu

It was from Kosaku Matsumora that Choki learned many kata. Motobu still challenged others to fights often and was eager to develop and improve his fighting skills. He eventually asked Matsumora to teach him kumite. Matsumora said of him: *"for a young man, he is extremely talented in the martial arts"* (*Ryukyu Shimpo*, 1936). Ryosho Kin asked Motobu a question: *"My father, Mr. Ryōjin Kin, used to tell me very often that you are a real bushi. My father also told me that Matsumora remarked about you, that 'When the man called Choki Motobu came to my place, we practiced kumite. Motobu punched my face one time during kumite training. I really thought this Motobu had great martial arts skills for such a young man.' Matsumora Sensei praised your skill greatly. Was this story true?"*

Motobu answered: *"It happened when I was 19. I went to Matsumora's place with Tamashiro from Kariya who was a Sumo wrestler, and I received kumite training there. Matsumora Sensei threw a punch at me. My hand blocked the punch and hit straight into Sensei's (Matsumora's) face. His teeth immediately begun to bleed. I took one step back and said, 'I am very sorry, Sensei.'*

"But Sensei insisted, 'Don't stop, just keep punching and hitting me continuously.' Then I felt great, becoming more excited and kept on training. This was a true story. I never told anyone about this incident, but Yabu used to tell me that he knew about it."

He formulated his own formidable style of kumite and began to get much attention in Okinawa and in Japan on his trips to the islands. One day while in Kyoto he witnessed a contest where people were asked to match skills with a foreign boxer. A friend coaxed Motobu to give it a try. The boxer was arrogant and goaded Motobu constantly. For two rounds Motobu just avoided the boxer's attacks. In the third round he knocked the boxer out.

The boxer has been identified as the historically documented Jan Kentel.

Motobu said: *"I think it was around 1923* [actually probably 1922]. *I went to watch a match with the foreign boxer John 'somebody'* [note – Jan Kentel] *in Kyoto. The boxer fought against a Judo stylist for the first match. This boxer fought very sluggishly. He looked like an amateur. I applied to challenge this boxer and bet money on the match. I was already over fifty years old at that time. I didn't have a chance to fight that day, so I went back there the next day. When I said (to the referee) that I would fight without gloves, this boxer despised me, because he was much taller than me. And he treated me like a child, as he held my nose and twisted my cheek.*

"I did not fight seriously during the first round and we took a break. When I got up to fight the second round, I suddenly thought, 'If I am defeated by such a foreign boxer, it will shame both Karate and Okinawa. I want to beat this opponent.'

"I determined to win the fight. As soon as the boxer came forward to attack with his full power, I hit his temple very hard with one punch in a rage. He collapsed right there.

"All the spectators got very excited, and with a thunderous round of applause, started to throw their floor cushions, cigarette holders, drawstring coin purses, and other things toward me. It was such an exciting event, because such a big boxer (about 6 feet tall), and was knocked out by a Karate technique.

"Many newspaper articles stated that I hit the boxer with a flat (open) hand. However, I did not use the flat of my hand to hit him. I hit him with my fist, but the spectators thought my hand was flat since I hit him so fast; it was lightning fast.

"The essence of Karate is to move gently or casually, then immediately and explosively hit the enemy when the opportunity presents itself. This is Karate jissen, actual fighting."

Needless to say, Motobu quickly gained a reputation as a master and many curious people came to learn this mysterious new art. Soon, Motobu became a full time teacher. During this time, Motobu gained great respect for his fighting ability. He was hailed as the greatest fighter in Japan. Many Sensei advised their students to go and train with Motobu and learn his kumite techniques (for obvious reasons).

He was also asked to teach at several universities. Because of this, many great instructors of today's styles, such as Hironori Ohtsuka of Wado Ryu, had the benefit of his instruction.

He arrived in Osaka in 1921, before Funakoshi Gichin arrived in Tokyo. Motobu had been living in Japan a couple of years when he made the acquaintance of a Judo teacher named Doi, who encouraged him to try to teach Karate in Japan. Motobu subsequently began giving demonstrations and teaching in the Kobe-Osaka area, but development of the art was slow. After a couple of years he thought of giving it all up, but then in the mid-1920s interest in the art slowly began to grow. Among Motobu's students in Osaka were Mikio Sindo and Fujiwara. Motobu then left Osaka and moved to Tokyo where Funakoshi was teaching. He strongly stressed the importance of makiwara training and became as enthusiastic about kata as he had always been about kumite.

In 1936, at the age of 65, Motobu left Tokyo and went back to Okinawa to visit his instructors to talk about the state of Karate in Japan and to make sure that he was teaching the kata and techniques in their original, unaltered form. Oddly enough, there is a story of Choki, full of confidence, challenging his brother Choyu to a fight. It is said that Choyu threw Choki around like a rag doll but others doubt this.

I would suggest he may have engaged in a friendly game of push hands with his brother. I cannot imagine them fighting in earnest.

Motobu Choyu

After the experience, Choki is said to have humbled himself and adopted more of his family's Ti forms. Later in life, Motobu seemed to stress the importance of tradition in training.

Subsequently, he returned and continued teaching in Tokyo. Shortly before World War II, he returned to Okinawa and died in September of 1944 of a stomach disease at the age of 73.

Motobu's mystery Kung Fu master

According to American Karate pioneer Robert Trias, Motobu Choki cross-trained with a Chinese master named Tung Gee Hsing. According to Trias, Motobu taught and graded Tung 3rd Dan and in exchange Tung taught Motobu the art of Hsing-I. Trias, who told this story in numerous sources including *Black Belt* magazine, stated that Hsing was a student of Sun Lu Tang. It may be that the name 'Hsing Gee Tung' is actually a corruption of 'Sun Lu Tang' and Trias somehow considered that Tang and Motobu had met and learnt from each other. There is no evidence that I know of, other than the recollection of Trias, that Motobu trained with Tung/Tang but given the time the two men lived – Tang was just 10 years older than Motobu – it is not impossible.

Sun's martial arts system 'Sun style' is a combination of three Chinese internal martial arts – Taijiquan, Hsing-I and Pakua. Sun Lu

124

Tang was born in 1860 or 1861 and his father died when he was very young meaning the boy had to go out and provide for his family. The rich landowner he worked for beat him, and would only pay him in food. In order to defend himself against beatings the young Sun Lu Tang sought out a Shaolin instructor to teach him to fight. He was fired for fighting and so to ease the burden on his family he would forage for food.

His life then turned around when he met Li Kuiyuan and began learning Hsing-I Chuan, a boxing style based on five fists and 12 animals. He then graduated to learning with Li's father Guo Yunshen. Guo was known for having united Hsing-I with Pakua by fighting the Pakua founder Dong Hai Chuan.

Sun studied with Kuo for eight years before graduating. Upon graduating, Sun went to study Pakua with the famous master Cheng Tinghua under whom he trained for three years. Sun travelled to Beijing when he met the famous Tai Chi master Hao Weizhen, whose master Wu Yu-hsiang studied under both Yang Lu Chan (head of Yang style) and Chen Ching Ping (head of Chen style).

Sun Lu Tang was actually one of the first Chinese to suggest the common themes found in "internal" martial arts and in Taoism. Therefore the idea of the eight trigrams, the five elements and other such concepts were widely introduced by Sun. He said:

"There is a central idea. Merely practicing is not understanding. Seek to understand the human ability. Study diligently for deep ideas. The result after a long time is that one is able to know. The natural course of things is always followed. This prevents one from harming their post-heaven strength. Focus is on beneficial cultivation of one's natural life force as the core of training. All people – men, women, the old, and the young – may practice in order to replace temerity with bravery; and stiffness with pliability. Those of you who are weak, who suffer from fatigue and injury or illness, or who have weakened your qi from the practice of other martial arts to the point that you no longer have the strength to train, all of you may practice Tai Ji Quan. With practice, the qi will quickly return to a balanced state and will become strong, while the spirit naturally returns to a state of wholeness. Disease will be eliminated and the length of life increased."

Trias wrote:
It is believed that King Sho Tai of Okinawa sent Matsumura (1806-

1895), Master of Shuri-te and martial arts weapons, to China to increase his knowledge of the Chinese arts. Upon his return, he was appointed personal bodyguard to the king. Matsumura brought back invaluable techniques and methods from the Chuan-fa and Hsing-yi (hsing-i) systems, which at that time were the foremost accepted forms of the Chinese art in China. Shuri-te was the original style of the Okinawan masters Sokon Matsumura, Yasutsune (Ankoh) Itosu; and later Choki Motobu, Kentsu Yabu, Chosun Chibana, Chotoku Kyan, Kanken Toyama, Yasuhiro Konishi, and others. Through the decade of 1874-1884 traveling monks were being robbed and killed between Canton, Namoi and Tong-king, by roving bands of robbers and cutthroats. Many of these were Chinese rebels or ex-rebels who had been driven across the frontier during the suppression of the Yu-Nan and Taiping rebellions. At the Hai Chiwang Sze Temple, Shang Tsao-Hsiang (Tsao Hsing) had studied the internal systems of Chuan-fa, Hsing-Yi and Pakua, and the external systems of Shaolin-chun and Hung-kun, from the most formidable fighters of that time, Masters Li T'sun Yi (1849-1924) and Sun Lu T'ang (1859-1932). He taught these skills to the monks to enable them to defend themselves against the highway robbers and cutthroats. The elder Hsiang died, leaving to his nephew/son T'ung Gee Hsing (Tong Gee Hsing or Hsiang) the secrets of Hsing-yi. Hsing later settled in the Chinese settlement of Kume Mura in Okinawa. While Master Hsing lived in Kume Mura, he met Master Choki Motobu. The incorporation of their two noble systems became the basis of modern Okinawan Shuri-te and the entirety of the Shuri-ryu system as taught today.

Author's note: American Goju Ryu pioneer Peter Urban said that Choki was a giant of a man, standing 7'4". Trias claimed this was an exaggeration and Choki only stood around 6'8". In the author's opinion 5'6" would be generous and Motobu himself talked about the 6'0" Jan Kentel towering over him.

Shito Ryu in Kansai

Mabuni Kenwa, a student of Shorin Ryu (Itosu) and Naha Te (Higaonna) established the Shito Ryu style in Osaka. Mabuni was like an oracle of kata and in some respects Shito Ryu was intended as a universal system that brought together all the different factions of

Okinawan Karate. Even today Shito Ryu has far more kata than its cousins like Shotokan and Goju Ryu. Among Mabuni's most notable students in Osaka was Tani Chojiro, the founder of a branch called Tani-ha Shito Ryu, which is today better known as Shukokai.

One of Tani's co-students was Hiroshi Fujimoto. They were also co-students with Tomiyama, Yamashita and Ueshara at the Doshisha university Karate club where they trained under Shito Ryu founder Kenwa Mabuni.

One of Mabuni's notable students was Kanyei Uechi, a distant relative of Uechi Ryu founder Kanbun, but the two should not be confused stylistically. Kanyei studied Karate under his father and uncle in Okinawa and then moved to Osaka in 1924 looking for work. There he befriended Mabuni and by 1935 was given the unusual grade of "2nd Dan Shihan". He opened his own Shito Ryu Karate club in 1937 and closed it three years later when he returned to Okinawa.

Mabuni Kenwa

Mabuni was the founder of Shito Ryu Karate and early in his martial arts studied Shuri Te, Naha Te and Quan Fa. He started his Karate training with Shorin Ryu at the age of 13 under Master Anko Itosu (1830-1915).

While still in his teens, Mabuni was introduced by his friend, Miyagi Chojun (the founder of Goju Ryu Karate) to Higaonna Kanryo (1853-1915). During the 1920s Mabuni participated in a Karate club operated by Miyagi and Motobu Choyu, with help from Chomo Hanashiro and Juhatsu Kiyoda. Here the masters picked each other's brains. Mabuni learned some White Crane from the legendary Gokenki.

Mabuni had become a highly respected police officer and made several trips to Japan. He spent many of his early travelling years with Koyu Konishi, a friend and sometimes student who later founded Shindo-Jinen-Ryu Karate. In 1925 Mabuni and Konishi visited Japan's Wakayama prefecture where Kanbun Uechi, the founder of Uechi-Ryu, was teaching.

Shito Ryu master Mabuni Kenwa

Mabuni actually spent most of his time in Osaka, where he taught at various Dojo. In 1929, Mabuni moved permanently to Osaka. Mabuni called his style hanko-Ryu (half-hard style), but by the early 1930s Shito Ryu was the official name. Mabuni also studied Shinden Fudo Ryu Jujutsu and was listed as the art's Soke and was friendly with the last historical Ninja, Seiko Fujita.

Students of Mabuni Kenwa:

Mabuni Kenei
Kankei Uechi
Ryusho Sakagami
Iwata Manzo

Chojiro Tani
Hiroshi Fujimoto
Katsumi Fujiwara
Shogo Kuniba

Uechi Ryu in Kansai

Kanbun Uechi (1877) was an Okinawan Karateka who like his peers
Kanryo Higaonna and Norisato Nakaima studied Quan Fa in Fujian. It
seems the styles they studied were related. Patrick McCarthy has
conjectured that Higaonna studied Whooping Crane, but it seems as
likely that the styles were Pangainoon and Kingainoon. In 1922 Uechi
moved to Wakayama near Osaka and in 1923 started teaching Karate
to a few friends. By 1932 he was teaching a well established Karate
academy. He only returned to Okinawa in 1946 at the age of 69 and
died two years later.

Uechi's son Kanyei Uechi lived with his father in Japan and in
1937 opened an Uechi Ryu Dojo in Osaka which he ran for two years
until he returned to Okinawa in 1939. Fujimoto Hiroshi was a master
of both Uechi Ryu and Kushin Ryu Karate Jutsu. His teacher was
Seijiro Sakihama who studied Uechi Ryu under the founder Kanbun
Uechi, and Kushin Ryu he studied under its joint founder Kanemori
"Kensei" Kinjo.

The author demonstrates one of the secret fist forms of the
Motobu Ryu's 'Ryukyu Oke Hiden Bujutsu' called Kasshin-di

Kushin Ryu in Kansai

Kushin Ryu was jointly founded by Kanemori and Kiyotada Sannosuke Ueshima. Kanemori had studied two styles of Karate, the Shorin Ryu (Kobayashi Ryu) of Chosin Chibana and the Goju Ryu of Chojun Miyagi.

Ueshima (1893-1987) had studied Karate from the age of 9 under an Okinawan man named Sugaya who was presumed to be an early student of Itosu, since he taught the Channan and Kushanku forms. Ueshima had also from the age of 3 trained in a style of Jujutsu called Koshin Yujoyitsu in the Academy of Matsubara in the city of Akou, under his teacher Kiyotada Kajei Matsubara. In 1918, at the age of 25, Ueshima received the title of professor of Konshin Yujoyitsu from professor Matsubara and professor Guikyo Mazai Akada. After receiving his title Ueshima transferred to the city of Osaka, where he opened the academy Konshin Ryu Yujoyitsu.

After opening his academy in Osaka several teachers of Karate arrived from Okinawa to the city of Osaka. On arrival in Osaka they visited Ueshima's academy to practise and teach martial arts. These masters were Chōki Motobu, Kanemori Kinjo and Chosin Chibana. According to Mark Bishop it was Ueshima who visited Kinjo's Dojo in Osaka, but regardless the two became friends and founded Kushin Ryu together (Ku can also be pronounced Kara and Shin from Konshin).

Motobu Chosei (son of Choki) told Graham Noble of Ueshima training with his father (A Meeting with Chosei Motobu, *Classical Fighting Arts*). It recorded: *"Regarding Yasuhiro Konishi, the founder of Shindo Jinen Ryu Karate, Chosei confirmed that he had been a great help to Choki Motobu in Japan... There was also Sannosuke Ueshima, a Jujutsu instructor who had been one of Motobu's early students in the 1920s. Takeji Inaba had actually been to meet Ueshima, who told him that when he had first gone to meet Choki Motobu they had exchanged ideas on technique. Ueshima recalled that each time he tried a move, Motobu would anticipate it, then neutralise or counter it... Ueshima was somewhat shocked by this... although many people said bad things about Choki Motobu he really was an exceptional martial artist."*

In 1932 Ueshima founded the style of Kushin Ryu Karate, as he combined his Jujutsu with his Karate. In 1933 Ueshima received the title of Kyoshi (Judo) from the Dai Nippon Butokukai and in 1935 and for the first time in Japan, the Dai Nippon Butokukai conferred the title of professor of Kyoshi (Karate) to Ueshima with other two teachers, Miyagi and Konishi. In 1940, Kinjo was awarded the title of Renshi.

In 1960 Kinjo's top student Shintaro Yoshizato introduced Kushin Ryu to Okinawa. In 1965, Ueshima received the title of 8th Dan in Judo from the Kodokan. Kanamori Kinjo returned to Okinawa where he spread the Kushin Ryu style. In 1987 at 94 years of age, Soke Kiyotada Sannosuke Ueshima, founder of the Kushin Ryu style, died in the city of Osaka.

Part Five: Karetedo

Shoto Ryu

In 1922 Gichin Funakoshi, aged 53, travelled from his home in Okinawa to the Japanese mainland to give a demonstration of the little known art of Karate.

A school teacher by profession, Funakoshi was the favourite student of Anko Azato and also studied under Anko Itosu and to a lesser extent their teacher Sokon Matsumura.

While Yasutsune Itosu is the most famous of Matsumura's students, Itosu was actually more of a Tomari stylist. Matsumura's style was more closely represented by Funakoshi, via the Azato line. Funakoshi stated: *"Azato followed Matsumura and Itosu followed Gusukuma."*

He reiterated: *"Masters Azato and Itosu were students of Matsumura and Gusukuma respectively. Masters Azato and Itosu were the teachers who instructed this writer and to whom the writer is greatly indebted."*

Funakoshi Sensei lived in a small room in the Meisojuku, a boarding home for Okinawan students, and to make ends meet he had to take odd jobs around the hostel as a caretaker. Funakoshi Sensei had actually made an earlier visit to Japan, giving a demonstration of the art in Kyoto in 1917, but it was not until Crown Prince Hirohito visited Okinawa in 1921, and a Karate demonstration was given in his presence, that Funakoshi was "noticed". The Okinawan captain of the prince's ship suggested to Funakoshi that Karate should be introduced to the Japanese mainland.

Funakoshi was also asked to give a demonstration at the Kodokan Judo hall, in front of Judo founder Jigoro Kano himself and his senior instructors. To assist him, he took along Shinkin Gima, a twenty-five-year-old Okinawan living in Tokyo, who had studied Karate under Kentsu Yabu and Anko Itosu. Funakoshi demonstrated Kushanku (now called Kanku Dai in Shotokan) and Gima demonstrated Naihanchi (Tekki Shodan) and the two demonstrated Bunkai. Gima recalled: *"When I arrived at the Kodokan with Funakoshi Sensei not only were the seniors there to greet us but the Director, Jigoro Kano himself. More than 80 members of the Tomishinsoku Kodokan branch were there too, so there were over 200 people assembled for the demonstration. We were both overawed. It was natural we should feel nervous because the Kodokan was considered to be the mecca of Japanese budo.*

"Kano Sensei was eager to learn about Karate and he asked such detailed questions that Funakoshi Sensei sometimes had difficulty in answering them. I believe that because we demonstrated at the Kodokan, Karate was more easily introduced into mainland Japan. In other words, the fact that Kano Sensei recognized Karate meant that in turn Karate was recognised by the Japanese budo world."

In July 1922, Funakoshi began teaching his Karate to a small group of students who had heard about him by word of mouth. For a Dojo he was allowed to use the lecture hall of 20 tatami (mats) in the Meisojuku.

Shinkin Gima was himself one of those early Meisojuku Karateka. There were no Karate uniforms and students would simply take off their coats and jackets to train. Another early student was the Shindo Yoshin Ryu Jujutsu instructor Hironori Ohtsuka. Later Gima would go on to head the original Karate branch known as Shoto Ryu, and Ohtsuka founded Wado Ryu. This was before the advent of Shotokan and Shotokai. Funakoshi taught classes of around 8 students and taught mostly kata. By the 1930s, his son Yoshitaka (Gigo) assumed most of the teaching responsibilities. These are the roots of the original Shoto Ryu Karate Jutsu before students like Nakayama and Egami conquered the world with the Shotokan movement.

In 1930, Funakoshi established an association named Dai-Nihon Karate-do Kenkyukai to promote communication and information exchange among people who study karate-do. The Kenkyukai eventually became Shotokai, and in 1939, Funakoshi built the first Shotokan Dojo in Tokyo. We should note that Funakoshi himself never referred to his style as Shotokai, Shotokan or Shoto Ryu. He called himself Shoto as a nickname but only ever wanted his art to be called "Karatedo" in the way that Jigoro Kano only referred to Judo not "Kano Ryu Judo."

Another early student of Funakoshi's was Minoru Mochizuki, later founder of Yoseikan, and the only Budoka considered to have mastered Judo, Aikido, Karate, Kendo, Iaido and Kenjutsu. It is possible Mochizuki received a Karate lesson as early as 1924 since his Judo teacher Toku Sanpo was Okinawan. We might suggest that an Okinawan martial artist would have been very likely to have known at least a little Karate.

In the 1920s another Okinawan began teaching in Japan; he was

Mabuni Kenwa. Like Funakoshi he was also a student of Itosu. If we can say anything about Mabuni it is that he was a walking directory of kata. Studying almost every style on Okinawa, under Itosu, Higaonna, Aragaki and Gokenki, he may have known upwards of 70 kata.

Even Funakoshi sent his own sons to train with Mabuni to learn new kata (possibly Nijushiho, Gojushiho and Wankan) since Funakoshi only seemingly knew in the region of about 12-15.

According to Terry Wingrove, the key to Funakoshi's Karate being accepted was Yasuhiro Konishi. Wingrove Sensei knew Konishi and Gima in Japan and explained that Konishi's influence was critical. He said: *"I was very fortunate to have contact with Shinken Gima Sensei almost on a daily basis when I was working at FAJKO from 1968 and he would often have lunch with [Hideo] Tsuchiya Sensei and myself and tell us stories of the early days of Karate in Japan.*

"We must not forget that in those days of the rise of Imperial Japan the formal introductions and who-you-knew was a key element in the development of any enterprise, not only in Martial Arts. In the case of Gichin Funakoshi the "fixer" without doubt was Yasuhiro Konishi as the first demonstration at the Kodokan, apparently did not impress Jigoro Kano, as he criticised it for not being an organised system as Funakoshi and Gima gave a disjointed display.

"It was at Konishi Sensei's Dojo that Funakoshi formalised his "style" for general consumption. Also do not forget that an application was made via the Kodokan for Karate to be accepted as a division of the Kodokan by the [Dai Nippon] Butokukai in 1923. This was not acceptable to Funakoshi so no further action was taken."

Funakoshi's art was beginning to be known as Shotokan (much to his dismay), Chojun Miyagi's Naha Te based art was now called Goju Ryu (via his Japanese representative Gogen Yamaguchi), Hironori Ohtsuka's mixture of Jujutsu and Karate was now called Wado Ryu and Kenwa Mabuni's mixture of Itosu and Higaonna styles was now called Shito Ryu. Minoru Mochizuki would later follow with Yoseikan Ryu, Kanbun Uechi with Uechi Ryu and so on. However this was mostly happening in Japan. Karate was very much still thriving in Okinawa. Men like Hanashiro Chomo (Shorin Ryu), Chojun Miyagi (Goju Ryu) and Choki Motobu (Motobu Ryu) saw what was happening in Japan and it would seem their views were mixed. On one side, they didn't seem to appreciate Funakoshi and Mabuni standardising Karate and making it popular. On the other side.... they wanted in.

Notable students of Gichin Funakoshi:
Makoto Gima
Gigo Funakoshi
Hironori Ohtsuka
Minoru Mochizuki
Masatoshi Nakayama
Shigeru Egami
Hidetaka Nishiyama
Mitsusuke Harada
Hirokazu Kanazawa
Keinosuke Enoeda

The New Shuri Te, Tomari Te and Naha Te Karatedo in Okinawa

As far as I know the only styles that have been handed down from the past are the Goju Ryu of Master Miyagi and the Shito Ryu of Master Mabuni. I have never given a name to the Karate I am studying but some of my students call it Shotokan Ryu." – Gichin Funakoshi

In 1936, a local newspaper in Okinawa held a meeting of the island's leading Karate masters. They included: Chomo Hanashiro (Shorin Ryu senior student of Itosu); Kyan Chotoku (Tomari Te student of Matsumora and Itosu); Choki Motobu (Tomari Te student of Matsumora, Itosu and Matsumura); Chojun Miyagi (Goju Ryu. Student of Higaonna); Juhatsu Kyoda (To-on Ryu student of Higaonna); Choshin Chibana (Shorin Ryu student of Itosu); Shimpan Gusukuma (Shorin Ryu student of Itosu, not to be confused with earlier Gusukuma); Genwa Nakasone (representing Kanken Toyama); and Chotei Oroku.

Nakasone remarked that the instructors in Tokyo (ie Funakoshi) were calling Tode Jutsu (also pronounced Toshu Jutsu or Karate Jutsu) "Karate" (empty hand rather than Chinese Hand) and he thought that was a good idea. Hanashiro Chomo, concurred, saying lots of people just called it Te anyway.

Chojun Miyagi stated he called it Chinese Hand but saw no problem changing, considering Jujutsu and Hakuda had changed to Judo. He said: *"We use "Toudi" because it is in general use. However, it is a term used casually. Most people who come to my place wanting to learn usually just ask if I can teach them "te." Judging by that, I would say that "te" seems to have been used before. I believe that the term karate is a good name because of what it represents. As Mr. Shimabukuro pointed out, Judo evolved from Jujutsu. In China, they used to call kempo, Baida or Hakuda."*

He added: *"Although I didn't begin training in China, I went there after realizing that it was the place I had to go for more advanced gongfu studies... The Chinese seemed to be familiar with the term "Toudi."* Kyoda however felt most Okinawans would oppose calling it by a new name and felt more research was needed. But Chomo said he himself had used "empty hand" as early as 1905.

Gizaburo Furukawa, Supervisor of Physical Education of Okinawa Prefecture, stated that he thought Okinawan Karate should be unified, saying: *"There are a lot of Ryu or styles in karate now. I think we have to unify them at any cost. I hear there are small differences between Shuri style karate and Naha style karate. I think both styles should be unified and we should make Kata of Japanese Karate-do. In the old days, we had about 200 styles of Kendo (= swordsmanship), but now they have been unified and we have the standard Kata of Japanese Kendo. I think karate would become popular all over the country if we*

136

had the unified Kata. For example, we can newly establish ten Kata as Japanese Karate. The name of each Kata should be changed into Japanese, such as Junan-No-Kata (soft and stretch kata), Kogeki-No-Kata (= offensive kata) and so on." Miyagi said he agreed with some things, such as a standardised uniform, but didn't just want to invent new kata, saying: "As to karate clothes, we also would like to make karate uniform soon as we often have problems. As for terminology of karate, I think we will have to control it in the future. I am also advocating it, and I have been making new technical words and promoting them. Regarding Kata, I think traditional Kata should be preserved as old or classic Kata." Miyagi said of Shorei Ryu and Shorin Ryu: "They say that karate has two separate sects: Shorinryu and Shoreiryu. However, there is no clear evidence to support or deny this. If forced to distinguish the differences between these sects, then I would have to say that it is only teaching methods that divides them. Shorinryu's fundamental training (kihon) and open hand techniques (kaishu) are not taught in any clearly defined way. However, the Shoreiryu kaishu and kihon are taught according to a clearly established method. My teacher taught us according to the Shoreiryu method." But Chibana said of Shorin Ryu: "Our teacher taught Naihanchi for fundamental development."

Shortly after this meeting new styles of Karate emerged in Okinawa along with the already strong ones like Goju Ryu and To-on Ryu. Chosin Chibana called his style Shorin Ryu, basing it entirely on Itosu's teachings. The characters Shorin can also be read Kobayashi. Shoshin Nagamine, a student of Choki Motobu and Chotoku Kyan, also called his art Shorin Ryu, but used the syllable Sho (Matsu) rather than Sho (Ko) in order to pay homage to Matsumura and Matsumora. Therefore this school is also called Matsubayashi Ryu.

Chotoku Kyan

Therefore among the original Karate styles and their founders were, in no particular order:

- Goju Ryu (Chojun Miyagi. Largely based on Naha Te)

- To-On Ryu (Kyoda. Largely based on Naha Te)

- Ryuei Ryu (Norisato. Largely based on Naha Te)

- Shoto Ryu (Funakoshi and Gima. Largely based on Shuri Te)

- Kobayashi Ryu (Chosin Chibana. Largely based on Shuri Te)

- Matsubayashi Ryu (Shoshin Nagamine. Largely Shuri Te)

- Wado Ryu (Hironori Ohtsuka. Largely based on Shoto Ryu)

- Yoseikan Ryu (Minoru Mochizuki. Largely based on Shoto Ryu, Aikido and Judo)

- Uechi Ryu (Kanbun Uechi. Largely based on Naha Te and Pangainoon)

- Shudokan (Kanken Toyama. Largely based on Itosu, Higaonna and other arts)

There were also notable derivative styles, such as Kyokushin (largely a mix of Shotokan and Goju Ryu) and Shukokai (originally

138

Chojiro Tani's branch of Shito Ryu) as well as Malaysian Budokan which was developed by Chew Choo Soot, a student of Takamizawa whose main teacher was Kanken Toyama. Two styles that came later were founded by descendants of Sokon Matsumura. They were Chito Ryu, founded by Tsuyoshi Chitose, and 'Matsumura Seito Shorin Ryu', founded by Hohan Soken. There were other martial arts of course arriving later in Okinawa and Japan which resembled Karate, including Shorinji Kempo, Taikiken and Akio Kinjo's Jukendo, but the above are the main arts from which other styles developed.

The Dai Nippon Butokukai

Much of what is taken for granted in Karate today comes from the Dai Nippon Butokukai. The Kyoto institution was a powerful governing body for Budo and shaped all styles.

The Dai Nippon Butokukai was originally established in 1895 in Kyoto under the authority of the Japanese Government and the endorsement of the Emperor Meiji to solidify, promote, and standardise martial disciplines and systems throughout Japan. It aimed for the preservation of traditional Budo and the nobility associated with samurai culture. It was the first official and premier martial arts institution sanctioned by the government of Japan.

The Dai Nippon Butokukai subsequently became the centre for the proud heritage and elitism of Japanese Budo. It stressed the martial virtues of the samurai warrior and incomparable historical excellence in martial disciplines.

In 1911, the Butokukai opened its martial arts college the Budo Semmon Gakko or Busen for short. One of Kano Jigoro's top disciples, Isogai Hajime (teacher of Mikonosuke Kawaishi), served as the first director of the Butokukai's Judo department. The Butokukai not only sanctioned martial arts, it also awarded teaching titles such as Renshi and Hanshi.

The first Okinawan Karate master who truly embraced the concept of Japanese Budo was Funakoshi Gichin. The diminutive Okinawan brought Karate to Tokyo's attention and especially the attention of Kano.

Kanken Toyama: Godfather of Okinawan Karate

While the likes of Gichin Funakoshi and Mabuni were pushing Karate on the mainland, in Okinawa, many Karateka looked to Kanken Toyama for leadership.

Kanken Toyama was born in Shuri, Okinawa on the 21st year of Meiji, September 24, 1888. His given name was Kanken Oyadamari and he born into a noble family. In 1897 Toyama Kanken began his formal training in Toshukuken (Toshu Jutsu or Karate) under Master Itarashiki. Later, he apprenticed himself to Anko Itosu, who then became his primary teacher. He continued studying under Itosu until Itosu's death in 1915.

In 1907 Toyama was named Shihandai (headteacher) by Itosu at the Okinawa Teacher's College in Shuri City, and in 1914 he held a high office at the Shuri First Elementary School. Toyama was one of only two students to be granted the title of Shihanshi (protege); Gichin Funakoshi was the other to receive this title from Itosu. In 1924 Toyama Kanken moved his family to Taiwan where he taught elementary school and studied related systems of Chinese Ch'uan Fa (Kempo).

According to students of Toyama (see for example *Kanken Toyama* by Miller, Vandome & McBrewster), this included Taku (Hakuda),

140

Makaitan, Rutaobai, and Ubo. Here Toyama was making a concerted effort to return Karate back to his roots – and that was Hakuda.

Taku is one of central China's Hotsupu (northern school) Ch'uan Fa and is further classified as Neikung, an internal method. This would support our earlier theory that Hakuda came from a Northern system like Bazi Quan.

Makaitan and Rutaobai, from which the techniques of nukite (spear hand) came, and Ubo, all belong to the Nampa (southern school) Quanfa and are external methods or Waikung.

These later three styles hail primarily from Taiwan and Fukuden, China. Toyama Sensei was also known to have studied and taught Tai Chi.

Early in 1930 Toyama moved again from Taiwan to mainland Japan and on 20 March 1930 he opened his first Dojo in Tokyo. He called his Dojo Shu Do Kan meaning "The Hall for the Study of the Way" (in this case the Karate-way).

In 1946, Toyama Kanken, now a Dai Shihan, founded the All Japan Karate-Do Federation (AJKF). Toyama's intention when establishing the AJKF organisation was to unify the Karates of Japan and Okinawa into one governing organisation, providing a forum for the exchange of ideas and technique. Toyama's specialties in Karate were strong gripping methods, Useishi No Kata [Gojushiho] and the Aku Ryoku Ho of Itosu and Itarashiki and similar Chinese methods of finger and hand strengthening. He was the author of books *Karate-do Taihokan* and *Karate-do*. In 1949 Toyama was awarded a special title of honour by the Governor of Okinawa, Mr. Shikioku Koshin. Aside from learning Shorin-Ryu from Itosu, Toyama studied and mastered other styles of Karate from other notable masters of Naha-te and Tomari-te which also included Okinawan Kobudo. A few of his other teachers were Aragaki, Azato, Chibana, Oshiro, Tana, and Yabu. It is also thought that when the Korean (Ch'uan fa) master, Yoon Byung-In, came to train at his gymnasium, he also studied Northern Manchurian Kwan-bop with him. Toyama therefore was also an ancestor of Taekwondo.

Shorinji Ryu

Chotoku Kyan trained under Matsumura, Matsumora and Oyadomari. His notable students include Joen Nakazato, Tatsuo Shimabukuro (Isshin Ryu), Ankichi Arakaki, Shōshin Nagamine, Tsuyoshi Chitose, Kori Hisataka and Zenryo Shimabukuro (Seibukan).

Shorin Ryu (Kobayashi Ryu)

Chosin Chibana's Shorin Ryu is probably the closest style to the teachings of master Itosu. His notable students include Arakaki Ankichi, Katsuya Miyahira, Shūgorō Nakazato, Nakama Chozo and Yuchoku Higa who also taught Shotokan master Hirokazu Kanazawa.

Matsumura Seito (Shorin Ryu)

Hohan Soken claimed his uncle Nabe Matsumura was a student of his grandfather Sokon Matsumura but the Seito style bears clear hallmarks of Chosin Chibana's influence. Kata include Pinan, Naihanchi, Chinto, Rohai, Bassai and Hakutsuru. His notable students include Fusei Kise.

Motobu Ryu

The Motobu family style was passed on to Seikichi Uehara. Another school somewhat related to the Motobu Ryu is the Kishimoto school. Soko Kishimoto was a student of Bushi Takemura who was a contemporary of Bushi Matsumura.

Matsubayashi Ryu

Shoshin Nagamine, a prolific author, trained under Choki Motobu and Chotoku Kyan. His style, also sometimes called Shorin Ryu, combines Shuri Te and Tomari Te. He worked with Chojun Miyagi on creating the Gekisai (Fukyu) kata.

Goju Ryu

Chojun Miyagi's best known students include Gogen Yamaguchi, Seiko Higa, Seikichi Toguchi, Tatsuo Shimabuku, Ei'ichi Miyazato, Meitoku Yagi, and Seigo Tada. The most prominent Goju Ryu teachers in Okinawa currently include Hokama Sensei who runs the Okinawan Karate Museum, and Morio Higaonna a world respected 10th Dan who claims his teacher Aniichi Miyagi was the favoured student of Chojun

Miyagi. His former teacher Eiichi Miyazato somewhat disputed this.

Ryuei Ryu
Similar to Goju Ryu, Ryuei Ryu was founded by Norisato Nakaima who like Higaonna Kanryo claimed to have trained under Ryuryu Ko. It uses kata such as Sanchin, Seisan, Sanseiryu and Seyunchin, but also others.

Students of Chotoku Kyan:

Ankichi Aragaki
Taro Shimabuku
Shoshin Nagamine
Joen Nakazato
Zenryo Shimabukuro
Tatsuo Shimabuko
Eizo Shimabuko

Ankichi Aragaki not to be confused with the earlier Seisho Aragaki

Isshin Ryu

Isshin Ryu founder Shinkichi Tatsuo Shimabuko was a student of both Shorin Ryu master Chotoku Kyan and Goju Ryu master Chojun Miyagi. Andy Sloane (Renshi 6th Dan) in Okinawa submitted this extensive biography of his style's grandmaster:

Shinkichi Shimabuku was born on September 19, 1908 in Gushikawa Village, Gushikawa City (present-day Uruma City), Okinawa to Ura and Nabe Shimabuku. The eldest of 10 children, he came from a farming family.

Beginning at about age 13 (c. 1921), he became an apprentice sanjinso (fortune teller) under his maternal uncle, Shinko Ganeko, who was a school principal in Ishikawa City (now part of Uruma City) and lived in the neighbouring village of Agena. In addition to this training, his uncle taught him the rudimentary martial arts techniques he had once learned in China. Thus began the young Shimabuku's informal introduction to the martial arts.

Shimabuku's formal training in martial arts began, approximately, at the age of 16 (c. 1924), when he briefly trained with Choyu Motobu (1857-1928) - the distinguished heir to the Motobu family and the Motobu family martial art (Motobu Udundi)—at the Karate Kenkyukai (Research Club) in Wakasa, Naha City.

In January 1927, at the age of 18, Shimabuku married Uto Oshiro, and together they would have 5 children: Haruko (c. 1927-c. 1960), Matsuko (c. 1934), Yukiko (b. 1937), Kichiro (b. 1939), and Shinsho (1942-c. 2004).

In the same year of his marriage, Shimabuku's maternal uncle introduced him to the famous master Chotoku Kyan (1870-1945), known as Chan Miguwa in the Okinawan dialect. Kyan's Karate, today classified as Shorin-ryu, was largely Tomari-te with a slight Shuri-te influence.

Shimabuku trained with Kyan at his home in Makibaru Village, Yomitan Town—just across the Hija River Bridge from Kadena Town—until 1939, at which time he relocated to Davao City in the Philippine Islands for work. Shimabuku returned to Okinawa in mid-1941 and, in late 1942, briefly trained at the Nishi, Naha City Dojo of the renowned Choki Motobu (1870-1944), the younger brother of Choyu Motobu. To better support his large family, Shimabuku relocated once more and worked in Osaka as a security guard until

1944. With the money he'd earned on the mainland, Shimabuku invested in horses and carts and bought property in Kyan Village, Gushikawa City upon his return.

Japan, by this time, had determined that a full-scale attack on the main islands was inevitable, with a high probability of an invasion of Okinawa beforehand, and the Boetai—a civilian labour corps—was created by the Imperial Japanese Army. Shimabuku was among those forced to help build and reinforce the airfield at Kadena as part of the defence of Okinawa. When America first bombed Okinawa on October 10, 1944, the airfields were destroyed and Shimabuku was left virtually penniless. Along with thousands of his countrymen, he and his family were evacuated to Takaharu, Miyazaki Prefecture in Kyushu shortly thereafter. Consequently, they were among those fortunate not to have had to endure the atrocities of the 82-day Battle of Okinawa the following spring and summer. The Shimabukus were eventually repatriated to a war-torn Okinawa in late 1946.

After returning to his homeland, Shimabuku made ends meet by performing bo kata at weddings and festivals, fortune telling, and by working as the Kyan Village tax collector. He also began teaching Karate publicly for the first time. Chotoku Kyan, his most influential teacher, had never truly named his art, so Kyan's students all called their interpretations of Kyan-style Karate different names. Shimabuku initially decided upon the name Chan Miguwa-te (Small-eyed Kyan's Hand) for what he taught in his Dojo.

At about age 38 (1947), not long after he began teaching, Shimabuku took on the masculine nickname by which he came to be known worldwide: Tatsuo, meaning "Dragon Man"—and he also devised his own personal Karate kata that he called Sun nu su (later shortened to Sunsu).

Additionally at this time, Shimabuku had the opportunity to train briefly with Goju-ryu founder Chojun Miyagi (1888-1953) when Miyagi would visit his daughter in neighbouring Taba Village, and Shimabuku added elements of Naha-te to his repertoire.

Shimabuku had his own ideas about Karate and didn't always agree with his teachers. In about 1948, he began to blend the two styles together and renamed his art Sun nu su-te after his personal kata.

Shimabuku's innovative style of Karate adopted a higher stance to facilitate both balance and ease of movement. In a great departure from most other Karate styles, it also showcased vertical-fist punches and blocks with the muscles of the forearms. He felt that a non-twisting punch was not only stronger, but faster, and that blocking with the entire forearm was more advantageous in real application. He modified Kyan's and Miyagi's kata to fit with his vision of a more streamlined mode of self-defence.

By the early 1950s, Shimabuku's style included the empty-hand kata: Seisan, Seiunchin, Naihanchi, Wansu, Chinto, Kusanku, Sun nu su, and Sanchin.

Kobudo (weapons) kata included Tokumine nu Kun and Chan nu Sai, a short sai kata that Shimabuku had devised based on basic sai techniques taught to him by Chotoku Kyan. Shimabuku held the *Kenpo Hakku* (8 philosophical poems regarding combat) from the Bubishi (a Chinese martial arts text) in high regard and passed their mysteries along to his students as gokui (essential principles).

Abandoning the typical Karate kata designed for novices, Shimabuku instead opted for a set of 30 upper- and lower-body kihon (basic strikes, punches, blocks, kicks, stretches, and exercises) as a way of teaching the principles of his style to beginners. A codified series of self-defence techniques (kumite), striking post (makiwara) practice, and forearm conditioning (kotekitai) training rounded out his curriculum. Shimabuku, later still, created a second sai kata— Kusanku Sai—which eventually supplanted Chan nu Sai.

On January 15, 1956, after much contemplation, Shimabuku announced to his students that his Karate would thenceforth be called the Isshinryu (Wholehearted/Complete style). His style—a representation of all of Okinawa's martial arts traditions—soon became immensely popular with the American Marines who found themselves stationed on Okinawa. In late 1957, Shimabuku acquired a contract with the Marine Corps to teach Karate to the Marines as an after-hours activity to promote friendship and understanding between the two nations, and he relocated his Dojo from Kyan to Agena to be closer to the two main Marine Corps bases of the day.

From 1958 to 1960, Shimabuku furthered his weapons training with the illustrious Shinken Taira (1897-1970), and, after leaving his unique mark on them, he added the kobudo kata Chatan Yara nu Sai, Urashi nu Kun, Shishi nu Kun, and Hamahiga nu Tuifa to his curriculum.

Shimabuku visited the United States twice—in 1964 and 1966— and marvelled at how his creation had taken root in the homeland of his Marine students. He retired from active teaching in 1971 and allowed his eldest son, Kichiro, to become the second soke (headmaster) of Isshin-ryu karate. Tatsuo Shimabuku—the Dragon of Isshin-ryu—died of a stroke on May 30, 1975 at the age of 66 after experiencing a brief period of illness.

- Andy Sloane Renshi

Japanese Teaching Titles

In old Japanese martial arts there were three teaching titles which recall the days when a Sensei was someone who trained soldiers (rather like a drill sergeant). The title of Renshi was awarded first. In modern terms this would be at say 4th Dan. The Renshi title meant "polished teacher" and meant one who had honed their teaching skills through teaching many students.

Next came Kyoshi which would be equivalent to say 6th or 7th Dan and Hanshi equivalent to around 8th Dan. Prior to Shotokan, Shotokai and Wado Ryu, Karate master Gichin Funakoshi of the Shoto Ryu school received the title of Renshi in 1938. It was awarded by the Dai Nippon Butokukai.

The character "Ren" means "polished, tempered" and "shi" means "person". Thus Renshi indicates a "polished instructor" or expert. The "Kyo" in Kyoshi means "professor" or "philosophy". Therefore, Kyoshi equals a "professor" capable of teaching the philosophy of the martial arts. The "Han" in Hanshi means "example, model" and indicates "a teacher that can serve as an ideal model for others", or a "senior master".

The First Karate Blackbelts

The first black belts were simply given to Funakoshi's top seven students (including Ohtsuka and Gima). A few days later a formal certification process took place where these members received their Shodan rank. Apparently Gima's cousin Tokuda received Nidan.

Choki Motobu, Chosin Chibana, Chomo Hanashiro, and Shiroma Shimpan were also pictured in the late 1920s to 1930s wearing black sashes or belts.

It seems in the early days of Shoto Ryu and Shito Ryu Funakoshi and Mabuni regarded the highest attainable grade to be 5th Dan.

147

Funakoshi Gichin, Funakoshi Gigo and Kenwa Mabuni were awarded the Renshi title.

However in 1937 the Butokukai acknowledged Karate and Chojun Miyagi was given the title of Kyoshi at the age of 49 which would imply a grade of around 7th Dan.

The other who received recognition of the same rank was Konishi Yasuhiro at 44. He was reputed to have started training in Karate around 1920. The implication here was that Funakoshi was regarded as senior to an implied 7th Dan. In 1939 Ueshima of Kyushin Ryu was awarded the title of Kyoshi by the Butokukai.

The Dai Nippon Butokukai pictured in around the 1930s

The Return of Dai Nippon Butokukai

In 1946, after the end of the Pacific war, the Dai Nippon Butokukai was dissolved of its organisational charter. But then in 1953 the Dai Nippon Butoku Kai was reestablished with a new charter and the new philosophical vision. Kumao Ohno was instrumental in this process while he served as the vice chair, with Jigo Higashifushimi, the uncle of Emperor Hirohito, becoming the chairman of the new society.

In 1972, with the endorsement of the late Hanshi Kumao Ono and the Honbu, the first official division outside Japan was established in Virginia and the east coast USA and the likes of Richard Kim became prominent officials. In 1992 the Honbu of DNBK officially established the International Division under the leadership of Tesshin Hamada overseeing all international members. In 2000, the first UK

Butoku Sai was conducted in Manchester England coordinated by Allan Tattersall.

The Renaissance of Okinawan Kobudo

If Funakoshi Gichin can be said to have introduced Karate to the mainstream, then his student Taira Shinken must hold that honour for the Okinawan weapons arts of Kobudo.

Taira was born in 1897 and begun his martial arts studies under his grandfather. He then began studying with Gichin Funakoshi.

In 1929, Funakoshi introduced Taira to Kobudo master Yabiku Moden (1882-1941). Yabiku had established the Ryukyu Kobujutsu Kenkyukai in 1925 leading study of Kobudo in Okinawa.

With the official permission of Funakoshi and Yabiku, in 1933 Taira opened a Shotokan Dojo in Gunma Prefecture where he also taught Kobudo. In around 1934 he also began studying Shito Ryu under Mabuni Kenwa who stayed with him for six months before returning to Osaka. In 1940 Taira returned home to Okinawa and accelerated his research in the traditional weapons of his homeland such as bo, tonfa, nunchaku, sai, tinbei, tekko and kama. In 1955 he established the Ryūkyū Kobudo Hozon Shinkokai as a continuation of Yabiku's Ryukyu Kobujutsu Society.

Hanshi Terry Wingrove guiding the author through an original copy of the Ryukyu Kobudo Taikan, by Taira Shinken, published in 1964

In 1964 the president of the *Zen Nihon Kobudō Renmei*, imperial Prince Kaya Tsunenori, granted to Taira the title of Hanshi and that year Taira published his greatest work the *Ryūkyū Kobudō Taikan*. The book includes the basics of Bojutsu, the Sai Jutsu and Tonfa of Hama Higa and basic nunchaku kata. In his foreword he thanked Sakagami Ryusho, the principal director of the Ryukyu Kobudo Hozon Shinkokai, Kanto district, for his assistance, as well as Inoue Motokatsu. Sakagami's most famous student is Fumio Demura.

Okinawan Kobudo Weapons

Rokushaku Bo	Quarterstaff (literally six shaku staff)
Nuntei Bo	Bo with a heavy metal end
Jo	Staff (broom handle size)
Sai	Hand held metal trident shaped truncheon.
Jutte	Single prong sai often used by Japanese police
Tonfa	Side handled baton
Kama	Hand held sickles. Often used in pairs
Kusarigama	Kama on the end of a cord or chain
Rokushakugama	Kama on the end of a bo
Nunchaku	Rice flails. Two batons with a cord
Sansetsu Kun	Three sectioned flails
Yumi	The longbow or bow. The weapon of Kyudo
Yari	Spear. The weapon of Sojutsu
Katana	Japanese-style longsword
Tanto	Japanese-style short sword
Kogatana	Otherwise known as aikuchi. A small knife.
Yamagatana	Curved sword resembling a Dao
Ryobagatana	Two edged straight sword resembling a Jian
Naginata	Japanese style halberd
Kwan Dao	Chinese style halberd
Timbei	A shield. Often made from a turtle shell
Rochin	A thrusting blade
Toyei Kama	A 'dockers hook'
Kuwae	A gardening hoe
Tekko	Knuckle dusters
Tessen	Fan
Kanzashi	Hair pin
Kiseru	Tobacco pipe

Surujin	The bolas
Eku	Boat oar
Zei	Bamboo or rattan cane
Tan kon	Police style truncheon
Hashi	Chopsticks
Tichu	Also a Yawara held with a ring
Mutsuba Yari	Trident
Tuja	Harpoon
Sanshaku Jo	Walking stick ('three foot stick')
Teppo	Firearms

Kokusai Budoin

After the war and the re-organisation of Budo, Kokusai Budoin was launched as a Japanese organisation promoting international Budo. It is significant to the history of Karate because it awarded teaching and mastery titles to style founders like Hironori Ohtsuka, pioneers like Yamaguchi Gogen and present day masters like Kanazawa Hirokazu.

The organisation, founded in 1952, has headquarters in Tokyo, Japan and has branches in around 17 countries. Kokusai Budoin is dedicated to the promotion and development of the martial arts worldwide. Many of Japan's most legendary martial artists have been members as well as members of the Imperial and Shogun families.

It was founded by a group of some of Japan's most prominent martial arts practitioners including (their final grades indicated):

- Kyuzo Mifune Hanshi 10th Dan Judo
- Master Kazuo Ito Hanshi 9th Dan Judo
- Shizuya Sato Hanshi 10th Dan Nihon Jujutsu, 9th Dan Judo
- Hakudo Nakayama Hanshi 10th Dan Kendo
- Hiromasa Takano Hanshi 10th Dan Kendo
- Hironori Otsuka Hanshi 10th Dan, founder of Wado Ryu Karate

First Chairman: Prince Tsunenori Kaya (uncle of Emperor Hirohito)
Second Chairman: Prince Higashikuni (Prime Minister of Japan).

Other members have included:

- Gogen Yamaguchi, Hanshi 10th Dan, founder of Goju Kai Karate
- Hirokazu Kanazawa, Hanshi 10th Dan, Shotokan Karate
- Kazuo Sakai, Hanshi 10th Dan Wado Ryu Karate
- Katsuo Yamaguchi Hanshi 10th Dan Iaido
- Kisshomaru Ueshiba, second grandmaster of Aikido and son of the founder
- Minoru Mochizuki Hanshi 10th Dan Aikido, 9th Dan Nihon Jujutsu
- Katsuo Yamaguchi Hanshi 10th Dan Iaido
- Kenji Tomiki Hanshi 8th Dan Aikido
- Gozo Shioda Hanshi 10th Dan Aikido
- Tadao Ochia, Hanshi 10th Dan Iaido
- Seirin Tsumaki, Hanshi 9th Dan Kobudo
- Terukata Kawabata, Hanshi 9th Dan Kobudo

History of Kokusai Budoin

In 1951, a group of Japan's most prominent martial artists from a variety of disciplines gathered in November of that year to discuss the first, large-scale open demonstration of Japanese martial arts since the end of World War II. In January the next year, The National Japan Health Association was founded. It would later be called the Kokusai Budoin, International Martial Arts Federation.

IMAF was officially founded in January 1952 by Master Kyuzo Mifune, Master Kazuo Ito and Shizuya Sato of Judo; Master Hakudo Nakayama and Master Hiromasa Takano of Kendo; Master Hironori Otsuka of Karate-do; and Kiyotaka Wake and Sueo Kiyoura. The first Chairman was Prince Tsunenori Kaya (uncle of Emperor Hirohito, and former lieutenant general in the Imperial Army), and was followed by Prince Higashikuni (the first post World War II Prime Minister, the only member of the Japanese Imperial Family to have held this post). After the first exhibition in Hibiya Park in 1952, members of IMAF continued to promote the practice of Japanese martial arts throughout

Japan. In 1953, the 2nd All-Japan Budo Exhibition was held in Okayama Prefecture, Japan. Spectators came from many cities to watch these prominent martial arts perform.

In 1958 the name Kokusai Budokai was adopted but later changed in 1965 to Kokusai Budoin IMAF shortly after the 4th Annual All-Japan Budo Exhibition in Tokyo. Prince Higashikuni became the second Chairman of IMAF in 1965. In 1968 Master Kazuo Ito and Shizuya Sato travelled to 12 countries promoting and demonstrating traditional Japanese martial arts. This was the first Kokusai Budoin World Tour. A few years later in 1970, the Government of Panama invited Master Kazuo Ito to introduce Judo to Central America. Since then, a variety of different Judo and Nihon Jujutsu styles have evolved throughout Central and South America. In 1973, Sueo Kiyoura was appointed the first President of IMAF.

IMAF continued to grow and spread the knowledge of Japanese martial arts throughout the world, and in 1975 the first international branches opened in Belgium, France, Great Britain, India, West Germany and the Netherlands. In 1976, delegates from these branches arrived in Tokyo for the 1st International Kokusai Budoin Conference. Three years later in 1979, the 1st European Congress was hosted in Paris, France.

In 1981 Denmark, Austria and Taiwan became branch IMAF countries. Later, in 1983, Gunzo Fukuhara was appointed the second President of IMAF. In the next year, the United States established an IMAF Branch and hosted the 1st IMAF Americas meetings and seminars in 1985. In that same year, the 10th Annual All-Japan Budo Exhibition was held along with a celebration in honour of Prince Higashikuni's 99th birthday in Tokyo, Japan. In 1986, Shinsaku Hogen was appointed as the third President of IMAF. In 1988, Italy and Switzerland become IMAF Branch Countries, and the 7th European Congress was held in Torino, Italy with seminars in France and the UK.

In 1983 the European faction of Kokusai Budoin headed by Minoru Mochizuku became an autonomous federation, so there was Kokusai Budoin in Japan headed by Shizuya Sato and the International Federation of Nippon Budo (IFNB) representing IMAF Europe headed by the legendary Mochizuki.

Minoru Mochizuki is one of the most highly graded masters of all time, with grades including 10th Dan Aikido, 9th Dan Nihon-den Jujutsu, 8th Dan Iaido and 8th Dan Judo. He also paved the way for

IMAF in Europe and the UK.

Mochizuki awarded Judoka Kevin Murphy (a student of Kenshiro Abbe) with the grade of 7th Dan Kyoshi in Judo and Nihon-den Jujutsu (Murphy was the only Englishman to receive this award from Mochizuki) and Murphy became the inaugural IMAF UK Director.

As a result of disorders in Japan two trends arose, the Kokusai Budoin Headquarters and the International Federation of Nippon Budo (IFNB). During the IMAF World Congress in Turin Austria, Denmark and France chose the side of the Japan Headquarters, Kokusai Budoin. The Netherlands, Belgium, Italy and England chose the side of the IFNB. Kevin Murphy was succeeded under Sato's IMAF by his two students Dave Wareing (UK Director) and Colin Hutchinson (UK Secretary).

In 1991, Europe celebrated its 10th Anniversary European Congress, an event held in Belgium with seminars in Germany. In 1992, IMAF celebrated its 40th Anniversary along with the 17th Annual All-Japan Exhibition. Later, in 1994, IMAF Americas celebrated its 10th Annual Meetings & Seminars. Since 1995, IMAF Headquarters has sponsored tours featuring Branch Representatives worldwide. This is a special time for all members to get together, practise Japanese martial arts and share ideas in organisation. Branches in Europe and the Americas have hosted numerous Exhibitions and Seminars throughout the years.

2002 was a very special year for IMAF. This marked the 50th Anniversary of the organisation. With celebrations in Tokyo, several prominent guests from government, industry and the martial arts community in Japan attended along with worldwide IMAF members. IMAF Americas celebrated its 20th Annual Meetings & Seminars while IMAF Europe celebrated its 22nd Annual Exhibitions & Seminars in 2004. The European seminar was hosted in Charleroi and saw Shizuya Sato teach Nihon Jujutsu, Tadanori Nobetsu teach Nisseikai Karate and Iwasa Sensei teach Iaido.

The author with Tadanori Nobetsu 9th Dan at a Kokusai Budoin European Congress

Gogen Yamaguchi (10th Dan IMAF)

Chojun Miyagi was teaching Karate at Kyoto Imperial University and there he was introduced to a young Karate student, Gogen Yamaguchi, who was studying at Ritsumeikan University (also in Kyoto), and he invited Miyagi to come and teach there.

Yamaguchi was born in 1909. Like Karateka of previous generations Yamaguchi actually began his studies in Jigen Ryu. According to his own writings he was shown Karate by an Okinawan named Murata from the age of ten, for ten years, then started up a club at Ritsumeiken with some tutelage from Yogi. Although Yamaguchi is one of Chojun Miyagi's best known students, it seems likely that

Yamaguchi only trained with Miyagi between about 1928 and 1931.

Yamaguchi claimed that when Miyagi saw what the young Japanese had accomplished, he left him in charge of Japanese Goju Ryu. It is likely that Yamaguchi continued to train making visits to Okinawa to "top up" his Goju Ryu.

Peter Urban, in his book *Karate Dojo*, tells a story about how Yamaguchi had killed a tiger bare-handed when he was imprisoned in a cage. This however pales in comparison to a story in Yamaguchi's own book were he single handedly took out an armed battalion of 20 Chinese soldiers in a 40 minute battle:

"Bandits on horses stopped in front of our office. I took cover as I fired my revolvers through the window, until both guns were empty. Twenty bandits with guns and Chinese swords rushed our defence. Five or six bandits broke the door down with the butts of their guns and rushed into the room.

"With my guns empty, I resorted to Goju school of karate for my defence. I adjusted myself with breathing and was ready to fight.

"The room was dark and the bandits could not use their guns freely without possible injury to each other. I had trained myself to see in this amount of light and knew I would be able to withstand the onslaught of four or five people at a time. Under such a situation, I had to dispatch the enemy, one by one.

"I avoided the first bandit who tried to strike me with his gun, and turning quickly to the right, struck him between the thighs with a roundhouse kick. He cried and fell to the ground. Another fired his gun at me from behind, but he missed. My elbow found the pit of his stomach with great force. A bloody Chinese sword slashed at me as I struck, with my right fist, the man who was wielding this sword. The fighting was confused but the narrow room was to my advantage. They rushed at me in the close quarters, which made it easy for me to fight them. When they drew near, I knocked them out using nukite (finger strikes), hijiate (elbows), shuto (sword hand) and seiken (fists), against the guns, I used tobi-geri (jumping kicks) and yoko-geri (side kick). I was able to fight more freely than in practice because I did not have any regard for my opponent's welfare.

"Luckily, only my left arm had been injured by the slash of a dagger. I went upstairs to obtain a better view and observed the bandits fallen back with stolen weapons, gun powder and supplies. It was now 7 o'clock in the morning."

Hironori Ohtsuka (10th Dan IMAF)

Hironori Ohtsuka was born on June 1 1892 in Shimodate City, Ibaragi, Japan. He was the first son of Dr. Tokujuro Ohtsuka and his first teacher was his great uncle Chojiro Ebashi, a member of the samurai class and Jujutsu teacher of the Shindo Yoshin Ryu. From the age of 13 he studied the art under Shihan Shinzaburo Nakayama Sensei who was also adept in Jikishin Kage Ryu swordsmanship.

He began attending the famous Waseda University in 1910 and continued his Jujutsu studies. In 1917 Ohtsuka joined the Kawasaki Bank, during the year he met Morihei Ueshiba Sensei, the founder of Aikido, and this began a deep influential friendship.

Shindo Yoshin Ryu was founded by Katsunosuke Matsuoka (1836 – 1898) making it a very young style as Koryu go. Matsuoka originally studied Yoshin Ryu Jujutsu and was also a student of Jikishin Kage Ryu Kenjutsu and Hokushin Ittoryu Kenjutsu as well as being a certified teacher of Tenjin Shinyoryu Jujutsu. It was in 1864 that Matsuoka formed his own style of Yoshin Ryu Jujutsu, calling it Shindo Yoshin Ryu Jujutsu. The next generation was Matakichi Inose (1852 – 1921) and finally Ohtsuka Sensei's teacher Tatsusaburo Nakayama (1870 – 1933). It is sometimes stated that Ohtsuka was the 4th grandmaster of Shindo Yoshin Ryu – but this is probably not the case. Tatsusaburo Nakayama was not the 3rd headmaster of Shindo Yoshin Ryu as is frequently stated. In 1917, the 2nd headmaster, Motokichi Inose, awarded Tatsuo Matsuoka, grandson of Shindo Yoshin Ryu's founder, a menkyo kaiden and handed over the Sokeship. Tatsuo Matsuoka died without formally appointing a successor.

In 1922 Ohtsuka met the Karate master Gichin Funakoshi. Ohtsuka had become Chief Instructor of Shindo Yoshin Ryu Jujutsu at the age of just 30, and an assistant instructor at Funakoshi Sensei's Karate Dojo. In 1924 the two met Yasuhiro Konishi who would become the next piece in the Karate puzzle. Konishi was a well respected Kendoka and had studied Muso Ryu Jujutsu at the age of six and then in high school switched to Takenouchi Ryu Jujutsu – he was therefore a natural Karate practitioner.

In the 1920s Ohtsuka also trained with Choki Motobu. It has been suggested Motobu had no respect for Gichin Funakoshi, but it seems he did respect the young Ohtsuka. Motobu taught his version of Naihanchi (Tekki) to Ohtsuka, who may well have reciprocated with

Jujutsu teachings. At this time Ohtsuka also had the chance to train with Shito Ryu head Kenwa Mabuni. The "Nihon Budo Taikei" tells of a meeting at Yasuhiro Konishi's Dojo in 1929, between Choki Motobu and Gichin Funakoshi. Also present were Hironori Ohtsuka and a Judo fourth Dan who was accompanying Motobu. Motobu arranged a challenge in which the Judoka took a grip on Funakoshi's collar and sleeve. Motobu then said, "Now you are so proud of your basic kata, show me what value they have in this situation. Do what you wish to escape." It is obvious that the odds were greatly against Funakoshi, the much younger Judoka having established a firm grip. He reportedly tried to disengage with Soto-uke and Uchi-uke with no success and he was lifted up and thrown against the wall of the Dojo. Ohtsuka Sensei was then asked to try his luck. He rose to the challenge and because of his Jujutsu background had no difficulty in dealing with the situation.

His desire to adapt Funakoshi Sensei's Karate by introducing more kumite elements caused him to grow apart from his teacher. In 1929 Ohtsuka left Shotokan to form his own style of Wado Ryu with the full blessing of Funakoshi. Ohtsuka admitted in later years that it took him another 10 years before what he wanted was actually formulated into Wado Ryu as we know it today. At this point, in 1929, he had studied Karate for eight years and was around 38 years old.

His approach to Karate and Jujutsu was extremely progressive. In 1934 his son Jiro was born and he also registered his style of Karate as Wado Ryu.

Kata of Wado Ryu:
- Pinan Nidan (known in Shotokan as Heian Shodan)
- Pinan Shodan (Heian Nidan)
- Pinan Sandan (Heian Sandan)
- Pinan Yondan (Heian Yondan)
- Pinan Godan (Heian Godan)
- Kushanku (Kanku Dai)
- Naihanchi (Tekki)
- Seishan (Hangetsu)
- Chinto (Gankaku)
- Bassai (Bassai Dai)
- Jion (Jion)
- Niseishi (Nijushiho)

- Jitte (Jutte)
- Rohai (Meikyo)
- Wanshu (Empi)

In 1938 aged 46 he was awarded the Renshi title, implying a grade of around 4th or 5th Dan. In 1942 Ohtsuka Sensei was awarded the rank of "Kyoshi Go" suggesting a grade of at least 6th or 7th Dan. In 1963, a three man team left Japan to demonstrate Wado-Ryu Karate to America and Europe. The team was composed of Arakama Sensei, Takashima Sensei and Suzuki Sensei.

Tatsuo Suzuki introduced Wado Ryu Karate to England, although technically it had already been taught here by Hiroo Mochizuki, who began his studies in Yoseikan/Shotokan but then trained with Ohtsuka Sensei. Among the early British pioneers in Wado were Ticky Donovan and John Smith. Other Japanese Wado Ryu instructors of the time were Shiomitsu Sensei and Takamizawa Sensei.

In 1966 Ohtsuka Sensei was awarded "Kun Goto Kyokujitsu Shou" (something like an OBE) by Emperor Hirohito for his dedication to the introduction and teaching of Karate.

On October 9, 1972, the Kokusai Budoin (International Martial Arts Federation) awarded Ōtsuka the title of *Shodai Karate-do Meijin Judan* (first-generation Karate master 10th Dan); this was the first time this honour had been bestowed on a Karate practitioner.

Earlier in this book we theorised a link between Yoshin Ryu's Hakuda and Okinawan Karate. Hakuda aspect refers to southwestern Japanese Jujutsu such as taught by Akiyama. This was a percussive art and in many ways was a mainland Japanese version of Karate.

Hironori Ohtsuka wrote about that link: *Every year, for purposes of promoting the Japanese martial-arts, the Butokuden in Kyoto held a national festival. In 1938, the festival focused on the originators of each martial art, however, no originator of Japanese Karate had been identified. I named the originator of the first true Japanese style of Karate-Do as Shiro-Yoshitoki Akiyama (the founder of Shinto Yoshin-ryu Jujutsu) and named this new style of Karate-Do, 'Wado-Ryu' meaning: 'Japanese-way school' or also 'Peaceful-way school' since the Kanji lettering for 'Wa' can mean both."*

Ohtsuka considered the founder of Yoshin Ryu Jujutsu (Hakuda) to be the originator of his style of Karate.

Yukiyoshi Takamura, head of the Takamura Ha Shindo Yoshin Ryu Jujutsu, a branch of the Ryu descended through from Shigeta Ohbata, said in *Aikido Journal* 117, Autumn 1999: *"The Wado-Ryu Jujutsu Kempo headquarters dojo still teaches Shindo Yoshin-Ryu in Tokyo. Wado-Ryu founder Hidenori Otsuka held a Menkyo Kaiden in Shindo Yoshin-Ryu. He received his license from Tatsusaburo Nakayama Sensei around 1921.*

"My grandfather knew Otsuka only slightly but thought highly of him. He was a man of exceptional reputation.

"I hope that Wado-Ryu does not lose its Jujutsu roots which makes it one of very few Karate styles to have a Bujutsu heritage.

When he died in 1982, Ohtsuka's son Jiro took the name Hironori Ohtsuka II and succeeded him as headmaster of Wado Ryu.

Shizuya Sato (10th Dan IMAF)

One of the systems that owes its origins to Wado Ryu is Shizuya Sato's Nihon Jujutsu. Sato Sensei was assistant to Ohtsuka Sensei in the 1950s. Sato also trained in Judo with Mifune and Ito, in Kendo with Nakayama and in Aikido with Kenji Tomiki. Born in 1929 in Tokyo, Japan, Sato began his lifetime study of Judo during middle school at age 12. Sato's father learned Judo while in the Imperial Japanese Navy during World War I, and was a senior Judo instructor for the Tokyo Metropolitan Police. Sato's father's friends and Judo compatriots included many preeminent pre-WWII Kodokan instructors, including Mifune Kyuzo, Nagaoka Hidekazu, Sumiyuki Kotani, and Ito Kazuo. When Sato Sr. died in 1948, the young Sato came under the care of these senior Judoka who lent their personal guidance and lifelong support, which greatly influenced the development of Nihon Jujutsu.

Upon graduation from Meiji Gakuin University in 1948, he joined the International Section at the Kodokan. Prior to the end of WWII, in 1945, regular Kodokan training included self defence, kata, randori (sparring), taihojutsu, and, to a limited extent, weapons training such as Kenjutsu, Jojutsu, Tanbo, and Bojutsu. This multi-disciplinary approach was in keeping with Kano Jigoro's philosophy that budo naturally evolves and grows in accordance with human experience. Postwar, a large number of non-Japanese entered the Kodokan for the first time. The majority of these young men, along with a few women, were US military personnel of the Occupation forces. Many established lifelong bonds of friendship and cooperation with Sato-

Sensei and other budo instructors, and some eventually became the pioneers responsible for introducing Japanese martial arts to the West. Significant American budoka who began their studies at the Kodokan, and later played large roles in the ensuing development of budo worldwide, particularly in North America, include Donn Draeger, Dan Ivan, and Walter Todd.

The core curriculum of Nihon Jujutsu incorporates the practical, decisive throwing, choking, and immobilisation methods of Judo; the entering and striking of Aikibujutsu; the restraining techniques of taihojutsu; and the taisabaki (evasive movement), open hand, and armed self-defence principles expounded by Dr. Tomiki Kenji. When Tomiki became the Aikido director of the Kodokan's Strategic Air Command (SAC) martial arts program (1952 – 1956), Sato became the assistant Aikido instructor, and remained so for the duration of the program.

Until mid-WWII, Aikibujutsu hand-to-hand combat instruction (as directed by Ueshiba Morihei, and Tomiki Kenji, in Japan and Manchuria respectively, as well as other instructors) comprised the core of combative training for elite Imperial Japanese military personnel. During this period, the fundamental methods of aikibutsu, Kodokan goshin jutsu, and aikido were refined and compiled.

While Tomiki taught the Imperial military in Manchuria, Ueshiba Morihei directed training in Tokyo at the Toyama School (Army officer training school), the Nakano School (site of the famous Army intelligence officers' program), and at the Navy officer candidate school in Etajima.

In 1952, the US Air Force Strategic Air Command (SAC) sent two initial groups of airmen to the Kodokan to study Judo, Karatedo, Aikido, and police techniques. This program was expanded through 1956, and by its end hundreds of US Air Force martial arts instructors had trained under Sato Sensei, who instructed both Aikido (under head Aikido instructor Tomiki) and taihojutsu techniques (under taihojutsu head instructor and senior Tokyo Metropolitan Police Taihojutsu /Judo instructor Hosokawa Kusuo).

In the early 1950s, Sato Sensei began teaching Judo and self-defence at US military facilities around Tokyo.

In 1957, Sato Sensei founded the US Embassy Judo Club where he continued to develop and refine the techniques that ultimately evolved into his Nihon Jujutsu.

Author's note: Fumio Demura told me that he too studied at this site and was keen to point out that he considered Shizuya Sato was teaching Judo rather than Jujutsu. I suspect that after Jun Osano and Minoru Mochizuki, previous heads of the Nihon Jujutsu division, left Kokusai Budoin, that Shizuya Sato took the job on himself. It was at this point that the Nihon Jujutsu division became essentially the practice of pre-war Judo and Tomiki Aikido.

Minoru Mochizuki (10th Dan IMAF)

Minoru Mochizuki was born April 7, 1907 in Shizuoka. His grandfather was the last descendant of a line of samurai and taught Kenjutsu.

Mochizuki began his martial arts training in around the 1910s. His first style was Gyokushin Ryu Jujutsu under the grandmaster Sanjuro Oshima. After this he studied many other arts but in his advanced years, recognised as a 9th Dan Nihon Jujutsu by IMAF, he tried to assemble all his knowledge into bringing back Gyokushin Ryu and wrote a manual on Nihon-den Jujutsu.

Mochizuki's first Judo teacher was Toku Sanpo. Because Toku was Okinawan and was known to perform breaking demonstrations it is not too much of a stretch to think he may have taught Mochizuki Karate as well. Although Toku was feared and revered Kyuzo Mifune was held in even greater regard and he became Mochizuki's next teacher. The young Mochizuki even came to the attention of Judo founder Jigoro Kano who asked Mochizuki to go and learn other arts and bring his knowledge back to the Kodokan.

Mochizuki went to study Daito Ryu Aikijujutsu under Morihei Ueshiba and stayed a student of Ueshiba all of his life. Mochizuki was awarded a mokuroku (similar to 2nd or 3rd Dan) in Daito Ryu and later awarded the 10th Dan Aikido by IMAF on the authority of the Ueshiba family.

Mochizuki's Karate studies are not so well documented but it has been claimed he trained with Gichin Funakoshi and may have received the grade of 5th Dan. Mochizuki taught the first ever European Karateka and among the first European Aikidoka in Jean Alcheik and Claude Urvois and later he sent Hiroo Mochizuki, Mitsuhiro Kondo (9th Dan IMAF), Shoji Sugiyama and Tetsuji Murikami to teach in Europe.

Mochizuki studied Japan's oldest extant martial arts school the Tenshin Shoden Katori Shinto Ryu, and so impressed the headteacher that according to some sources he was offered marriage to the headmaster's daughter so he could become the new Soke. Mochizuki also held the Budo grade of 8th Dan in Kendo. Mochizuki studied Muso Shinden Ryu with Hakudo Nakayama (10th Dan IMAF) and achieved the grade of 8th Dan.

Mochizuki trained under headmaster Takeji Shimazu in Shindo Muso Ryu (a school focussed around the Jo) and attained the grade of 5th Dan.

The JKA is Formed

By the end of the war there were no 5th Dans in Shotokan under Gichin Funakoshi. His favoured son, the dynamic Gigo Funakoshi, had died a 4th Dan in 1945.

The Japan Karate Association (JKA) was formed in 1948 with Iaso Obata as Chairman.

In the early 1950s, Shigeru Egami was promoted to 4th Dan and Masatoshi Nakayama to 3rd Dan. Nakayama, who had been a 2nd Dan at the start of World War 2, was elected Chief Instructor in 1955 and unlike some of his peers was a professional Karateka. Nakayama advanced through the Dan grades very quickly. In 1946 he was 2nd Dan, in 1955 he possibly double graded and achieved 5th Dan; between 1956 and 1960 he took his 6th and 7th Dans, and in 1961 he was 8th Dan.

He was assisted by the likes of Nishiyama who took his Shodan in 1946, his Nidan in 1948 and his Sandan in 1950.

Many instructors left the JKA in the early 1950s and formed the Shotokai organisation which stuck to Funakoshi's original 12 Kata and 5th Dan grading cap.

The JKA system of gradings led to the formation of WUKO and then FAJKO. This was an effort to modernise and standardise Karatedo around the world regardless of style and to unify the arts in the way that Olympic sports like Judo had been.

Terry Wingrove, the only foreigner in the front office of either recalled training at this time.

He said: *"This was a unique opportunity for me to see firsthand the genro (elders) up close and compare their attitudes and intentions on a daily basis. I felt privileged to see Ohtsuka (Wado), Yamaguchi (Goju), Nakayama, Ito & Takagi (Shotokan), Ito, Hayashi, Sakagami (Shito), Konishi (Shindo Jinen Ryu) all up close outside the Dojo plus the Okinawan masters such as Kinjo, Gima and Mabuni and many other leaders all on a near daily basis as they were very keen to find out the latest news and not miss the boat while at the same time sniping in a Japanese way at their peers."*

Talking about his role at FAJKO that saw him working alongside Kanken Toyama's student Hideo Tsuchiya, he said: *"I found in my job I was continually being asked by each and everyone to contact their local groups all round the world to answer the local queries and at the same time get the local news to see what their rivals were up to.*

"After a couple of years I formed an objective opinion re the masters that were genuinely friendly and those that were aloof and very difficult to deal with."

Wingrove is an English Karateka with an Italian mother, had trained in France and was now living in Japan, so he was well-placed to work in an international role. He explained: *"I had one big thing in my favour as the linguistic skills of the masters were very limited I slowly built up a position of trust with most of them and as I travelled the world with the FAJKO and WUKO admin."*

Terry Wingrove in Japan in 1972 with Karate Jutsu master Hiroshi Fujimoto who introduced him to the Motobu and Uechi traditions.
[Pic courtesy of Terry Wingrove.]

164

He said it was a time when many of the masters, perhaps including Nakayama and Yamaguchi but also perhaps the likes of Aikido master Ueshiba, were re-writing their tatemae to suit post-war Budo.

Wingrove said: *"I realised the petty jealousies that filtered through and the 'Japanese way' of dealing with that very difficult period from 1936 to 1945, when it seemed magically all the masters were in no way involved in the fighting and killing of the period but were 'meditating or working on the land in Manchuria', this was possibly believable when told to us on an individual basis but how could all these devotees of Budo be so far away from the action? In truth they weren't and had reinvented their past after WW2 and the rebirth of Karate internationally as sports Karate in its new guise to the world.*

"I listened for years to the stories between these elders late at night in their cups when we were overseas especially as they relived their WW2 activities and I realised that some of them were running protection rackets or collecting bad debts or beating up the locals in China, Manchuria and SE Asia and much closer to home within Japan. I would sit quiet in the corner listening saying nothing then when I was one to one at a later date I would mention a specific event I heard and try to get them to expand on it."

Terry Wingrove and his mentor Hideo Tsuchiya on the board of WUKO in 1974 [Pic courtesy of Terry Wingrove]

Hirokazu Kanazawa (10th Dan IMAF)

Kanazawa Sensei teaching in Portugal [Pic: JP Casainho]

"Enoeda was the powerhouse, Shirai was the leader, Kanazawa was the technician" were the words Hanshi Terry Wingrove used when I asked him his first impressions of the Shotokan masters when they arrived in England in the early 1960s. And Kanazawa was indeed the technician.

Kanazawa is known for being a Shotokan disciple of Funakoshi and Nakayama but actually his first Karate teacher was an Okinawan Shorin Ryu practitioner named Yamashiro who had befriended Kanazawa's brother. It was this that attracted him to learning further in Tokyo. Kanazawa Sensei was one of the "university generation" of Shotokan students studying at Takushoku.

He was not of the first generation of students like Makoto Gima (Shoto Ryu) or Hironori Ohtsuka (Wado Ryu); he was one of the youngsters who, led by masters like Masatoshi Nakayama, studied the art as a sport.

Kanazawa however was training at a time when master Funakoshi was still overseeing classes. Kanazawa recalled: *"Funakoshi Sensei didn't want so much Jiyu Kumite but the seniors, they liked it very much."*

In the 1950s Kanazawa was fighting in the first ever Japanese Karate championships and broke his hand. With a bandaged broken hand he went into the finals and won, using just his kicks and his other hand.

He researched the origins of Shotokan by training in Shorin Ryu in Okinawa. One of the styles most closely related to Shotokan's origins is Shorin Ryu (Kobayashi Ryu) established by Itosu's student Chosin Chibana. Kanazawa and Enoeda went to Okinawa to study the style with Yuchoku Higa but only Kanazawa was accepted to train. This training gave Kanazawa a new dimension and saw him creating new forms based on older kata like his Koryu Gankaku.

In an interview with Graham Noble Kanazawa said: *"The first time I saw* [Yuchoku Higa on the makiwara] *I thought he wasn't very good. I thought he was missing the target. But I misunderstood. After four or five times I understood. He would hit each corner of the makiwara then the centre. Then on the last punch he would hit so the makiwara sheaf was knocked off the makiwara. Special technique."*

He is a strong advocate of Tai Chi in his Karate training. He also integrated Kobudo into Karate chiefly the nunchaku.

Kanazawa teaches a number of Goju Ryu forms including Suparimpei. He seems to be close friends with Goju Ryu master Morio Higaonna and it may be that the two have trained together.

Kanazawa Sensei runs his own organisation SKIF, and now the father of Karateka, he is referred to as Soke. He is also director of Kokusai Budoin IMAF's Shotokan Karate division and was awarded the title of Meijin (enlightened master) by Tokugawa Yasuhisa – the only living master to hold that title.

A student of Kanazawa, Phil Handyside (now 9th Dan) recalled meeting his teacher: *"I met Kanazawa Sensei at the railway station and my initial reaction was 'what a gentleman.'*

"He even offered to take me for a cup of tea and of course I said, 'no, no Sensei, please let me buy you a cup of tea.'

"We picked him up in a Japanese car which he loved and he put on a great course for us. In terms of internal power he was like nothing I'd ever seen before.

My greatest inspiration, a real master and a gentleman."

Kanazawa taught generations of students. Another student of Kanazawa in the 2000s, Kicki Holm of Denmark said: *"He is such an inspirational man. That he could move so quickly even at the age of 80. He is so generous as a person with his time and teaching."*

The author teaching Bojutsu to Kicki Holm who graded under Hirokazu Kanazawa

Kenneth Funakoshi

It is remarkably fitting that one of Kanazawa Sensei's most well known students was a relative of Gichin Funakoshi.

Kenneth Funakoshi was born in Honolulu in 1938. His father, Yoshio, was apparently Gichin Funakoshi's third cousin and practised Karate with him in Okinawa from 1915 until he left for Japan.

The young Kenneth Funakoshi studied Kempo under a student of William Chow. Chow, in turn, was a student of Masayoshi James Mitose. In 1960, Funakoshi began to train in Shotokan Karate under Hirokazu Kanazawa, who had been sent to Hawaii by the Japan Karate Association. After three years, Kanazawa was followed by Masataka Mori, and Tetsuhiko Asai. In 1969, after Mori left Hawaii, Funakoshi was named as the chief Shotokan instructor of Hawaii.

Key JKA Shotokan events

When was Gichin Funakoshi born?
The son of Gisu Funakoshi, Gichin was born in 1868 in Shuri.

Who were Funakoshi's teachers?
His primary teacher was Azato. His secondary teachers were Itosu and Matsumura. He also trained with Kiyuna, Niigaki [thought to be Aragaki] and Toono. It might be said he also learnt from Jigoro Kano.

When was the first Funakoshi demo to Japan?
Funakoshi gave a demo in Shuri in 1921 for the Emperor Hirohito.

Where was the first Funakoshi Dojo in Japan?
Funakoshi taught a small class at the Meisei Juku in Tokyo in 1922.

When were Funakoshi's first writings published?
Ryukyu Kempo Tode was published in 1922. The revised edition *Rentan Goshin Tode Jutsu* was published in 1925.

Who were the first black belts?
Funakoshi awarded black sashes to seven of his students including Shinkin Gima in around 1924.

When was Shotokan established?

The original Dojo the Shoto Kan was built in 1936. It was destroyed in in a 1945 air raid.

Who ran the Shoto Kan?

Funakoshi was assisted by his youngest son Gigo who died young in 1945.

When was the JKA formed?

The Nippon Karate Kyokai (Japan Karate Association) was founded in 1949.

When did Funakoshi die?

He died on April 26 1957.

Who have been the senior graded Shotokan Karateka?

Shinkin Gima held 10th Dan in Shoto Ryu (old Shotokan); Hirokazu Kanazawa holds 10th Dan awarded by IMAF; Masters Nakayama, Nishiyama, Asai, Kase and Enoeda held 9th Dan. Nakayama, Asai and Nishiyama were awarded 10th Dan posthumously. Many others held 10th Dan which they claimed were in Shotokan but may have only been recognised by smaller associations. Ken Funakoshi holds 10th Dan. He is not thought to be a close relative of Gichin Funakoshi. Others may have been considered 10th Dans by virtue of grades in other arts, such as Vernon Bell.

What became of the old Shoto Ryu Karate?

The school was passed from Shinkin Gima to Ikuo Higuchi who currently holds the grade of 9th Dan within Kokusai Budoin (IMAF).

When were the first JKA All Japan Karate Championships?

They were held in 1957 in Tokyo. Kanazawa won the Kumite and Hiroshi Shoji won the Kata. Kanazawa also won both Kata and Kumite in 1958. Notably, Asai won the Kumite in 1961 and 1963, Shirai won Kata and Kumite in 1962 and Enoeda won the Kumite in 1963. Contrary to the claims of various Westerners, all the All Japan Kata and Kumite champions between 1957 and 1990 were Japanese.

Who was the first Karate instructor in Europe?

There may have been several people come to Europe who had

experienced Karate. For example Judo founder Jigoro Kano had discussed Karate with Gichin Funakoshi. But the first actual Karate instructor was Hiroo Mochizuki in July 1956. He was followed by Tetsuji Murakami in November 1957 and then Mitsuhiro Kondo and Shoji Sugiyama.

Author's note: I was lucky to attend training with Mitsuhiro Kondo in around 2003, almost 50 years after he started teaching Karate, and to my amazement he demonstrated the agility of a teenager, as he jumped into athletic Kani-basami scissors takedowns. I also noted Kondo Sensei's careful precise movements even when doing something as mundane as kneeling. Around the same time, a teacher of mine trained and graded under Ikuo Higuchi, successor to the old school of Shoto Ryu established by Funakoshi and Gima.

Goju Ryu: Miyagi's successors

Seiko Higa

A notable early student of Chojun Miyagi was Seiko Higa, especially notable to historians as he also trained with Miyagi's teacher Higaonna.

Higa was born in Naha and at age 13 he began to study under Higaonna until the master's death four years later. Higaonna had three students at the time: Juhatsu Kyoda (1887-1968), Chojun Miyagi (1888-1953), and Seko Higa (1898-1966). Kyoda went on to create his style, To On Ryu, and Miyagi assumed the mantle of Higaonna's legacy, later founding Goju Ryu. Higa, a policeman at the time, continued his studies with Miyagi for 38 years until Miyagi's death.

In 1931, Higa retired from the police force and opened his Dojo in the Kumoji section of Naha. Only three students of Miyagi's were allowed to open a Dojo while the master was still alive: Seko Higa, Jin'an Shinzato, and Jinsei Kamiya. In 1935, Higa went to the island of Saipan to teach Goju Ryu but later returned to Okinawa.

One of the most prominent Goju Ryu teachers in Okinawa today is Tetsuhiro Hokama. He was born in Taiwan in 1944 to parents of Okinawan descent. He began training informally under his grandfather, Seiken Tokuyama, in 1952. In 1961 his formal training began at the Naha Commercial High School Karatedo club, which was under the supervision of Chiyokutani Irashi, a student of Seiko Higa. That same year he began training with the legendary Seiko Higa himself.

It was at Higa's Dojo where Hokama met Shinpo Matayoshi and began learning Kobudo and Kingai Ryu.

Another prominent Okinawan Goju teacher from the Higa lineage is Yoshio Kuba, a 10th Dan black belt and the head of the Kenpokai in Okinawa. He was a direct student of Seikichi Toguchi Sensei, who was a student of Chojun Miyagi Sensei and Seiko Higa Sensei.

He runs a full time acupuncturist practice in Okinawa and is head of the Acupuncture Association in Japan.

Miyazato, Anichi Miyagi and Morio Higaonna

Possibly the most famous Karate master in the world today is Morio Higaonna. It is particularly fitting given that Chojun Miyagi, who learned from someone called Higaonna (Kanryo), for someone called Higaonna (Morio) to learn from someone called Miyagi (Anichi).

Morio Higaonna was born 25th December 1938 and began training in Karate when he was 14. He studied Shorin Ryu with his father and at 16 began to train in the Goju Ryu style. In 1955 the young Higaonna was training in the garden Dojo of the late Chojun Miyagi Sensei. His instructor was Anichi Miyagi Sensei.

In 1957 the garden Dojo moved to a permanent building. This was called the Jundokan, and he continued his training there, training up to five hours every day. After his instructor Anichi Miyagi Sensei moved away to work on an American oil tanker Higaonna Sensei gained a place at the Takushoku University in Tokyo, and it was around this time that the first official Dan grading was organised. Higaonna Sensei was awarded 3rd Dan. The year was 1960. It was in Tokyo that Higaonna Sensei taught at the famous Yoyogi Dojo. Many thousands of students passed through this Dojo, some of the more notable being Senseis Ogawa, Todano and Terauchi and from the West Ernest Brenech, James Rousseau, Bakies Laubscher and from Shotokan Karate Terry O'Neill.

In an interview published in Terry O'Neill's *Fighting Arts International*, Higaonna described the situation after Miyagi's death.

Higaonna said: *"After Chojun Miyagi Sensei died, Eiichi Miyazato took his position as chief instructor, but nobody considered Anichi*

Miyagi [again, not thought to be a close relative of Chojun]. *I believed in both and followed both. In 1970 they separated which was a hard blow to me. I had a very difficult time trying to decide whom I should follow. I decided to continue with Anichi Miyagi Sensei, since he had always taught me."*

When asked who he believed was the successor to Chojun Miyagi, he replied: *"My honest opinion about this… is that the successor of Chojun Miyagi Sensei is Mr Anichi Miyagi."*

Higaonna Sensei's view is far from unanimous however. In his last interview, Miyazato said: *"Anichi Miyagi was my student. He came to Miyagi Chojun to study with him, but he only trained for a short time and Miyagi Chojun died. Anichi Miyagi came to train under me. He trained with Miyagi Chojun under my direction for maybe one year. During that time if you add up the number of days it came to about one month training in one year. Anichi Miyagi was never recognized as a student of Miyagi Chojun. He was only 22 years old at the time of Miyagi's death. In the Goju Ryu society in Okinawa few know the name Aniichi Miyagi. No one other than Morio Higaonna has ever heard of him."*

When I asked one senior Karateka who knew Higaonna and Miyazato for their view on Higaonna, they replied: *"Higaonna to me is faultless and anyone that criticises him is more than likely jealous. He is a master who outshone his former teacher."*

During the late sixties and early seventies Higaonna Sensei began to travel to several of the countries that were practising Okinawa Goju-Ryu. He was invited to perform a demonstration at the World Karate Championships in Paris in 1972 and his reputation as one of the strongest Goju-Ryu practitioners in the world was growing. In 1979 in Poole, England with the help of his senior international instructors the IOGKF was set up.

Tadanori Nobetsu and Kai Kuniyuki

Tadanori Nobetsu (9th Dan Hanshi Goju Ryu Karate, 6th Dan Kobudo), born in 1935 in Kyushu, is the present chief director of Kokusai Budoin and reportedly studied Goju Ryu under Ei'ichi Miyazato and Tomoharu Kisaki. Other teachers, for whom the author can find little information, are listed as Kuge Baisho, Isamu Asada and Taiwanese Feeding Crane master Chin Mei Long. In 2014 he celebrated 50 years of teaching the Nisseikai club in Saitama Prefecture. Nobetsu, who reportedly cycles to work every day, is also an enthusiast of herbal remedies, nutrition and poetry.

Another Kyushu-born Goju Ryu master is Kai Kuniyuki (10th Dan). Kai was born in 1943 and began his training aged 13 under Mori Kyu before training under Miyazato. Kai also studied Yoshinkan Aikido under Shioda Gozo, Muso Jikiden Eishin Ryu, Shindo Muso Ryu and Asayama Ichiden Ryu, among many other styles.

RyuTe

RyuTe is a classical form of Karate Jutsu emphasising life protection by controlling an opponent without the use of excessive force. It is related to the Tuite of Motobu Ryu and the Matsumura but also includes striking techniques common to the likes of Uechi Ryu.

RyuTe includes Tuite, grappling, locking, and escape techniques; Kyusho Jitsu, striking techniques that exploit the body's weak points; Kobudo, weapons techniques and Bogu Kumite, protective gear sparring. It was founded by Taika Oyata.

Taika Seiyu Oyata, born 1930 in the island of Henza near Okinawa, was the founder of RyuTe and was one of the masters responsible for introducing Tuite and Kyusho Jitsu to the West. RyuTe, originally called Ryukyu Kempo, is a blend of Tode, Shuri Te, Naha Te and Tomari Te. In a 1983 letter, Oyata said: *"During my studies I accidentally happened upon a couple of techniques while analytically researching a kata. I approached one of my teachers and asked him… He made a couple of corrections concerning the two techniques I had worked out from the kata but he would not tell me of the others. He only encouraged me to work out the other techniques hidden within the katas. This hidden art is known as Tuite by the very few who have been introduced to and practice it. This unravelling of Tuite techniques took many years with much experimentation as the old masters hid the art very well, with turns and twists which were designed to throw off the person trying to interpret the grappling art from the striking techniques. I found after many years that there were over 500 Tuite techniques hidden within the various kata. After understanding these grappling techniques I came to understand why the old Karate masters were virtually undefeated, for they did not use only Karate but also Tuite."*

Oyata was a descendent of Zana Oyakata, a high ranking official of the Shuri Government before the Satsuma invasion Okinawa. Due to his heritage, Oyata received instruction from a direct descendent of the Okinawan Warrior class, Uhugushuku No-Tan-Mei. According to Oyata, the Uhugushuku family were retainers of the Okinawan Monarchy serving as guardians for the Shuri Kingdom, a relationship dating back before the 14th Century. Uhugushuku was known as a kakurei bushi "hidden warrior", meaning he did not teach Karate Jutsu publicly.

Under Uhugushuku's tutelage, Oyata learned the principles of weapons fighting, weapons kata and theory of technique. Uhugushuku introduced Oyata to Wakinaguri, a descendent from the ancient Chinese families sent to Okinawa as emissaries. Wakinaguri continued to instruct Oyata after the death of Uhugushuku and was responsible for his deep understanding of martial arts principles. After the death Wakinaguri, Oyata trained with Nakamura, Shigeru and other famous Okinawan instructors. Chosin Chibana was one of the instructors that Taika went to early on after both Uhugushiku and Wakinaguri died. The RyuTe website claims that Taika trained with him for about three months until they argued over the Naihanchi kata. Chibana told him that these kata were for fighting on rice paddies which Taika thought was funny and laughed. Apparently this offended Chibana and Taika was asked to leave.

Taika also participated in a research group with Seikichi Uehara who eventually inherited the Motobu family system, where they compared tuite.

Part Six: International Karate

Early Karate for the Gaijin

William Adams (1564 –1620), known in Japanese as Miura Anjin or 'Samurai William', was famously the first 'English Samurai' and quite possibly the first Englishman to set foot in Okinawa.

In 1600 he was the first Briton to reach Japan during a five-ship expedition for the Dutch East India Company. Adams was the first ever (of a very few) Western samurai and became a key advisor to the shogun Tokugawa Ieyasu. In 1614, Adams stayed in Okinawa from 27 December 1614 until May 1615.

In 1616 Japan banned trade with foreigners. The only exception was that traders in Nagasaki bay were entitled to import from China. The powerful Dutch East India Trading Company got round the ban in 1634 by partitioning off part of Nagasaki with ditches to in effect make their own island called Dejima.

In 1667 the first Swedish book about Japan and China was written by two Swedish sailors who had been there on Dutch ships. In 1731 the Swedish East India Trading Company was created, inspired by the likes of the Dutch East India Company to trade with the Far East as far as Japan and Guangzhou and in 1745 the Swedish Ship Gotheborg was famously sunk on the way back from China.

As well as importing spices, Sweden was also exporting steel to Japan. Swedish steel from railway sleepers was used to make the legendary Japanese sword.

Richard Fuller describes nine manufacturing methods for pre war Japanese swords. One of these is Gendaito: *"Fully hand forged from mill steel or (more often) 19th century railway tracks made from Swedish steel. Differentially hardened in the traditional manner using water as a quenching agent. Possesses an active hamon and hada."*

Ryujin Swords states: *"The best 'mill steel' gendaito are made from mid-19th century railway tracks that were manufactured from Swedish steel and exported to Japan. Swedish steel has been highly prized for its excellence and purity for centuries. The use of good Swedish steel therefore meant that the smith could make a blade that was potentially in the same category as the highest performing traditional blades. Furthermore, the presence of manganese means that the metal is tougher than straight carbon steel."*

The company got a 15-year monopoly on the trade, and the goods exchanged were Swedish timber, tar, iron and copper against tea, porcelain and silk. The company was situated in Gothenburg. The company existed for 82 years and its vessels made 132 expeditions with 38 different ships. Even though the company in the end went bankrupt it made an enormous profit in most of its years of operation and it has influenced Swedish history in several ways.

In the 1750s the art of China was the height of fashion in Sweden. A small Chinese palace was even built in Sweden. Count Carl Fredrik Scheffer, who was the governor to the young crown prince Gustaf (Later King Gustaf III), was well informed about the Confucian ideas. He had as a six-year-old boy acted at the inauguration of a small Chinese pavilion presented to his mother Queen Louise Ulrica of Prussia on her birthday the 25th of July 1753. The small palace was built secretly at Drottningholm, the royal summer palace, in Chinese taste.

In 1759 Anders Ljungstedt was born in Sweden. He later worked for the Swedish East India and in 1820 was appointed Sweden's first consul in China. He was well loved in Macao where he was called Long Sital.

By 1774 90% of tea in Sweden was imported from China. In 1775 Swedish physician Carl Thunberg moved to Dejima near Okinawa. In 1776 he met the Shogun in Edo, and in 1779 he returned to Sweden. Thunberg was a student of the earlier Swedish physician Carl Nilsson.

One 19th century Karate master named Matsu Kinjo was the son or grandson of a European. Kinjo can also be pronounced Kanagushiko and he had the nickname Itoman Bunkichi. His name Matsu was also in the Okinawan dialect Machiya.

It may be that the European country that adopted primitive Karate skills the most prominently in the 1800s was France - and this is seen today by the Karate influence on the art of Savate.

A French naval expedition under Captain Fornier-Duplan onboard Alcmène visited Okinawa on April 28, 1844.

Trade was denied, but Father Forcade was left behind with a Chinese translator, named Auguste Ko. Forcade and Ko remained in the Ameku Shogen-ji Temple near the port of Tomari.

After a period of one year, on May 1, 1846, the French ship Sabine, commanded by Guérin, arrived, soon followed by La Victorieuse, commanded by Rigault de Genouilly, and Cléopâtre, under Admiral Cécille.

The Ryukyu court in Shuri (now part of Naha) complained in early 1847 about the presence of the French missionaries, who had to be removed in 1848.

Admiral Guérin landing with his troops in Tomari, Okinawa in 1855

France would have no further contacts with Okinawa for the next 7 years, until news came that Commodore Perry had obtained an agreement with the islands on July 11, 1854, following his treaty with Japan.

Subsequently sailors developed a style of boxing based on Chuan Fa or Tomari Te called Chausson.

Chinese Martial Studies states: "*A precursor of modern French Boxing called "Chausson" is said to have been popular with French sailors in Marseilles and was later adopted by the French Navy. This style of kickboxing featured higher kicks and open hand slaps rather than punches.*

"These facts have been expanded upon to introduce a nautical element into the modern mythology of French Boxing. Some commentators claim that these arts were actually shaped by their origins on the cramped spaces of a ship. They assert that the hands were left open so that they could steady a sailor on the deck of a pitching ship. Of course it could also be that punching someone in the

178

face with a closed fist without boxing gloves is not always a great idea (ergo the frequency with which a wide variety of global fighting systems use open hand strikes). Such traditions will of course sound vaguely familiar to students of the southern Chinese martial arts, which are also sometimes said to have been shaped by their nautical precursors."

The emperor Napoleon III, nephew of Napoleon Bonaparte, famously proclaimed that "The Empire means peace" ("L'Empire, c'est la paix"), but the French Navy were involved in various foreign campaigns at that time.

Napoleon's challenge to Russia's claims to influence in the Ottoman Empire led to France's successful participation in the Crimean War (March 1854–March 1856).

The French frigate La Guerrière commanded by Admiral Roze was the lead ship in the French Campaign against Korea, 1866. Napoleon took the first steps to establishing a French colonial influence in Indochina.

In China, France took part in the Second Opium War along with Great Britain, and in 1860 French troops entered Beijing. The French Navy also had a mild presence in Japan in 1867-1868, around the actions of French Military Mission to Japan, and the subsequent Boshin war.

Although the beginnings of Savate came from the Paris slums, formalisation of a fighting style using predominantly kicking, rather than punching (as was the case in English boxing at the time) began with the French Navy developing Chausson— meaning "slipper," in reference to the sailors' footwear at the time. Chausson soon became a local street game about Marseille, Aubagne and Toulon and was named jeu Marseillais (game from Marseilles).

During the Napoleonic Wars the average Frenchman's exposure to Chausson increased as they were conscripted into fighting, which served to spread the fighting style and perhaps was influential in exposing Chausson and Savate practitioners to each other. At the time both Savate and Chausson did not involve striking the opponent with the fists, probably due to fist fighting being outlawed by the French government. Instead, they preferred to use open-hand techniques such as slapping to defend against kicks and to strike opponents. Again, another influence on Savate came during the Napoleonic Wars with French prisoners of war being exposed to boxing by their British captors, but it was not until much later did boxing make its way into the fighting style.

Savate began to be regulated with the opening of the first salle (official training school) by the famous instructor Michel Casseux (1794-1869), also known by his nickname of le Pisseux. Disallowing such techniques as head butting, eye gouging and grappling, Cassaux created a system of Savate and added la canne (cane fencing), calling it the "Art of Savate." He went on to teach many famous members of French society.

Formal Karatedo was introduced to France in the 1950s when Jean Alcheik and Claude Urvois studied at the Yoseikan under Minoru Mochizuki and along with Henri Plee set up Dojo in Paris.

Author's note: My maternal great great grandfather August Nilsson was a sailor in the Swedish Navy, as was his father Nils Johann. August's son coached his sons in boxing. I have records of a branch of the family from two generations earlier sailing to Canton in 1784 and staying in Okinawa. My paternal great great great grandfather Herve Briant was a sailor in the French Royal Navy at the time Napoleon III sent his marines to Tomari, and they came back with 'chausson'. Both August and Herve came to Liverpool in the 1800s; this is just an example of the cultural mixing pot cities like Liverpool were, and it is also the oldest China Town in Europe.

Karate in the USA

Karate may have been formally introduced to what is now the United States by Kentsu Yabu (1866-1937) when he visited Hawaii – which was not a US state until later.

Yabu arrived in Honolulu in 1919. Giving lectures, classes and seminars on Karate he reportedly taught 700 people at one demo.

Various Karate masters made their way to the American state of Hawaii but in terms of the continental United States the first instructor is thought to be Robert Trias, head of the States Karate Association. Trias started martial arts in 1942 and claimed to have studied with a Chinese master named Hsiang who lived for a time in Okinawa.

The story goes that while serving in the United States Naval Reserve as a Metalsmith First Class during World War II, Trias was stationed on or around Tulagi in the Solomon Islands from June 1944 to November 1945, and was a Navy champion middleweight boxer.

There he met Tung Gee Hsiang, a Chinese missionary of Chan (Zen) Buddhism. Hsiang often watched Trias work out and imitated his boxing footwork, and he asked to practise with Trias. Trias refused because Hsiang was "just a tiny little guy," but Hsiang was persistent and at last Trias agreed to spar with him. Hsiang gave Trias "the biggest thrashing of his life" and Trias then asked Hsiang to instruct him in the martial arts.

Hsiang taught Trias some Hsing-I as well as some Okinawan Shuri Te Karate, which Hsiang had learned from Choki Motobu in Okinawa.

He later opened the first public Karate school run by a Caucasian in the United States mainland in Phoenix, Arizona, in 1946 and in 1948 he founded the United States Karate Association.

Jointly with John Keehan, Trias hosted the first national Karate tournament in the United States, called the 1st World Karate Tournament, at the University of Chicago Fieldhouse in 1963 in Chicago, IL.

Trias claimed his 9th Dan in 1964 had been awarded by Konishi. He later claimed his 10th Dan had been awarded by Shinkin Gima.

Ed Parker was born in Hawaii in 1931 and began training in the martial arts at a young age in Judo and later boxing. Some time in the 1940s, Ed Parker was introduced to Kempo by Frank Chow and William Chow, a student of James Mitose. It seems likely that Mitose had briefly trained under Choki Motobu or at least been inspired by him. Mitose began teaching Kempo and Jujutsu in Hawaii in the 1930s, Chow perhaps in the 1940s, and Parker opened up a celebrity-friendly Dojo in California in the 1950s, where he taught everybody from Chuck Norris to Elvis Presley.

Jim Mather is now the chairman of the United States National Karate Association and head of one of America's oldest Karate schools, the California Karate Academy. His primary instructor was the legendary Tak Kubota.

Mather Hanshi has studied Karate since 1955, beginning under Hiro Nishi, a Japanese black belt in San Jose. Mather also trained at the Pacific Judo Academy under Bill Montero and studied Kempo under Sam Brown, a student of William Chow.

Serving in Korea, he worked in Army Intelligence and did reconnaissance. While there, he studied the martial arts with Dr. N.B. Lee, who awarded him his black belt.

He returned home after his discharge and opened a Dojo near San Jose. In 1965, Mather hosted the US Winter Nationals Karate Championships at the San Jose Civic Auditorium. Chuck Norris won his first grand championship title and Mather's friend, the then relatively unknown Bruce Lee, performed one of the demonstrations that would soon make him famous.

Mather also hosted the Pacific Coast Karate Championships at Foothill College as Ron Marchini of Stockton defeated the nationally ranked Joe Lewis.

While a graduate student at Stanford, Mather taught tennis, weight training, and volleyball in Stanford's physical education department, as well as continuing to teach Karate at his Dojo, the California Karate Academy. He was also goalie coach for the Stanford water polo team, which was one of the top four teams in the US at the time. In addition, he served as start coach for the sprinters on Stanford's top-rated swimming team, which included two of the world's top sprinters.

He authored hundreds of articles for various national and international publications. For several years, he wrote a monthly column for *Black Belt* magazine, the world's most read martial arts publication.

One of his students, Tom Sadowski, was selected to represent the United States at the World Karate-do Championships in Los Angeles in 1975. Several of his other students have been selected over the years for the national team. In the late '80s, he joined the USAKF, the official national governing body for Karate under the US Olympic Committee (USOC), and was soon named one of five martial arts instructors comprising the National Coaching Staff for the official US Karate Team, which led the US team into international competition. He was one of a group of coaches who worked with the USA Karate Team at its first training session at the US Olympic Training Center at Colorado Springs.

Mather was also known as the Arrow Catcher for his speed and reflexes. Bill Zarchy, a graduate film student at Stanford and award-winning filmmaker, heard of Mather's arrow catching ability. With access to an extremely high-speed camera, Zarchy filmed Mather catching arrows at Felt Lake, behind Stanford. He edited some of the footage into a demo print he sent out to get film work. PBS saw it and was intrigued. They interviewed Mather and, using Zarchy's footage, created a short feature entitled *The Arrow Catcher*, which ran on PBS for many years. Ray Anders, stunt coordinator for *The John Newcomb Show* saw the feature and invited Mather to appear on his show, calling his arrow catching "One of the 10 greatest visual stunts he ever witnessed". Anders later became stunt coordinator for a show entitled *The Guinness Game*, in which participants tried to set a new Guinness World Record while a panel of contestants bet whether or not it could be done. Mather succeeded in setting a new world record. He later appeared twice on ABC's *That's Incredible!* The first time, he caught arrows. The second, he broke an arrow in mid-flight with a Shuto. In 1985, the BBC invited him to appear on *The Paul Daniels Show*, its top rated variety show. Knowing this would be his last performance, Mather demonstrated several new skills – including shattering an arrow in mid-flight with a pair of nunchaku and cutting one in two with a katana.

Fumio Demura: The Kobudo master of California

Fumio Demura is a Shito Ryu Karate master largely responsible for spreading Kobudo in the West. He was famously Pat Morita's (Mr Miyagi) martial arts stunt double in the first four *Karate Kid* movies and taught Bruce Lee to use the nunchaku. He holds the rank of 9th Dan in Shito Ryu Karate.

Demura was born on September 15, 1938, in Yokohama, Japan. At the age of nine, he began training in Karate and Kendo under an instructor named Asano. At the age of 12 he started training under Ryusho Sakagami in Itosu-kai (Shito Ryu) Karate. Demura received his 1st Dan black belt in 1956, and won the All Japan championship in 1961. In 1959, he began training in Kobudo under the direction of Taira Shinken. He has also trained with Shorin Ryu (Kobayashi) grandmaster Chosin Chibana, Matsubayashi Ryu grandmaster Shoshin Nagamine, in Judo with Shizuya Sato and Yoshinkan Aikido grandmaster Gozo Shioda. In 1965, Demura came to the United States, representing the Japan Karate-do Itosu-kai. From his base in southern California, he became well known for his Karate and Kobudo skills. In 1971, he was ranked 5th Dan, and he remained at that rank until at least 1982.

Through the 1970s and 1980s, Demura wrote several martial arts books, including: *Shito-Ryu Karate* (1971), *Advanced Nunchaku* (1976, co-authored), *Tonfa: Karate weapon of self-defense* (1982), *Nunchaku: Karate weapon of self-defense* (1986), *Bo: Karate weapon of self-defense* (1987), and *Sai: Karate weapon of self-defense* (1987).

British Martial Arts

Jujutsu was the first commonly taught martial art in Britain and its introduction dates back some 60 years prior to the advent of Karate and Aikido.

There are a few examples of Westerners studying oriental combatives prior to the 1890s: members of the Dutch and Swedish East India Trading Company in Canton and Nagasaki; army officers (typically French) in Japan at the start of the Meiji Restoration, Portuguese and Jesuits in Japan; Napoleon III's navy ships being sent to the Orient and the sailors returning with Savate; and cities like Liverpool hosting a Chinatown whereby Kung Fu could have been practised. So we cannot say that before the 1890s, no Westerner ever performed a Jujutsu throw or held a katana; but those that did have not been recorded in a Dojo teacher-student setting.

Most of the early practitioners were in Jujutsu – with one exception – an army officer, whose name is recorded as Mr Norman, went to Japan in the 1890s to teach the Japanese about British military systems. He took up Kendo and became proficient. He later taught the art in England.

For a true record of Japanese martial arts as we know them being practised in the West, we must turn to British Jujutsu and Judo. 1892 is an excellent starting point. That year a Mr Takashima Shidachi gave a Jujutsu demonstration in London for the Jujutsu society and that same year Rudyard Kipling wrote about British sailors in Yokohama encountering the Meiji police.

We should point out that at this point Kodokan Judo had only been established for 10 years and the Dai Nippon Butokukai was still three years away.

In 1897, Manchester newspaper sub editor Ernest J Harrison arrived in Yokohama and was accepted into the Tenjin Shinyo Ryu school of Jujutsu, one of the principal styles that influenced the development of Kodokan Judo.

EJ Harrison subsequently became the first Western Judo blackbelt. Harrison was one of the earliest martial arts authors in English and his books are still highly sought after. It is fair to consider Harrison the pioneer of English Judo.

In 1898, Edward William Barton-Wright, a British engineer who had spent the previous three years living in Japan and studying the Shinden Fudo Ryu in Kobe, returned to England and announced the formation of a "New Art of Self Defence".

This art, he claimed, combined the best elements of a range of fighting styles into a unified whole, which he had named Bartitsu (Barton-Jujutsu). He combined Jujutsu with English boxing, French Savate, French cane fighting and more to create an Edwardian self defence method. Of course the most famous Bartitsu practitioner who never lived was Sherlock Holmes who practised "Baritsu".

It is interesting that the Koryu Barton-Wright studied in Japan was Shinden Fudo Ryu, because that means he could have shared training partners with Mabuni Kenwa.

The *Bugei Ryuha Daijiten (Great Encyclopaedia of Martial Arts Schools)* says Mabuni was the 17th generation Sôke of the school and passed it on to his son Kenei, who then taught Ueno Takashi, another colleague of Sato Kimbei.

Barton-Wright arranged for Japanese master Yukio Tani (perhaps from the Fusen Ryu) to come to England. At the time the equivalent of the proverbial "Britain's Got Talent" was the music hall shows.

Customers might see a strongman like William "Apollo" Bankier, a Jujutsu man like Tani, a wrestler like George Hackenschmidt or some combination – the Jujutsu and wrestlers would challenge members of the audience and put on a show 'stretching' them.

In 1900 Sanda Uyenishi arrived in England from the Tenjin Shinyo Ryu and by 1904 joined with Tani in establishing a Jujutsu school.

Another man of interest is one Harry Hunter, who taught "Super-jujitsu". Hunter learned his Jujutsu while stationed in Japan with the British Navy in 1904. He became the self styled "Jujitsu Champion of Europe". At some point it seems that he taught William Green of Liverpool and also taught the police unarmed combat.

In 1903 Theodore Roosevelt was graded to 1st Dan in Judo. Presumably this was an honorary grade.

In these early days a few books were written on the subject. William Garrud wrote *The Complete Jujitsuan* in 1914, Bruce Sutherland wrote *Jiu Jitsu Self Defence* in 1916 and Leopold McLaglen wrote *Jiu-Jitsu: A Manual of the Science* in 1918. Mrs Emily Watts and Raku Uyenishi produced a book entitled *The Fine Art of Jiu-Jutsu.*

In 1906 Gunji Koizumi left Japan and sailed via Bombay and North Wales to Liverpool. There he saw advertised the post of chief instructor to Kara Ashikaga's school of Jujutsu.

Ironically the Kara Ashikaga was the north of England's first known martial arts school and Mr Ashikaga himself probably never existed – he was just a Japanese-sounding marketing ploy. 110 years later even the most brazen McDojo might think twice about pulling that stunt!

And so Koizumi took up the post and taught in Liverpool until his departure to London. His club remained and Arnott St School in Walton, where my great uncle studied Judo, became the Northern base of the BJA.

In 1918 Gunji Koizumi created the Budokwai as a society to teach Jujutsu, Kendo and other Japanese arts to members of the public. He founded a Dojo at 15 Lower Grosvenor Place, Victoria, London SW1 and the club officially opened on Saturday, January 26, 1918 with 12 members, making it one of the oldest Judo clubs in Europe. Koizumi became the first president of the Budokwai and Yukio Tani the first chief Judo instructor.

According to the Budokwai: *"The first Englishman to join was O.D. Smith as member number thirty-seven: Yukio Tani was member number fourteen, and W.E. Steers number fifty-two. Steers was to introduce Ernest John Harrison in May 1919; they had been friends in Japan. The first woman member, number sixty, Miss Katherine Cooper-White, joined in April 1919. Following her lead other women joined and within a few years there was a regular women's section."*

It has been claimed that the Budokwai is the oldest martial arts club outside Japan but according to the club itself this is not the case:

"It is often said that The Budokwai is the oldest judo society outside of Japan. This is not the case. The oldest club outside Japan is the Seattle Judo Club on the west coast of America, which dates back to at least 1903 or even earlier. Recent information has come to hand to prove that the oldest club in Europe is the Cambridge University Ju-Jutsu Club, formed by ECD Rawlins, of Trinity College, in 1906. This was and is a closed organisation limited to members of the University."

In July 1920, Dr. Jigoro Kano (the founder of Judo) visited Britain and the Budokwai for the first time. He was accompanied by Hikoichi Aida who stayed in Britain and instructed at the Budokwai for two years. A member named Tanabe received his first Dan, becoming the Budokwai's first home-grown black belt.

Tani and Koizumi were promoted to Nidan, despite technically never having studied Judo, but clearly their Jujutsu was up to par.

Professor Jack Britten was a London born student of Yukio Tani who moved to Liverpool in about 1920. He established the Alpha Jujutsu school in the Kensington area which we suspect was Liverpool's (and therefore the north of England's) second public martial arts club. Britten was a respected Jujutsu instructor and many leading martial artists such as Bob Clarke, Ronnie Colwell and Andy Sherry began their training under him in the 1950s.

In 1928 another Japanese master came to England. His name was Mikonosuke Kawaishi. Like Koizumi and Tani he was originally a Jujutsu man who later converted to Judo.

He had studied under a master named Yoshida Kotaro who was hereditary grandmaster of Yanagi Ryu (a branch of Yoshin Ryu Hakuda or Jujutsu) and was also one of the top students of Daito Ryu headteacher Takeda Sokaku.

Kotaro famously introduced Takeda to his most famous student Morihei Ueshiba, later the founder of Aikido. Kawaishi also studied Judo with Isogai Hajime.

It is said the Judo of Kawaishi was that taught in Kyoto (Dai Nippon Butokukai) which differed from the Kodokan Judo of Tokyo.

Kawaishi began teaching in Liverpool, and like Tani he subsidised his income by acting as a professional wrestler, named Matsuda.

He taught his Jujutsu, Aikijujutsu and Judo to a small group of students, the only name of which we know is Gerald Skyner who established the Kawaishi Ryu, in Liverpool. His teacher then departed for Europe and became a famous Judo teacher.

The spread of Jujutsu in England naturally stagnated during 1939-1945, but in this time many members of the merchant navy sailed to places like Japan and Singapore and brought back with them exotic methods of pugilism.

During World War II the British Army enlisted WE Fairbairn and EA Sykes to come up with an unarmed combat system. Both were seasoned veterans of the Shanghai Municipal Police, with Fairbairn having experience of Judo and 33 years experience in the police. Fairbairn created his own martial art, Defendu.

Other martial artists who claimed to have studied Jujutsu during the Second World War include Jim Blundell and Vernon Bell. The history of Jim Blundell (who trained with William Green) is documented by the British Ju Jitsu Association which he founded.

By the time Vernon Bell introduced Karate to England in 1956, the arts of Jujutsu and Judo had already been taught here some 60 years. The Edwardian music halls were no strangers to the sight of Japanese

Jujutsu players grappling with wrestlers and strongmen and eventually, thanks to masters like Gunji Koizumi and Yukio Tani, these arts spread through cities like London and Liverpool. It was not until the 1950s however that Karate appeared.

The start of European and British Karate

A Frenchman, Claude Urvois, and a French-Algerian, Jean 'Jim' Alcheik, trained in Shizuoka, Japan at the Yoseikan Dojo of Minoru Mochizuki, a master who has studied all of the main Japanese martial arts (mostly with the founder of each of these arts no less) and they convinced Mochizuki to introduce the arts of Karate and Aikido to Europe.

Alcheik was of Algerian and Turkish descent and did military service in Tunisia. He was awarded 1st Dan in Judo in 1952 from Raymond Sasi and in 1954 he and Urvois were invited to the Yoseikan where they not only trained with Mochizuki but in Judo under Kyuzo Mifune, Aikido under Kisshomaru Ueshiba and in Shito Ryu with Masaji Yamaguchi (no relation to Gogen as far as it is known). They also studied Kendo, Jujutsu and Iaido.

Urvois and Alcheik joined with their friend, Judo instructor Henri Plee, in establishing a base for European Karate, and on July 12 1956, Minoru's son Hiroo Mochizuki arrived in Paris, later followed by Mitsuhiro Kondo to Switzerland, Shoji Sugiyama to Italy and Tetsuji Murikami, who would end up in England. At this point Alcheik held a 4th Dan in Aikido, a 2nd Dan in Karate, a 2nd Dan in Kendo and a 3rd Dan in Judo.

In around 1960 Alcheik was recruited by the French government as an agent and sent to Algeria to fight against the OAS Organisation Armée Secréte, a paramilitary organisation seeking Algerian independence from France – the background to this is documented in *The Day of the Jackal*. Alcheik was sadly killed in a parcel bomb explosion in a villa.

In 1956 Vernon Bell, a 3rd Dan Judo instructor under instructors like Kenshiro Abbe, began corresponding with Henri Plee and attending his classes in France, soon after Bell started what would today be called a "study group" at the tennis courts of his parents' back garden. We should note this was around eight years before Japanese masters like Kanazawa, Enoeda and Suzuki ever came to this country.

We should note that while many Jujutsu schools such as Jack Britten's may have taught atemi waza or strikes that had much in common with Karate or Kempo, this chapter will only deal with official Karate-Do schools derived from the main Okinawan schools.

We should also note that Bell's Judo teacher Kenshiro Abbe – a great master who seemingly studied every art BUT Karate – did begin to advertise his credentials as including Karate. Abbe was a master of Jujutsu, Judo and Aikido so his repertoire of strikes was likely impressive, but since Abbe had not actually studied Karate, we do not class it as such.

To help understand the 'dark ages' of British Karate, from 1956-1963, we will analyse the historical records of the British Karate Federation and other sources.

The early history of British Karate

Michael Manning and Terry Wingrove giving a Karate demo in the early 1960s before the JKA masters arrived

What kind of Karate was first brought to the UK?

Yoseikan founder Minoru Mochizuki studied Karate with Gichin Funakoshi and some suggest he was awarded the grade of 5th Dan. The Karate of Yoseikan resembled old style Shotokan. Mochizuki was also a master of Aikido under Ueshiba, Judo under Mifune (and briefly Kano) and many other styles. We can safely say that Mochizuki's varied training will have 'coloured' his Karate. At his Yoseikan Dojo a Shito Ryu instructor named Yamaguchi also taught there, so Yoseikan also had this influence. Reading Henri Plee's Karate book, the Karate of Yoseikan was good, basic Karate.

190

Kata were initially fewer, but then Plee added several of his own Taikyoku kata. At one time six Taikyoku kata were taught before Heian Shodan. In 1962 Plee wrote: *"A 1st Dan knows 2 or 3, a 2nd Dan 4 or 5, a 3rd Dan 6 or 8."* Here it is assumed he was including Heian kata in his calculations, so estimated that a 3rd Dan would know perhaps only 5 Heians, Tekki Shodan, Bassai Dai and Kanku Dai. This may explain why Plee added extra Taikyoku kata.

Plee added: *"The 5th Ei-an [Heian Godan] is one of the most difficult Katas with the Katas of Tekki (which are three in all, all in Kiba Dachi). There are a great many other Katas, about twenty but they have nothing original about them. Master Funakoshi said that they could only be a combination of the Ei-an and the Tekki."*

Vernon Bell was adept at Jujutsu, Judo and to some degree Aikido before ever studying with the Yoseikan, so we may also assume these skills will have been transferable to his Karate to some degree. Bell was awarded 1st Dan after 18 months of study on March 13 1957, dated on his certificate April 1 1957. He was awarded his 2nd Dan on July 19 1959 under Tetsuji Murikami. Bell's group was called the British Karate Federation.

Vernon Bell's first Karate students on record were: Dennis Clarke (the earliest recorded on August 18 1956), Michael Manning and Gerald Tucker as well as a D Blake and P Byron. In this very first year other students included D Brandon, B Dolan, D Dyer, Kenneth Elliott, B Miles, L Pearson and Trevor Guilfoyle.

British Karate pioneer Vernon Bell and some of his earliest students

Author's note: In 2013, Michael Manning told me: *"I started having Judo lessons under Vernon at Thurrock Technical College in 1955, I was 18 years old. Things were very basic, coconut mat and a canvas sheet.... I finally reached the dizzy heights of 3rd Kyu. Mr Bell asked me if I would like to have Jujutsu lessons. He wouldn't teach anybody* [Jujutsu] *below green belt* [in Judo]. *I jumped at the chance.... Mainly our Jujutsu lessons consisted of a few basic locks, a few trips and sometimes a glimpse of Atemi Waza. It was this 'dirty fighting' that drew me in.... One morning Mr Bell showed us a scratchy film about Karate.... He had been visiting a Dojo in Paris..."*

When was the first Karate grading in Britain and who graded?

On April 30 1957, at Maybush Road, Vernon Bell awarded the grade of 6th Kyu to Trevor Guilfoyle and Gerald Tucker.

When was the second Karate grading in Britain and who graded?

On May 31 1957, at Maybush Road, Vernon Bell awarded the grade of 6th Kyu to Michael Manning, P Byron, DF Clarke and Ken Elliott.

Michael Manning said: *"We were really stumbling around in the dark. Vernon would make weekly visits to Henri Plee's Dojo in Paris, come back and pass on what he had learned.... Vernon would be so badly bruised he could only walk with a stick."*

When did the first oriental Karate instructor come to Britain?

On July 19 1957, Vietnamese Hoang Nam 3rd Dan (presumed to have studied some Kung Fu-like art prior to Karate and billed as "Karate champion of Indo China") taught his first class at Maybush Road. Michael Manning said: *"It was an eye-opening experience... Nam was very small, very lithe and most polite. He made allowances for our lack of even the most basic skills and it was a joy to learn from him."*

When was the first public Karate demo in Britain?

On July 20, 1957, Hoang Nam, Vernon Bell and his senior students gave a display of Karate at a village fete in Ilford.

When was the third Karate grading in Britain and who graded?

On July 21 1957 Hoang Nam awarded 6th Kyu to D Blake, P Brandon, B Dolan, D Dyer and B Miles; 5th Kyu to Mike Manning and Ken Elliott; and 4th Kyu to Trevor Guilfoyle and Gerald Tucker.

When were the first brown belts awarded in British Karate?

On December 21 1957 Vernon Bell awarded 3rd Kyu to Trevor Guilfoyleand Gerald Tucker.

Who was the first English woman to study Karate?

Doris Keane from Romford and a Miss Higgins have both been quoted as such at various times by Vernon Bell. It is possible that Higgins was the maiden name of Keane.

Where was the first UK Karate Dojo where Karate was taught?

The British Legion Hall, St Mary's Road, Upminster, Essex began classes in December 1957.

Who was the first Japanese to teach Karate in Britain?

Tetsuji Murikami (1927-1987) 3rd Dan Yoseikan under Minoru Mochizuki and 1st Dan of the JKA arrived in England in July 1959.

Michael Manning said: *"He began his first lesson by telling us that we were a load of rubbish. This didn't please Mr Bell, after all he was our Sensei and we were the product of his teaching. We practised full contact kumite and some of us wore cricket boxes with a thought to marriage in later life! Murakami sussed this out and ended this practice by delivering a Mae Geri to one unfortunate, completely splitting the box.....On another occasion...Murakami showed us a defence against a strangle hold and slammed Bob [Buckner's] head hard into a wall. There was really no need for that level of violence."*

Who was the first student to obtain 2nd Kyu and 1st Kyu?

Michael Manning was awarded 2nd Kyu on July 19 1959 and 1st Kyu on February 1 1960. In applying for Manning's 1st Kyu, Vernon Bell wrote to Minoru Mochizuki directly saying: *"He is in charge of beginners' classes and was graded to 2nd Kyu by Mr Murakami on July 18 1959. He has been doing Karate for four years regularly every week and has good execution of all five ippon and sanbon Kata and the first three Pinan Kata. He can defeat six lower kyu grades in succession in Shiai and his technique is very good."*

Who were the first students to obtain 1st Kyu under Murakami?

Three years after Michael Manning was awarded 1st Kyu by Vernon Bell, Tetsuji Murakami awarded the grade of 1st Kyu to Terry Wingrove and Jimmy Neal.

When and where was the first national weekend seminar?

The first Karate summer school was held at the Ippon Judo Club, Scarborough, above the Imperial Hotel in September 7th-12th 1959. It was funded by Judo enthusiast and local business magnate Peter Jaconelli. Tetsuji Murakami taught the seminar. The event was repeated the following year.

Author's note: As the mayor of Scarborough and the owner of an ice cream business Jaconelli was wealthy enough to pay for visiting instructors to stay in Scarborough. Some excellent instructors taught there, including Kenshiro Abbe, Norman Grundy and Kevin Murphy.

Where was the first Karate Dojo outside London/Essex area?

The Liverpool branch of the British Karate Federation was set up by Frederick Gille in around 1959 and officially recognised in 1961. Training was at Harold House Jewish Boys Club in Chatham Street before relocating to the YMCA in Everton where it became known as the Red Triangle. Early members included Andy Sherry who had previously studied Jujutsu with Jack Britten.

When was the first Karate Dojo in Scotland?

Edward Ainsworth, a blackbelt Judoka, set up the first Karate study group in Scotland having attended the third 'Karate Summer School' in 1961. The Dojo was at Auchen Larvie.

When was Karate introduced to Manchester and who by?

Despite nearby BKF Dojos in Liverpool (such as the Red Triangle) it is thought that Karate was introduced to Manchester in around 1960 by Martin Stott who had no affiliation with Vernon Bell. It appears Stott had trained with a teacher in Paris called Tam Mytho (alternatively Tham Ny Tho) who was Vietnamese and junior to Henri Plee. Stott, it seems, corresponded with Bell in 1961 over affiliation; it appears this did not go ahead, but Stott continued to teach anyway. In an interview with *Traditional Karate* magazine the late Danny Connor who trained with Stott said: *"My father saw an advert for a Karate club opening in Ashton-Under-Lyne, and so I went along to this Judo club that was called Kyushindokwai. There, Martin Stott was teaching Karate, and so, at last, I learned how to pronounce that word. The mats at the club were a series of bedspreads with sheets pulled over them. I started training there, alongside Roy Stanhope, Tony Hudson... This was about 1960. I trained at the same club for three years, and then Martin invited me to be his partner and we moved to central Manchester and opened a gym there. Now at this time, we thought that you only had to know three katas to get your black belt. They were Kata One, Kata Two and Kata Three. There were no names! Somehow we located a book called 'What is Karate?' by Mas Oyama, and I used to hold the book while Roy Stanhope executed the katas that were in it."*

Who was the first notable Brit to practise Karate to black belt level outside of Vernon Bell's organisation?

Charles Mack was graded 1st Dan Shotokan by Masatoshi Nakayama on March 4 1962 in Japan. His grading kata was Bassai Dai.

What was the next Karate style to come to the UK after Yoseikan?

Shotokai Karate was introduced to England in 1963 by Mitsusuke Harada in 1963. Harada was graded 5th Dan, a very senior grade at the time, by Gichin Funakoshi himself.

When was Wado Ryu Karate introduced to the UK?

Yoseikan inheritor Hiroo Mochizuki returned to Japan from France and studied Wado Ryu with the founder, so when he returned in about 1963 technically he introduced Wado Ryu to England. Officially however the art was introduced by Tatsuo Suzuki, a 6th Dan, in 1964.

When did official JKA Shotokan come to the UK?

Vernon Bell was ratified as a JKA blackbelt on February 5 1964 having corresponded with the JKA in Tokyo and relinquished his Yoseikan grade. Taiji Kase, Hirokazu Kanazawa, Keinosuke Enoeda and Hiroshi Shirai gave the first JKA demo at Kensington Town Hall on April 21 1965.

Why did JKA Shotokan replace Yoseikan Karate in the UK?

When Vernon Bell began teaching Karate in 1956, with Tetsuji Murakami and under Henri Plee and Hiroo Mochizuki, he was under the impression that the Yoseikan Dojo was the personal HQ of Gichin Funakoshi and that Murakami was a designated representative of the JKA. Eventually it came to light that this was not the case and so Bell contacted the JKA directly and asked for his grades to be ratified in Shotokan. The JKA obliged and Bell requested Hirokazu Kanazawa and other Japanese instructors to come and live in England. Murakami took umbrage and left the country, later re-emerging as a 5th Dan Shotokai under Harada. At this point Bell had already fallen out with Henri Plee.

Who were the first UK students to be graded brown belt in JKA Shotokan?

Jack Green was awarded 2nd Kyu by master Kanazawa on June 24 1965; Andy Sherry and Joseph Chialton were graded 1st Kyu around the same time; and Eddie Whitcher and Robert Williams were awarded 1st Kyu in February 1966.

Who were the first UK students to be physically graded black belt 1st Dan in JKA Shotokan?

Andy Sherry and Joseph Chialton of the Red Triangle, Liverpool were graded 1st Dan by master Enoeda on February 10 1966 and Blackpool area instructor Jack Green around the same time. Sherry, Green and

Whitcher were also the first to be graded 2nd Dan in 1967 at Crystal Palace. The first female blackbelt was Pauline Laville graded by Kanazawa in 1967.

Who were the first to be graded 1st Dan in Britain by Kanazawa?

Edward Whitcher on April 20 1966. He was followed by Robert Williams, Ray Fuller and Michael Randall.

Who were some of the other Liverpool Shotokan Karate pioneers?

Terry O'Neill, whose father trained in Jujutsu with Gerry Skyner before the war, began training with Andy Sherry in about 1960; Ronnie Colwell, who began studying Jujutsu with Jack Britten in 1953, was also an early Karate instructor teaching "Kempo" in the Southport area. He is not listed in the records of the BKF and it is assumed he augmented his Jujutsu training by training in the 1960s-70s with the likes of Terry O'Neill and later Budokan Karate with Chew Choo Soot; Charles Naylor was also a founding member of Andy Sherry's group.

Who was the pioneer of Shotokan in the Midlands?

Judo instructors Jonny Brown, Tommy Ryan and Les Hart began teaching Karate in around 1963 probably from a book. Their only notable student was Cyril Cummins who began studying with them in 1964. He also trained on seminars with Harada and was awarded 1st Dan in 1966 by 'Budo of Great Britain'. He later retook his Shodan with Hirokazu Kanazawa and was a prominent KUGB instructor, running the Birmingham Shotokan Karate Club.

Who were the early pioneers of Wado Ryu Karate in the UK?

Among the first 1964 students of Tatsuo Suzuki were David 'Ticky' Donovan, John Smith and Danny Connor. John Smith, who studied Wado Ryu Karate under Tatsuo Suzuki from 1964, began teaching in London in 1968. He later joined with Danny Connor to devise a system of Karate called Bujinkai which included influences from Connor's Kung Fu training including Preying Mantis. The Bujinkai Academy was launched in Plymouth in 1972.

Who was Britain's first Shukokai practitioner?

Scotland's Tommy Morris visited founder Chojiro Tani's Dojo in Kobe in 1967. Morris became Scotland's first blackbelt.

When did Vernon Bell lose control of British Karate and why?

According to *Shotokan Dawn* from around 1963 Bell's health began to deteriorate and he suffered a nervous breakdown, so for the two years 1963-1965 he took a back seat in the Dojo, both to his seniors Murakami and later Kanazawa and to his assistant instructors Terry Wingrove and Jimmy Neal. By 1965 many students were growing closer to Kanazawa than to Bell. Among those seniors worth mentioning are Nick and Chris Adamou, Michael Randall, Eddie Whitcher and Mick Peachey. In 1966, Kanazawa's contract with Bell ended and he went to teach in South Africa for a spell. Many London students (loyal to Kanazawa) and Liverpool students (loyal to Enoeda) decided to break away from Bell and form their own group called the Karate Union Great Britain (KUGB). Eddie Whitcher was the senior member of the KUGB at the time of the break in 1966. On the tournament scene the Liverpool Red Triangle Club was the most successful. In 1967, 1968, 1969, and 1970 Andy Sherry won the men's Kata; and every year from 1971 to 1978 Terry O'Neill did the same (with the exception of 1976 when Dave Hazard won.) Sherry and O'Neill also dominated the men's Kumite between 1967 and 1978. From 1979 to 1992, Red Triangle Karateka Frank Brennan dominated both the Kata and Kumite.

Keinosuke Enoeda: The Tiger of British Shotokan

Enoeda Sensei was born on 4 July 1935 on the island of Kyushu, Japan. As a youth, he trained in Kendo and Judo, and played baseball. By the age of 16, Enoeda had reached the rank of 2nd Dan in Judo. He entered Takushoku University and, being impressed by a Karate demonstration there, began studying that martial art and within two years was the proud holder of Shodan. Another two years found him Club Captain. One his teachers was Gichin Funakoshi. After graduating from university, Enoeda studied at the Japan Karate Association (JKA) in Tokyo under Masatoshi Nakayama, then the

JKA's Chief Instructor. He also trained in Kumite under the direction of Taiji Kase. In 1961, he fought a notable tournament match against Keigo Abe, winning by decision after six extensions. He won the JKA All Japan Championship in 1963 against Hiroshi Shirai. During this period, Enoeda acquired the nickname Tora ("Tiger" in Japanese), after Nakayama had described his fighting. On 20 April 1965, following the JKA's policy of sending instructors abroad to introduce Karate to the rest of the world, Enoeda travelled to England with JKA instructors Shirai, Kanazawa, and Kase. He began teaching in Liverpool and had a flat in Percy Street, in Liverpool City Centre, close to the Anglican Cathedral, and his transport was a bright orange Volkswagen Beetle. He taught British Shotokan Karate legends such as Andy Sherry, Terry O'Neill, Bob Poynton, Charlie Naylor, Cyril Cummins, Frank Brennan, Dave Hazard, Harry Cook, Bob Rhodes, Billy Higgins and many more.

Enoeda's grading dates:
1st Dan   November 27 1955
2nd Dan   November 23 1956
3rd Dan   June 13 1960
4th Dan   June 12 1962
5th Dan   March 8 1964
6th Dan   April 1 1970
7th Dan   April 1 1974
8th Dan   October 1 1985
9th Dan   March 29 2003

What became of Martin Stott's Manchester Karate school?

Stott's Karate teaching may have been quite basic but it did produce some notable Karateka in addition to Danny Connor and Roy Stanhope. In the early 1960s Stott's school became affiliated to Tatsuo Suzuki's Wado Ryu and it is thought Stott's Dan grades were automatically recognised.

In 1965 Billy Higgins and a friend witnessed a free-sparring session at the Wado-ryu class run by Martin Stott. They were so impressed that they joined Stott's club the next night. In 1970 Higgins had earned his 1st Dan in Wado Ryu Karate. In 1970 he represented Great Britain at the European Karate Championships held in

Hamburg, Germany. As part of the squad he was awarded a bronze medal in the individual Kumite event. By the time he was a 2nd Dan in 1972 the commute from Liverpool to London to train with Suzuki was becoming tricky so he moved over to KUGB Shotokan.

At the 1972 European Karate Championships held in Brussels, Belgium, Higgins was part of the British team that lost to the eventual winners, France, in the Team Kumite final. That same year he came second in the Kumite event at the WUKO All Styles World Championships held in Paris.

In 1975 Higgins captained the British All Styles Karate team, managed by Steve Arneil, at the World Championships held in Long Beach, California. The team also included Terry O'Neill, David 'Ticky' Donovan and Bob Rhodes. The team became the first non-Japanese team to be crowned Team Kumite World Champions.

Another early student of Stott was Steve Powell, who writes: *"I first started out training in Karate in the Wado Ryu style at Milton Hall on Deansgate, Manchester, this was early June 1968, this is the entrance as it is today. I spent most of the time picking splinters out of my feet and being bawled at."*

Powell told me that some members of the club were prone to bullying and the quality was poor at the time with Stott resorting to teaching out of a book.

He added: *"I noticed one of the brown belts had superior technique to the rest (Bill Taylor) and he was opening a class at the YMCA, so I left. I then moved to the YMCA on Peter Street, Manchester, under Bill Taylor, and in early 1969 we changed over to the Shukokai Style of Karate. I started teaching there late 1969 after Bill Taylor left, and continued teaching until 1984. I used to wake up in the morning and go straight to the gym, go home for dinner, and then return to teach. Little wonder the gym was full of Champions."*

In 1973 Powell was awarded 2nd by Shigeru Kimura and went on to attain 5th Dan before moving over to the Jeet Kune Do system in which he is now a senior instructor.

What became of Vernon Bell and his senior students after the KUGB was formed?

In 1966 Bell and Charles Mack (the first Briton to be awarded Shodan in Shotokan in Japan and the first to be awarded 5th Dan in Judo) set up the British Karate Control Commission with Alan Francis and chairman. Bell left the JKA and reverted to the Yoseikan method of Shotokan and even began inviting Hoang Nam back to teach.

By the late 1960s one of Bell's senior students, Terry Wingrove, was living in Japan and had become employed by the Federation of All Japan Karate Organisations (FAJKO) and through his many contacts arranged for various Japanese instructors to visit Bell as patrons of his organisation. Among the most notable patronage of Bell's organisation was Masafumi Suzuki of the Nippon Seibukan. Among Bell's loyal students who stayed with him after the split were Ted Clarry and his son Chris at the Upminster Dojo; and Trevor Jones in the Manchester area. Bell maintained his Jujutsu classes too and by the time of his death in 2004 aged 81 he was graded 10th Dan in what he described as Tenshin Shinyo Ryu Jujutsu.

One of Vernon Bell's senior students, Paul Masters, went on to train in Japan under the headmaster of the genuine Tenjin Shinyo Ryu and became the only Westerner to be awarded the Menkyo Kaiden in the system. Paul Masters has since awarded a Menkyo Kaiden in the system to his son Lee Masters.

Trevor Jones' Manchester Yoseikan/Seibukan Dojo was inherited by his student Mike Newton who in 2002 was graded 7th Dan Karate, Jujutsu and Kobudo by Vernon Bell and may have subsequently graded 8th Dan.

The British Karate Federation, which had been signed over in Vernon Bell's time, was resurrected in around 2007 as a member of the World Karate Federation and parent group of the English Karate Federation. Michael Manning, who may well be Vernon Bell's oldest (in the sense that he trained the earliest) student, continues his interest in the martial arts. In 2013 he told me: *"I managed to contact some of Vernon's old students, Brian Hammond, Jimmy Neal, Terry Wingrove and Bill McGee a real blast from the past.... I sometimes even get the chance to don a gi and get stuck in.... When we do get together, talk always seems to come around to Vernon Bell and the golden days of British Karate. The younger students' eyes glaze over, yawns are stifled... But we don't care we were the first!"*

Since the passing of Vernon Bell, Terry Wingrove is the UK's longest serving Karate teacher, the only one to be awarded the 9th Dan in Japan and one of the few in the world to have studied with a legendary generation of Bujutsu masters, living in Japan for 21 years. He was the captain of the UK's first ever Karate club and one of the first in the UK to study Shotokan, Aikido, Goju Ryu and Shito Ryu.

Wingrove was born in London in 1941 and began his martial arts studies at the age of 11 in 1952 with Judo/Jujutsu at the famous Budokwai. In 1957, at the age of 16, he began studying Karate in the UK's first ever Karate club, Vernon Bell's Yoseikan, having already joined the Jujutsu club. In 1963 Terry became captain of the first ever British Karate team. He also trained with Yoseikan masters like Tetsuji Murikami and Mitsuhiro Kondo and travelled to Europe to train with Jim Alcheik. In 1965 the JKA Shotokan masters came to England and Terry subsequently went to South Africa to study Shotokan with Hiroshi Shirai who graded him 1st Dan. In 1967 Terry arrived in Japan and later became a senior officer in FAJKO. He began studying Shito Ryu (Tani ha Shito Ryu, known as Shukokai) and was graded 3rd and 4th Dan by Chojiro Tani.

Terry's teacher for three years was Katsumi Fujiwara, a Shukokai master who had also trained under Choki Motobu. Here he was introduced to Yawara (old Koryu Jujutsu) by masters like Dr Kimbei Sato, and introduced to a plethora of Chinese martial arts including Pakua. Hideo Tsuchiya (a student of Kanken Toyama) became a mentor to him in FAJKO and the two remain close to this day.

He began to pursue the old Karate Jutsu methods, training with masters like Hiroshi Fujimoto, and was the Uke of the legendary Bujutsu headmistress Hideo Sonobe as well as training in Aikido under the founder Morihei Ueshiba. His FAJKO connections allowed him to train with and get to know a golden generation of masters such as Shinkin Gima. Fujimoto was the editor of the *Mainichi Daily* newspaper which Terry wrote for, so his Karate Jutsu teacher was also his colleague. He attended the first all-styles grading in 1972 in Chiba, near Tokyo, where he was awarded his 5th Dan. He later graded 6th Dan and 7th Dan Kyoshi under Goju Ryu master Masafumi Suzuki of the Seibukan. He demonstrated his art in major Japanese demonstrations including at the Budokan and had chance to train with Choki Motobu's student Mikio Sindo as the two reflected on an almost lost method of Karate Jutsu. In the 2000s, Terry paid for the England Karate team to compete in the world championships, arranged for the founding of the English Karate Federation and organised a series of events in 2007 to celebrate the 50th anniversary of the British Karate Federation. Wingrove Hanshi was awarded 9th Dan by Okinawan master Kinjo Hiroshi.

Who were the pioneers of Goju Ryu in Britain?

The controversial Terry Dukes of Mushindo taught a system that may have been related to Goju Ryu or Uechi Ryu. He was teaching in around 1967. It has been suggested he learned Uechi Ryu from a book. In 1972 Dukes started calling himself Shifu Nagaboshi Tomio.

British Goju Ryu pioneers include George Andrews, Bob Greenhalgh, Tony Christian, Dennis Martin, Len Sim, Mike Lambert and from Scotland Jimmy Johnston. Shotokan legend Terry O'Neill also studied Goju Ryu with Morio Higaonna.

Steve Morris and New Zealand born Gary Spiers are also Goju Ryu pioneers in Britain having trained under Gogen Yamaguchi.

South African James Rousseau began his Karate training in 1960/1961 and after training in Japan gained his Shodan in 1963. In 1966 he met Sensei Morio Higaonna and became interested on Okinawan Goju-Ryu Karate. He came to the United Kingdom in 1974, as a 5th Dan, and established two Dojos in Oxford before returning to South Africa some six months later.

After James returned to South Africa, his brother, Peter, led the British Goju-Ryu Karate-Do Association (BGKA). BGKA was the forerunner of the English Goju-Ryu Karate-Do Association (EGKA) which was formed under the guidance of Sensei James Rousseau.

In July 1979, along with Sensei Higaonna and Sensei Teruo Chinen, he founded the International Okinawan Goju-Ryu Karate-Do Federation (IOGKF) in Poole Dorset.

List of the earliest practitioners of British Karate

Founder of British Karate movement: Vernon Bell, Hornchurch, Essex.
Already a seasoned Jujutsu and Judo teacher, began corresponding with French Karateka Henri Plee in February 1956. His Shodan certificate, signed by Minoru Mochizuki was dated April 1957.
The first students in 1956, trained in Hornchurch, Essex:
1. Michael Manning (previously studied Judo)
2. Ken Elliott (previously studied Judo)
3. DF Clarke
4. Gerald Tucker
5. Trevor Guilfoyle

First students to grade in England (April 30 1957): All passed 6th Kyu:
1) Guilfoyle (see above)
2) Tucker (see above)

Second students to grade in England (May 31 1957): All passed 6th Kyu:
1) Manning (see above)
2) Elliott (see above)
3) Clarke (see above)
4) P Byron

First recorded grading officiated by Hoang Nam (July 26 1956): All passed as far as it is known:
1) Guilfoyle 4th Kyu (double graded)
2) Tucker 4th Kyu (double graded)
3) Elliott 5th Kyu
4) Manning 5th Kyu
5) D Dyer 6th Kyu
6) P Brandon 6th Kyu
7) B Dolan 6th Kyu
8) D Blake 6th Kyu
Also attending post-grading training was the first female Karateka who was named Higgins
6th Kyu grading October 1957:
1) Anderson (passed 6th Kyu)
2) L Pearson (failed?)

Grading December 1957 (including first brown belt grading in UK):
1) Guilfoyle 3rd Kyu
2) Tucker 3rd Kyu
3) Manning 4th Kyu
4) Elliott 4th Kyu
5) Dyer 5th Kyu
6) Blake 5th Kyu
7) Byron (failed and remained 6th Kyu?)

June 1958 grading (all passed 5th Kyu):
1) J Sen

2) H Rayner
3) J Russell,
4) R Armstrong
5) P Conlon

July 1 1958 special brown belt grading:
1) Michael Manning (3rd Kyu)

Early students of the new London Dojo (1958):
F Fox, C Musgrove, G Izzard, K Richardson, J Lydon, Revill

December 1958 grading:
1) Armstrong (4th Kyu)
2) Rayner (4th Kyu)
3) Russell (4th Kyu)
4) Sen (4th Kyu)
5) Conlon (5th Kyu)
6) Fox (5th Kyu)
7) Hughes (5th Kyu)
8) Clarke (6th Kyu)

Tetsuji Murikami (1927-1987) 3rd Dan Yoseikan under Minoru Mochizuki and 1st Dan of the JKA arrived in England in July 1959.
In July 1959, Terry Wingrove commenced formal Karate study having previously studied Jujutsu with Bell since 1956 and previously Judo in 1952. Around the same time Jimmy Neal commenced Karate training.

First Karate grading in UK, held under a Japanese instructor (Tetsuji Murakami) July 17 1959:
1) Armstrong (3rd Kyu)
2) Rayner (3rd Kyu)
3) Russell (3rd Kyu)

Two days later on July 19 1959 (note Vernon Bell was now 2nd Dan Karate):
1) Vernon Bell (2nd Dan – awarded by Murakami – the first man in England to be awarded this)
2) Michael Manning (2nd Kyu) – note the first man in England to grade for this

3) Trotter (6th Kyu)
4) Wardle (5th Kyu – double graded)

Subsequent students grading included:
Goss, McEvoy, P Milner, Carter, F Gille, Dougherty, Gunns, Farkas.

Author's note: It is not known if P Milner (who failed) was Phil Milner (later a notable Karateka)
Gille (who also failed) was Fred Gille (later a notable Karateka)

February and April 1960 gradings:
1) Michael Manning (1st Kyu) – note the first man in England to grade for this
2) AR Martin (failed 6th Kyu)
3) Lydon (failed 6th Kyu)

LIVERPOOL DOJO FROM 1959
The British Karate Federation's first Liverpool representative was Fred Gille, previously a Judoka who applied for membership on September 29 1959.
First Liverpool Karate students, 1959:
1) F Gille (see above)
2) Barry Juxon
3) Kenneth Caulfield (previously studied Jujutsu with Jack Britten)

FIRST NATIONAL GRADING UNDER MURAKAMI

August 1960 – Held in Scarborough
Terry Wingrove (London) 5th Kyu
Fred Kidd (Middlesborough) 5th Kyu
E Shaw (Stoke Dojo) 5th Kyu
A Tranter (Stoke Dojo) 5th Kyu
R Buckner (Essex) 5th Kyu
P Butler (Sunderland) 5th Kyu
C Cabot (London) 5th Kyu
T Laverick (Sunderland) 5th Kyu
V Maxwell (Essex) 5th Kyu
R Salmon (Essex) 5th Kyu

Followed by grading in Essex a few days later:
C Alibone (6th Kyu)
E Harris (5th Kyu)
R Richardson (4th Kyu)
Jimmy Neal (5th Kyu?)
J Wijesundera (5th Kyu?)
Michael Manning (ratified 1st Kyu by Murakami)

December grading in Essex by Murakami:
Mike Dinsdale (6th Kyu)
K Goult (6th Kyu)
K Mansfield (6th Kyu)
S Morgan (6th Kyu)
J Shepherd (6th Kyu)
G Stubbings (6th Kyu)
E Tillet (6th Kyu)
D Williams (6th Kyu)
R Buckner (4th Kyu)
V Maxwell (4th Kyu)
Jimmy Neal (4th Kyu)
K Richardson (4th Kyu)
Terry Wingrove (4th Kyu)
J Wijesundera (3rd Kyu)

April 1961 grading, Upminster:
J Alibone (6th Kyu)
K Goult (5th Kyu)
Brian Hammond (5th Kyu)
E Harris (5th Kyu)
S Morgan (5th Kyu)
Alan Ruddock (5th Kyu) – Note founder of Irish Karate
J Shepherd (5th Kyu)
E Tillet (5th Kyu)
D Williams (5th Kyu)
Bob Buckner (3rd Kyu)
Terry Wingrove (3rd Kyu)

LIVERPOOL DOJO FROM 1961
1961 members:
1) Andy Sherry (previously studied Jujutsu with Jack Britten)
2) Terence Astley (previously studied Jujutsu with Jack Britten)
3) Michael Walls (previously studied Jujutsu with Jack Britten)

Note: Juxon was the first Liverpool student to grade, being awarded 6th Kyu under Murakami in 1961. Technically this made him senior to his teacher Gille, who failed that grading (see above)

Other 1961 Liverpool students:
T Barry, G Bingham, Alan Dewar, G Dicker, J Donoghue, G Frodsham, G Galletly, K May, P Meir, Charles Naylor, Alan Smith, E Travis, T Wignall, F Wignall, J Wilson.

Representatives of other centres:
Buckinghamshire Dojo was established by Art Malia in 1961
Scottish Dojo by Edward Ainsworth in 1961
Lincolnshire Dojo by Douglas Pettman in 1961
Ireland Dojo by Alan Ruddock in 1961
Scarborough Dojo by Fred Kidd in 1961
York Dojo by Gordon Thompson in 1961
Stoke Dojo by Edward Shaw in 1961 (previously studied under Kenshiro Abbe)
Leicester Dojo by Robert Johnson in 1962 (previously trained in Singapore)

Note: Middlesborough Dojo was established by Fred Kidd and later Walter Seaton and it was at this Dojo that the UK's first female blackbelt Pauline Bindra (nee Fuller/Laville) commenced her training.

August 1961 Grading (Essex):
R Barker (6th Kyu)
S Dalton (6th Kyu)
D Flateau (6th Kyu)
B Juxon (6th Kyu)
R Lamport (6th Kyu)
G McLeod (6th Kyu)
Edward Ainsworth (5th Kyu – double graded)
D Pettman (5th Kyu – double graded)

C Cabot (4th Kyu)
K Goult (4th Kyu)
Brian Hammond (4th Kyu)
Alan Ruddock (4th Kyu)
J Shepherd (4th Kyu)
D Williams (4th Kyu)

First Grading in Liverpool conducted on September 24 1961 by Vernon Bell:
1) T Astley (6th Kyu)
2) G Bingham (6th Kyu)
3) C Butler (6th Kyu)
4) K Caulfield (6th Kyu)
5) G Dicker (6th Kyu)
6) J Donoghue (6th Kyu)
7) K McCaldon (6th Kyu)
8) P Meir (6th Kyu)
9) Andy Sherry (6th Kyu)
10) P Sloan (6th Kyu)
11) M Walls (6th Kyu)
12) T Wignall (6th Kyu)
13) F Williams (6th Kyu)
14) J Wilson (6th Kyu)
15) Fred Gille (Honourary 5th Kyu)
16) Barry Juxon (5th Kyu)
17) Charlie Naylor (5th Kyu)
18) B Patsky (4th Kyu)

Liverpool grading December 1961:
T Barry (6th Kyu)
A Dewar (6th Kyu)
G Galletly (6th Kyu)
K May (6th Kyu)
Alan Smith (6th Kyu)
E Travis (6th Kyu)
F Williams (5th Kyu)

Essex grading December 1961:
B Henn (5th Kyu)
S Dalton (5th Kyu)

E Harris (4th Kyu)

A Malia (4th Kyu)

J Shepherd (3rd Kyu)

Note: Buckinghamshire student Arthur Malia went on to become a senior practitioner of the Korean art of Mo Dok Kwan and Bell saw him as his US representative.

Early members of BKF Scotland:
P Bannerman, J Bell, H Hackett, J Kelso, j malley, E McGowan, J McLean, J Mitchell, R Park, J Shaw

THE MANCHESTER DOJO:
Martin Stott who had trained under a Vietnamese instructor in France launched a Manchester Dojo in 1961. He is the first Karateka listed so far that was not affiliated to Vernon Bell's British Karate Federation.

First Manchester members whose names are recorded:

1) Martin Stott (started approx 1961)

2) Danny Connor (started approx 1962)

3) Roy Stanhope (started approx 1962)

4) Tony Hudson (started approx 1962)

The first British JKA Blackbelt
Charles Mack may have studied Shotokan Karate as early as 1958, rivalling Vernon Bell as one of the UK's earliest Karate practitioners. However he did not study or teach in Britain at this time. He spent seven years in Japan where he trained under Masatoshi Nakayama. Although Bell was the first British 1st Dan, that was in the Yoseikan organisation. Bell was later ratified by the JKA but Mack was already graded 1st Dan JKA.

March 1962 BKF Grading at Buckinghamshire:
J Winichx (6th Kyu)

F Alonso (5th Kyu)

E Daniels (5th Kyu)

M Echeverna (5th Kyu)

R Norman (5th Kyu)

B Norris (5th Kyu)

G Sullivan (5th Kyu)

M Thornton (5th Kyu)

A Love (6th Kyu)

John Chisholm (6th Kyu)
Jimmy Neal (2nd Kyu)
Terry Wingrove (2nd Kyu)

May and June 1962 Liverpool gradings:
S Coy (6th Kyu)
S McConell (6th Kyu)
K Skinner (6th Kyu)
T Astley (5th Kyu)
F Cope (5th Kyu)
Joseph Chialton (5th Kyu)
J Galletly (5th kyu)
Charlie Naylor (4th Kyu)
A Smith (4th Kyu)
R Stephens (5th Kyu)
R Woolfall (5th Kyu)

Selected early 1962 grading results:
A Love (5th Kyu)
K Goult (3rd Kyu)
D Williams (3rd Kyu)
J Chisholm (5th Kyu)
Walter Seaton (6th Kyu)
Fred Kidd (4th Kyu)
T Astley (5th Kyu)
Andy Sherry (4th Kyu)

Scarborough Summer school grading results:
T Astley (4th Kyu)
A Dewar (4th Kyu)
A Smith (4th Kyu)
R Stephens (4th Kyu)
R Woolfall (4th Kyu)
Charlie Naylor (3rd Kyu)
Andy Sherry (3rd Kyu)
Upminster students:
J Chisholm (4th Kyu)
A Love (4th kyu)
Edwards Ainsworth (4th Kyu)

August 1962 gradings:
Liverpool:
S Moore (5th Kyu)
J Chialton (5th Kyu)
G Gallately (4th Kyu)
K McCaldon (4th Kyu)
North Yorks:
K Bauer (6th Kyu)
J Clark (6th Kyu)
J Gough (6th Kyu)
J Sparkes (6th Kyu)
F Higgins (5th Kyu)
Walter Seaton (5th Kyu)
Gordon Thompson (5th Kyu)

Final gradings on 1962 saw the following awards:
G Heyward (5th Kyu)
J Sparkes (5th Kyu)
F Higgins (4th Kyu)
Walter Seaton (4th Kyu)
Fred Kidd (3rd Kyu)
K Bloomfield (6th Kyu)
H Frost (6th Kyu)
J Chialton (4th Kyu)
F Cope (4th Kyu)
J Donoghue (4th Kyu)
R Stephens (4th Kyu)
R Woolfall (4th Kyu)
B Williamson (6th Kyu)
K Bauer (5th Kyu)

February 1963 gradings in Liverpool:
K Bloomfield (6th kyu)
H Frost (6th kyu)
E Travis (6th kyu)
J Galletly (4th Kyu)
K McCaldon (4th Kyu)
S Moore (4th Kyu)
P Sloan (4th Kyu)

M Walls (4th Kyu)
W Whitehead (4th Kyu)

On January 1 1964 the senior Karateka in Britain, recognised by the British Karate Federation were Vernon Bell (2nd Dan), Terry Wingrove (1st Kyu), Jimmy Neal (1st Kyu) and Michael Manning (1st Kyu).

Timeline of British martial arts pioneers

1892   Takashima Shidachi (Yoshin Ryu) gives a talk in London on Jujutsu

1892   Rudyard Kipling writes about Japanese "wrestling tricks"

1890s   EW Barton Wright studies Fudo Shinden Ryu in Kobe

1897   Manchester's EJ Harrison arrives in Yokohama and studies Tenjin Shinyo Ryu

1898   Barton Wright brings "Bartitsu" (Barton Jujutsu) back to the UK

1899   Yukio Tani arrives in England possibly from the Fusen Ryu.

1899   Tani's early students include William Bankier and William Garrud and his wife Edith

1900   Raku Uyenishi arrives in England

1904   Harry H Hunter, author of *Super Jujutsu*, studies Jujutsu while in the Navy

1904   Leonard McClagen, an army captain, claims to be a Jujutsu champion

1904   Taro Miyake arrives from Dai Nippon Butokukai

1905   EJ Harrison joins the Kodokan in Tokyo

1906   Tenjin Shinyo Ryu master Gunji Koizumi arrives in Prestatyn and later Liverpool and begins teaching at the Kara Ashikaga

1907   Koizumi leaves for America.

1910   Anglo Japanese Exhibition. Koizumi having returned gives a demo

1913   EJ Harrison publishes *Fighting Spirit of Japan*

1914   World War I begins. Koizumi joins the Home Guard

1917   EJ Harrison returns to England

1918   End of the war. Koizumi founds the Budokwai in London

1919   Inazo Nitobe, author of *Bushido* gives a talk at the Budokwai

1919   Kusarigama and Kenjutsu master Sonobe gives a demo at the

Budokwai

1920   Judo founder Jigoro Kano visits England and awards Koizumi and Tani 2nd Dan

1924   Jack Britten, a student of Tani, opens the Alpha Jujutsu school on Sheil Road in Liverpool

1928   Mikonosuke Kawaishi arrives in Liverpool. Kawaishi school of Jujutsu established at 67 Mount Pleasant, Liverpool run by Gerry Skyner and attended by Bill Nelson my great uncle

1930s   Captain Fairburn creates "Defendu" based on his training in Shanghai

1939   World War II begins

1941   Vernon Bell takes his first Judo lesson under Ray Keene

1948   Vernon Bell and Pat Butler found the Amateur Judo Association

1950   Koizumi recognises Arnot St Judo club as northern branch of the BJA

1950   Vernon Bell is awarded 1st Dan Jujutsu

1952   Vernon Bell is awarded 1st Dan Judo

1952   Terry Wingrove begins studying Judo at the Budokwai

1953   Charles Mack awarded 1st Dan in Judo

1955   Kenshiro Abbe, master of Aikido and Judo arrives in England

1955   Kenshiro Abbe's Aikido students include Ken and David Williams

1956   Vernon Bell becomes the first Englishman to study Karate

1956   Under Henri Plee and Hiroo Mochizuki, Bell launches first English Karate club in his parents' back garden tennis courts

1956   Charles Mack awarded 3rd Dan in Judo

1957   Vietnamese Hoang Nam is first oriental to teach Karate in UK

1957   Vernon Bell awarded 1st Dan Karate (he did not take a grading)

1957   Jujutsu and Judo student Terry Wingrove begins studying Karate with Bell

1958   Charles Mack moves to Japan to compete in Judo and begins studying Shotokan

1959   Future prime minister Harold Wilson opens Southdene Jujutsu club in Kirkby near Liverpool, run by Bernie Blundell, older brother of Jim Blundell. Students include David and Paul Keegan my father and uncle

1959   Tetsuji Murikami is first Japanese to teach Karate in England

1959   The first Karate Summer School, hosted by Peter Jaconelli at the Ippon Judo club in Scarborough

1959   Fred Gille launches Liverpool's first Karate club and the first in the north of England. Students include Andy Sherry and later Charlie Naylor and Terry O'Neill

1959   Michael Manning becomes first British Karateka to grade 2nd Kyu on the mat

1960   Manning first Brit Karateka to grade 1st Kyu on the mat in Britain

1961   Edward Ainsworth opens Scotland's first Karate club

1961.   Martin Stott opens Manchester's first Karate club after studying with Tam Mytho

1961   Steve Arneil begins studying Karate

1962   Danny Connor begins training in Karate with Stott

1962   Terry O'Neill begins studying Karate

1962   Charles Mack is awarded 1st Dan in Shotokan by Masatoshi Nakayama in Tokyo

1962   Alan Ruddock, training under Vernon Bell becomes first Irish Karateka

1962   Roy Stanhope begins studying Karate under Martin Stott

1963   Charles Gidley begins studying Karate

1963   Phil Handyside begins studying Jujutsu under Richard Butterworth

1963   Terry Wingrove and Jimmy Neal graded 1st Kyu by Murikami

1963   First England Karate team headed by Terry Wingrove

1963   Shotokai master Mitsusuke Harada arrives in England

1963   John Van Weenan begins studying Karate

1964   Stan Knighton, Michael Randall, Cyril Cummins and Peter Consterdine begin Karate

1965   Charles Mack awarded 2nd Dan Karate in Japan by Nakayama and 5th Dan Judo by Risei Kano

1965   Wado Ryu master Tatsuo Suzuki arrives in England

1965   Masters Kase, Kanazawa, Enoeda and Shirai arrive in England from the JKA

1965   Ticky Donovan, John Smith, Eddie Daniels, Phil Handyside, Peter Spanton, Tony Christian, Bob Poynton, Hamish Adams, Billy Higgins, Brian Fitkin and Philip Kear begin studying Karate

1966   The Karate Union Great Britain is founded

1966   Mike Newton begins studying Karate under Yoseikan instructor Trevor Jones, a student of Vernon Bell

1966   Sherry and Chialton awarded 1st Dan by Enoeda

215

1966   Bell and Charles Mack set up the British Karate Control Commission with Alan Francis as chairman

1967   First KUGB championships. Andy Sherry wins Kata with Empi. J Green wins Kumite

1967   Tommy Morris becomes first Briton to study Shito Ryu or Shukokai

1967   Terry Wingrove becomes only senior Foreign officer of FAJKO in Tokyo and while studying Shito Ryu/Shukokai in Kobe

1967   Sherry, Green and Whitchener awarded 2nd Dan by Enoeda

1967   Pauline Laville first female Karate blackbelt

1967   Mike Nursey begins studying Karate under John Van Weenan

1967   Terry Wingrove trains for three years under Karate Jutsu master Fujiwara and grades 4th Dan in Tani-ha Shito Ryu. He also commences Jujutsu (Yawara) study with Sato Kimbei

1967   Steve Morris begins studying Karate under Steve Arneil and Bob Bolton

1967   Andy Sherry becomes first British all styles champion

1968   Sherry wins gold in Kata and Kumite at second KUGB championships. Terry O'Neill is second for Kata. Sherry wins European title

1969   Wingrove begins studying Karate Jutsu under Hiroshi Fujimoto

1970   The first World Karate Championships are held in Tokyo and Osaka on October 10 and 13 1970. In Kumite (Shobu Ippon), the Gold is won by Koji Wada (Japan), Silver by John Carnio (Canada) and Bronze by Tonny Tulleners (USA) and Dominique Valera (France). The only Briton (or foreigner) working for FAJKO or WUKO was Terry Wingrove

1971   Keinosuke Enoeda appointed JKA chief instructor for Europe

1972   Terry Wingrove awarded 5th Dan in Chiba, near Tokyo under FAJKO, he is understood to be the highest ranking Briton in the art of Karate at the time

Karate Jutsu in Kansai 1960-1987

After the war the original Okinawan Karate Jutsu methods fell into the abyss as Japan pushed for its brand of Karatedo to be universally standardised and modern Okinawan styles followed suit. The styles of Shotokan, Goju Ryu, Wado Ryu and Shito Ryu were the first to be recognised. There were however some masters who privately taught the older pre-war Karate Jutsu methods, including Hiroshi Fujimoto (Motobu Ryu, Uechi Ryu and Kushin Ryu), Katsumi Fujiwara (Motobu Ryu and Shito Ryu) and Mikio Sindo (Motobu Ryu).

Hiroshi Fujimoto

Hiroshi Fujimoto was a great Karate Jutsu master of the 20th century who studied under such notable masters as Kenwa Mabuni and Seijiro Sakihama.

Fujimoto was born on September 23 1925 and started practising Kendo at the age of 13. When he was 18 he joined Doshisha University in Kyoto and signed up to its Karate club. At the time Kenwa Mabuni was teaching a Naha Te style he called Hanko Ryu because the club had been established by Goju Ryu founder Chojun Miyagi. It was only later Mabuni taught the full Shito Ryu curriculum at Doshisha when Miyagi returned to Okinawa.

In an interview with Harry Cook and Graham Noble, Keiji Tomiyama, a former student of Doshisha and junior to Katsumi Fujiwara and Fujimoto, told the story of how they began studying Goju Ryu and then progressed to Shito Ryu. He said: *"When Chojun Miyagi was going back to Okinawa he said to the students that his friend had recently come to Osaka so why didn't they learn from this friend while he was away. That was Kenwa Mabuni."*

In 1947 Fujimoto as captain of the club and eight of his team mates visited Tokyo where they did a demonstration in front of Shotokan founder Gichin Funakoshi. This led to a post war spirit of co-operation between Shito Ryu and Shotokan. Fujimoto was a few years junior to Chojiro Tani, who also trained at the club under Mabuni.

Tani later established his own branch called Tani-ha Shito Ryu, better known as Shukokai. In 1950 Fujimoto was awarded his Shihan title by Mabuni. Soon after, he began on the Karate Jutsu path through a chance meeting. Fujimoto saw an advertisement for an Okinawan festival in Osaka and went to watch the dancing and Karate. Fujimoto decided to try his luck on one of the Okinawans backstage. It was Seijiro Sakihama. His attack was easily thwarted, as Sakihama was a master of Karate Jutsu – rather than the modern Karatedo. He easily defended against the young Karatedo exponent and almost rendered him unconscious with a light touch. Fujimoto asked Sakihama to teach him but was told he only taught Okinawans. Fujimoto kept pestering and got the address of Sakihama from the festival organisers, and in the end Sakihama agreed to teach him Karate Jutsu.

Sakihama was the founder of Jugo Shizen Ryu (soft/hard and a complete opposite in philosophy to Goju priorities of hard/soft) and had studied Uechi Ryu under the founder Kanbun Uechi in its formative years in Kansai in the pre war period, and Kushin Ryu he studied under its joint founder Kanemori "Kensei" Kinjo.

Kanemori had in turn studied two styles of Karate, the Shorin Ryu (Kobayashi Ryu) of Chosin Chibana and the Goju Ryu of Chojun Miyagi. The other co-founder of Kushin Ryu, Ueshima (1893-1987) had studied Karate from the age of nine under an Okinawan man named Sugaya and a style of Jujutsu called Koshin Yujoyitsu. They were later taught by guest instructors Choki Motobu and Chosin Chibana. Fujimoto became one of Sakihama's top students, learning the essence of Karate Jutsu from him. He learned three katas from Master Sakihama: Uechi-Sanchin, Higaonna-Seisan and Sanrinryu, also called Santairyu.

Keiji Tomiyama said: *"Mr Sakihama practised with Kanbun Uechi. Mr Fujimoto and Mr Tani were both graduates of Doshisha university Karate club. Mr Tani was, I think, two or three years senior to Mr Fujimoto. Then Mr Fujimoto went to Mr Sakihama and became a Jugo Shizen Ryu man."*

After graduating from university, Master Fujimoto (who was fluent in English) became a journalist working for *Mainichi Daily News*, the English version of *Mainichi Shinbun* which is one of the three main quality newspapers of Japan. Among other things, he covered the Vietnam war. He eventually became the editor of the paper. When *Encyclopaedia Britannica* started its operation in Japan, Master Fujimoto was recruited as the CEO of the company Encyclopaedia Britannica Japan.

He did not believe in teaching Karate to the wider public and did not like the way Karate Do was evolving. He did however teach Karate Jutsu to a few students.

218

Terry Wingrove, who as we saw in the previous chapter was a British Karate pioneer in the early days, moved to Japan in the 1960s and was initially employed as a physical education teacher at the Marist International School in Kobe. He joined the biggest Karate Dojo in the area which was the Shito-Ryu Dojo of Chojiro Tani and eventually became secretary of the international Shukokai organisation, training with Tani who graded him 3rd Dan and 4th Dan.

In 1968 Wingrove became an officer for FAJKO. He was able to travel around, training with many different masters. Wingrove was then employed as a copy editor and began to write for the *Mainichi Daily News*, where Fujimoto was his boss, and one day he received a painful introduction to pre-war Karate Jutsu from his editor. Despite being tall, well built and in his competition prime, the young Karatedo 4th Dan was man-handled by the small Karate Jutsu master. Fujimoto explained that what he was demonstrating was pre-war Karate Jutsu, not the modern Karatedo Wingrove had learned so far.

In a repeat of earlier times, Wingrove pursued Fujimoto to teach him Karate Jutsu and after a two year period he agreed. Fujimoto taught Wingrove the essence of Jutsu, derived from the teachings of masters like Sakihama, Motobu, Uechi, Chibana and Miyagi.

Regarding Fujimoto's leaving public Karatedo teaching behind, Wingrove said: *"In the early 1970s, Fujimoto saw the writing on the wall re the evolution of modern Karatedo competition and like many of his peers stepped away from teaching and only resumed teaching again in 1982 after being constantly invited by his alma mater Doshisha."*

Tomiyama explained that Fujimoto had been a leading Shukokai teacher before he turned his back on Karatedo. Tomiyama said: *"At that time Mr Tani was busy developing Shukokai so Mr Fujimoto was actually our teacher at the university. But when I was at university Mr Fujimoto decided to stop teaching."*

Tomiyama agreed with Wingrove's recollection that Fujimoto was asked to begin teaching the arts publicly again. Tomiyama said: *"Mr Yamashita talked to Mr Fujimoto. He said 'you said you would never teach again but if you die your technique will be lost.' So Mr Fujimoto began to teach again in 1982."*

After some years, he retired from the newspaper and started teaching journalism and English at Doshisha University in Kyoto, then at Baika University in Osaka.

Wingrove recalled: *"Fujimoto continued to teach Karate Jutsu and even came to UK to teach a memorable group of courses in the 80s."* Tomiyama said that Fujimoto's Karate Jutsu was far more effective than the Karatedo of Mabuni and Miyagi. Using the Kata Sanchin as an example was far more effective for combat; he said *"how he did it was a different world."*

Master Fujimoto suffered a mild brain haemorrhage and a heart attack in 2010. Although he had a successful bypass operation, he had been weakened a lot by those events and died on June 6 2012. Tomiyama said of him: *"In my opinion, he was the best Karateka of his generation. I have never seen anybody better than him. He took Karate very seriously but never took himself too seriously. He was always kind and warm. I learned a lot from him, not just Karate but how to behave as a human being."*

Fujiwara Katsumi

Fujiwara Katsumi is a Shito Ryu legend best known as one of the founding fathers of Shukokai along with Chojiro Tani, and a primary teacher of Shigeru Kimura. However he had also trained under Choki Motobu and was adept in older forms of Karate Jutsu.

Choki Motobu came to Osaka in 1921. Motobu subsequently began giving demonstrations and teaching in the Kobe-Osaka area, but development of the art was slow. Subsequently Goju Ryu and Shito Ryu were taught in the area.

One of Motobu's young students who later moved over to Shito Ryu was Fujiwara Katsumi. He trained under Shito Ryu founder Kenwa Mabuni's student Chojiro Tani but never forgot the Karate Jutsu teachings of Choki Motobu. Like Hiroshi Fujimoto, Fujiwara was a student at Doshisha University.

Wingrove, who trained under Fujiwara, explains: *"Fujiwara was senior instructor at Chojiro Tani's Shukokai dojo in Kobe and was Kimura's teacher and mine for three years from 1967-70. He studied as young student with Motobu during his first stint in Kobe/Osaka (Kansai) in the mid-late 20s and was a goldmine of knowledge re early Karate in Japan."*

Fujiwara was in fact a key influence on Tani-ha Shito Ryu (Shukokai). Graham Noble interviewed Keiji Tomiyama (also student of Hiroshi Fujimoto) and asked him about Fujiwara:

GN: I believe Tani was helped in his ideas by Katsumi Fujiwara?

KT: I think so... After the war [Tani] started the Shukokai... Mr Fujiwara was there.... and they worked together to develop the technique.

GN: You said he was something of a legend in Shukokai.

KT: Yes.

GN: He was a strong personality? A strong fighter.

KT: Yes, a strong personality, a strong fighter.

GN: He was a bit like Mr Kimura?

KT: Actually Mr Fujiwara was like a hero to Mr Kimura Fujiwara, went to South Africa to teach and died at the age of around 55.

Kimbei Sato the master of Yawara

Earlier in the book we explored the notion that some Japanese Jujutsu (Yawara) schools had parallel development to Karate, in that they were influenced by Chinese Chuan Fa and Chin Na, and also developed fighting systems using makeshift weaponry. Among these schools were Yagyu Shingan Ryu and Asayama Ichinden Ryu. In the mid 20th century a Japanese master named Sato Kimbei received teaching licences in both of these schools. He also taught some of the Chinese martial arts that originally influenced Karate such as Hsing-I.

The significance of Sato to this work is that he re-introduced Yawara and Chinese martial arts to many of the Karate Jutsu masters in Kansai, such as Chojiro Tani. Sato gave public demonstrations of both Yawara and Kung Fu in Japan, attended by numerous Karateka.

Kimbei Sato was born in 1925 in Fukushima and graduated from Tohoku University Department of Medicine with a Ph.D. in medicine, which helped in his understanding of the human body as it relates to martial arts. As well as mastering several styles of Jujutsu, he was also among the first Japanese masters to be a recognised lineage holder in several Chinese martial arts. He became Chairman of the All Japan Chinese Martial Arts Federation, Honorary Chairman of the Beijing Ba Gua Zhang Research Society, Honorary Advisor to the Eastern Chi Gung Society (Beijing), and Advisor to the Beijing Martial Chi Gung Society.

Sato began teaching police officers at Japan Police College in 1954 and opened up his own Dojo in Itabashi, Tokyo in 1958. As well as the many traditional martial arts he mastered he also formulated a system based on his own clan traditions called Daiwa-Do.

Sato once said of his studies: *"I have expanded my studies from Jujustu, to Chinese martial arts, to qin na, to pressure points, to chi-gung, and finally to Taoism. Anybody can learn to combine the techniques of reversals, throws, locks, thrusts, and kicks. The integration of my Jujutsu with chi-na and other martial arts is slowly coming to fruition, and its completion as a method for bare-handed fighting or with weapons is near. Jujutsu and Chinese martial arts make up the path that I have pursued and that have guided my life."* Another style Sato studied was Tenjin Shinyo Ryu, famously one of the main styles that influenced Judo. Sato's daughter recalls: *"My father learned from Miyamoto Hanzo, who gained his license in the art after studying under Inoue Keitaro and Yoshida Chiharu; because the Iso family line came to an end, it was Miyamoto who became responsible for carrying on the style as the 5th generation lineage holder. My father also received teaching in the style from Ono Sokichi of Ooshu Iwanuma, who learned Jujutsu and bone-setting from Yoshida Chiharu. Also, Inoue Takeo, the grandson of Inoue Keitaro, asked for some instruction in the art from my father during World War II when he was evacuated to Sendai."*

Perhaps the style of Jujutsu most closely linked to Sato was the Yawara system Yagyu Shingan Ryu. Perhaps Sato's experience in Chinese martial arts gave him an advantage in learning this art which does appear to be derived from Chuan Fa. According to Sato, this style of Jujutsu was more deadly than any other. His daughter recalled: *"It was 1950 when my father Sato Kinbei received his licence to teach Yagyu Shingan Ryu, just after he returned from the war in China. According to him, Yagyu Shingan Ryu is different from other forms of Jujutsu in terms of its practicality on the field of battle and its unrivalled fierceness and ability to kill the enemy. It is said that the experienced practitioner can shatter an enemy arm with one blow."* Sato began studying Hsing-I in 1959, studying with Wang Shu Jin for eight years. He also studied Taiji, Bagua and Baji Chuan. Sato studied Baji Chuan under Zhang Zhong.

Sato's name nowadays is often linked to those of Takamatsu Toshutsugu and Ueno Takashi, who are well known for being the teachers of Bujinkan headteacher Masaaki Hatsumi. Sato was actually Hatsumi's senior and studied Asayama Ichinden Ryu under Ueno. This was solely an atemi (striking) and gyakute (reversal) art. Sato found that many of the techniques in this art were already known to him from Daito Ryu. In 1955 he became the art's grandmaster. As well as Jujutsu, this art also includes reversals with the Jo and Tessen. Sato also learned Tenshin-ryu and Bokuden-ryu from Ueno, but it was a two way relationship and he too taught arts to Ueno. From Takamatsu, Sato learned Kukishin Ryu Bojutsu, Takagi Yo Shin-ryu Jujutsu and Gikan Ryu Koppo.

It may be said that Sato also helped to resurrect some dormant styles including Araki Shin-ryu Jujutsu which his great grandfather had studied, and Itten Ryushin Tyuukai Ryu, which was an amalgamation art of three styles, Isshin-ryu (from Sakuma Katusuke), Ryushin Tyuukai-ryu (from Miura Yoshiemon), and Tenshin Shin Yo-ryu (from Iso Mataemon). Sato's daughter recalled: *"My father was living in Iwanuma around 1953-4, and learned the art from its beginning from Ono, later receiving the written transmissions of the art to become the second generation in its lineage."*

Karate Jutsu International

Terry Wingrove (b1941) studied Karate Jutsu under Fujiwara, Fujimoto and Sindo as well as Yawara with Sato Kimbei, making for a dangerous combination of pre-war Jutsu training.

Wingrove had previously commenced Karate study with Vernon Bell in 1957 (see chapter on British Karate) having studied Jujutsu/Judo for a few years. He had trained with Tetsuji Murikami, Hiroo Mochizuki and Jim Alcheik and held the grade of 1st Kyu. He declined to take his 1st Dan under Murikami as Bell advised him to grade under the JKA. Wingrove instead left Britain and took his Shodan under Shirai after almost eight years of Karate training. Given his training, he was quite "under graded" when he arrived in Kobe.

It may be that Tani informally considered him a 2nd Dan because in around 1968 he graded him right to 3rd Dan. In 1968 Wingrove became an officer for FAJKO. There he was able to travel around, training with many different masters. In around 1969 Wingrove was graded 4th Dan by Tani and along with Bryan Huddard and Peter Duffy competed in the 1969 Hiroshima West Japan Karate Championships. In 1969 he returned to England and he and Bryan Hammond taught Shukokai courses, including in Bournemouth; and that year he took famous pictures of Kimura's punching power being

223

tested at the medical faculty of Kyoto University in 1969 when Tani, Kimura and Wingrove, Huddard and Duffy were making the first real investigation using modern technology of the efficacy of punching, and Tani Sensei was trying to determine the most efficient way of punching using the Shukokai philosophy.

Training with Fujiwara and Fujimoto he was taught about pre-war Karate Jutsu and gave displays of Karate Jutsu at the Budokan Hall. He also trained at length with Sato Kimbei in Jujutsu/Yawara, in Aikido with Morihei Ueshiba and Bujutsu with Hideo Sonobe. Known for her ability with the naginata, Sonobe Sensei was the headmistress of a Koryu called Jikishin Kage Ryu.

He was present in Kobe for Sato's Yawara demonstration at Shukokai Championships in Osaka, Japan 1968, and his demonstration of Chinese Kung Fu and sword in Kobe in 1969. He also witnessed one of the greatest Chinese stylists of the 20th century Master Hung (who we met earlier), the exponent of Tang Shou Tao and a master of Pakua and Hsing-I.

Wingrove helped organise the first World Karate Championships in Japan in 1970. In 1972 he was part of a FAJKO all styles Karate grading and was awarded 5th Dan. Throughout the 1970s Wingrove also trained with Masafumi Suzuki in Goju Ryu in Kyoto and was subsequently awarded 6th Dan and says his mentor Hideo Tsuchiya helped him make the Shoto/Shito transition to Goju. He was pictured in Singapore in 1972 with Tsuchiya. He was awarded his 7th Dan Kyoshi in 1989, by Suzuki.

Fujiwara introduced him to Choki Motobu's elderly student Mikio Sindo and the various applications of Karate Jutsu began to come together into his present system of Karate Jutsu and Yawara.

Wingrove recalled: *The most confusing thing for me was the denigration of dead masters and a general misrepresentation of Karate in Japan prior to 1939. As soon as anything was mentioned about pre-war Karate it seemed that the 'facts' available were sanitised and centred on Funakoshi sensei in the Tokyo area, in the late 20s and 30s, but little was mentioned of Kenwa Mabuni, Choki Motobu, Chojun Miyagi or the very big concentration of Okinawans brought to work in Wakayama in West Japan after the First World War, who brought their culture of music, dance and Karate with them and provided such a fertile base to study Karate Jutsu and even gave birth to a new style (Uechi Ryu) in W. Japan. In the 70s there was a definite effort to promote the progressive image of Gichin Funakoshi in ways that were not only confusing but in my book were not true. With the development and phenomenal success of the first and second generation JKA instructors in the late 50s and 60s came a PR deluge that looked more like the work of Hans Christian Andersen than the life and work of Gichin Funakoshi.*

"The interesting thing for me was that in this period we still had with us Gima (Funakoshi's partner in the first 1922 demo in Tokyo) Konishi sensei (the mover, shaker and fixer of Japanese Karate from 1928) and Egami sensei (the Shoto genius and top student of Funakoshi). All of these agreed that the early history of Shotokan had been entirely rewritten and embellished by denigrating others and creating a hierarchy that were not what they seemed.

"Specifically I remember being told that Choki Motobu - my hero - was an illiterate bully that was more interested in wine, women and song than Karate and that he was intimidated by Funakoshi. When I asked Gima and Konishi sensei about this they laughed and said look at the few photos there are of Funakoshi and Motobu that exist and you will note the man in the middle (the most important in Japanese protocol) is always Motobu, and Motobu treated Funakoshi with disdain as teaching inferior Karate.

"Gima sensei actually told Tsuchiya sensei and I that Motobu had put Funakoshi down on two occasions just blocking him. Then I was so very fortunate to meet Mikio Sindo who had been a student of Motobu in Kansai for five years and he showed me a fabulous collection of photos and letters from Motobu showing his literacy and technique. Sindo was a very wealthy Kobe businessman and although ungraded had a superior knowledge of Karate Jutsu and was still showing me technique into his 90s."

Wingrove established Karate Jutsu International in around 1987 to pass on and preserve pre-war Karate Jutsu. He was awarded both his 8th Dan and 9th Dan by Okinawan master Kinjo Hiroshi.

Author's note: Master Hung taught a number of Karate masters in the late 1960s and I had suspected that Japanese Jujutsu master Kimbei Sato (who was a master of a number of Chinese styles) had a hand in inviting him over, but actually it was Suzuki Sensei of the Seibukan. Hanshi Wingrove, who was there at the time, clarified this and referred to Hung as the most impressive Chinese martial artist he had ever encountered in more than 60 years of martial arts. He told me: *"Kimbei Sato did socialise with them but it was Masafumi Suzuki* *the Goju master from Kyoto who hosted and bankrolled them and I could keep you up all night with the efficacy of their techniques and challenges to every Karate teacher they could.*

"In my opinion the brothers were the most dangerous and competent Chinese masters I have ever witnessed. Hung I-Hsiang would give an open challenge to any Karate teacher to punch him in the stomach even at the Budokan and he would just stand there smiling as very high grade Shotokan, Shito Ryu and Wado Ryu masters would all punch him and he flexed his body and not defend and they would all bounce off him like fleas off an elephant.

"In general they did not like the Japanese and weren't scared to say how ineffective Japanese Martial arts were compared to Chinese martial arts. For me it was their Pakua that set them apart. Long may their memory survive. "

Malaysian Budokan Karate

Following the first world Karate championships in 1970, the Budokan style of Karate was given official recognition in Japan. Somewhat related to Shotokan, the style was founded by a Malaysian named Chew Choo Soot (Chew being the surname) who created a Karate style that was closer to the art's Chinese origins.

Chew was born on February 7 1922. At the age of 15 he became interested in and involved in weightlifting and fitness training and became the Malaysian national weightlifting champion in 1939-1942. Through his training he struck up a friendship with a Karate practitioner and they taught each other. This was during the Japanese occupation of Malaysia, and the Japanese officer contacted Chew after seeing him on a magazine cover. The officer had trained in a style called Keishinkan and ultimately introduced Chew to his teacher Takazawa Masanao. The Keishinkan style was derived from the teachings of Kanken Toyama whose Karate contained the essence of Karate Jutsu.

Grandmaster Chew Choo Soot teaching in Preston, England.
Pic courtesy of PAJ Handyside

In addition to Kanken Toyama's Karate, Chew also studied Chinese Kung fu, Tae Kwon Do, Judo and several styles of Karate-do including Shito-ryu and Shotokan. However another profound influence was the Shuri Te that was derived from Chotoku Kyan's teachings. Mr Chew studied under Zenryo Shimabukuro, the then Grand Master of the Seibukan style, who was a student of Chotoku Kyan, who was a student of Matsumura, Itosu and many others.

Chew also went to Taiwan where many styles of Kung Fu were taught. He studied the tiger style of Hung Gar, Choi Lee Fut, Tai Chi Chuan, and Pa Kua. He learned and mastered many different ancient Kung Fu and Kobudo weapons and he was renowned for both the broadsword and straight sword but also the dragon stick. In 1968 he established his Kuala Lumpur headquarters.

The first official headquarters building of Karate Budokan International at the Lote Yew road, Kuala Lumpur was declared open on 26th May, 1968 by the honourable Encik Mohd. Khir Jhohiri, who was then the minister of Education of Malaysia. Chew parted from the Keishinkan in 1971 and the style began to demonstrate a more Chinese influence. But he also employed two Japanese instructors, T.

Yoneda and T. Ishikawa of the Shito Ryu style from Osaka, to further his research. While his son Tony carried on teaching in Malaysia, Mr Chew began to spread his art around the world. He visited England in around 1978. Budokan Karate in Britain was largely introduced by Shihan Mike Newton (Leigh) and Shihan Phil Handyside (Preston), who previously studied respectively Yoseikan and Shotokan Karate. The third school to host Chew was Skyner's Jujutsu (Liverpool).

Phil Handyside began his martial arts studies in 1963 when he studied Jujutsu/Judo. While he was out of action from Judo, Phil attended a demo of a "new" type of martial art called Karate. The man giving the demonstration was Sadashige Kato, a 5th Dan in Shotokan which was of course a very high grade for these shores at the time.

Phil said: *"He was amazing - I'd never seen anything like it. And Karate suited my body type. In Judo I was always thrown about by bigger heavier people but Karate suited me."*

He would travel down to Crewe from Preston to train with Kato Sensei and took his first few grades with the Japanese teacher. In the early 1970s the Karate Union Great Britain had a grip on British Karate and Phil wasn't attracted to the dictatorial approach of the group, or to its charismatic leader Keinosuke Enoeda. When there was a dispute between his and another club over the rights to the name "Rising Sun", the KUGB's heavy handed approach prompted him to look outside the union. And it was then he found his next teacher, the great Hirokazu Kanazawa, now a 10th Dan Meijin.

In the mid 1970s, while teaching a large class in Fulwood, Phil was contacted by Chew Choo Soot. Phil recalled: *"He did not come across like a Karate master. He wasn't confident and cool like Kanazawa and he was built more like a wrestler than a Karateka, but his Karate was brilliant."* Escorting Chew on his tour of England Phil grew close to the master and aside from Kanazawa now sees him as his greatest influence. In 1979 he was asked to organise the world championships of Karate Budokan International and hosted the event at the Guild Hall in Preston. Chew was also accompanied to Britain by his senior students Wong Sek Khar (now grandmaster of a branch of Budokan) and Ng Tang Pheng, who Phil also trained under.

Rowe and Takamizawa [Pic courtesy of Steve Rowe]

In British Wado Ryu Tatsuo Suzuki is often cited as the most influential teacher, but Toru Takamizawa is perhaps equally influential.

Steve Rowe began his Karate training in 1973 in Za Zen Karate under Jim Fewins and then Wado Ryu Karate under Toru Takamizawa (1942-1998).

Telling the story of his teacher, Steve wrote: *"He broke away from the other Japanese Wado Ryu Sensei to found and run the highly successful Temple Karate Centre in Birmingham and headed one the first ground breaking large multi style Karate groups in the UK called Tera Karate Kai. Many of our top Karate Sensei and organisations today, including myself, emanate from those roots and owe much of their training and success to him.*

"We went on to form the Takamizawa Institute of Karate (of which I was the first Chairman) to teach his unique concepts of movement in the martial arts, and relocated himself locally to me in the Medway

area of Kent. When the other splits of the Japanese Sensei came about in Wado he realigned himself to his original Sensei Jiro Ohtsuka and was happily able to get back to his roots before he died."

Steve published two instructional books with Takamizawa Sensei. He said: "In 1985 we published 'Concepts of Karate' through TAKRO (Takamizawa and Rowe) in two parts 'The structure of Tsuki and Keri' and 'The structure of Uke and Dachi'. We produced them on an old Amstrad computer and printed them on an old Gestetner printing machine in a friend's garage, but these books were Martial Arts goldmines and I'm sure that those who purchased them in the 80s treasure them now."

Further describing his teacher, Steve wrote: "Toru was the youngest of seven children born to a Samurai family in Nagano Prefecture Japan, who he claimed were disgusted at him taking up the foreign Okinawan art of Karate at university which he told me was regarded as a blue collar activity and practised by the Yakuza.

"He graduated from university with a degree in Russian and came straight over to the UK to assist Tatsuo Suzuki to teach Wado Ryu Karate."

Steve became secretary and subsequently chairman of the English Karate Council, the Sport England Governing Body for Karate, and represented Karate on the Martial Arts Commission. He trained with Okimitsu Fuji in Muso Jikiden Ryu Iaido and when Fuji returned to Japan he studied Muso Shinden Ryu Iaido and Jodo with Vic Cook.

He studied Yang Style Tai Chi with Simon Wyard in the beginning under Rose li and then with Jim Uglow and through Jim, with Ma Lee Yang in Hong Kong.

In 1988 he parted amicably with Takamizawa and founded Shi Kon Martial Arts. Blending his many years' knowledge working in the security trade and zen, buddhist and taoist studies with his martial arts training he formed his own training system. Disillusioned with the political world of Karate he registered it with the British Council of Chinese Martial Arts as a system of Kung Fu and now teaches that along with Yang style Taijiquan. He has written for the martial arts magazines monthly for over 30 years including *Combat*, *Traditional Karate* and *Martial Arts Illustrated*, and he wrote a book, *Karate Warrior*, and partly scripted a video with Austin St John, (the Red Power Ranger), and in 2015 published his book of martial poetry *Warrior's Mind*. He founded the association Shi Kon Martial Arts based on the 'shikon' concept of warrior's mind taught to him by Fuji

Sensei. Steve's Kung Fu system uses forms that reflect the techniques for each grade and the basics, combinations, padwork and pairs work are all extracted from the forms named kick boxing, close quarter, power hands, 16 gates, 13 Hands and Circles, before focusing on the internal system in a White Crane style version of Sanchin, the 5 Animals in Tensho and the fa jing in Naihanchi, finishing with his own form Taiki that is a roll up of all the earlier forms.

In 2017 Shihan Handyside was awarded 9th Dan by Shikon after 55 years in the martial arts. The presentation was officially made in 2018 by Freestyle Karate pioneer and multi time world champion Alfie Lewis 9th Dan at the author's Dojo in Manchester

The World Karate Federation and Olympics

Henri Plee had headed European Karate from 1956, and in 1961 Jacques Delcourt was appointed President of French Karate, which was at that stage an associated member of the Judo Federation. In 1963 he invited the six other known European federations (Italy, Great Britain, Belgium, Germany, Switzerland and Spain) to come to France for the first-ever international Karate event, and Great Britain and Belgium accepted the invitation. The event featured hard hitting contests officiated by Hiroo Mochizuki.

In December of that year, six of the seven federations gathered in Paris, in what was to be the first European Karate Congress, with the aim of improving and organising Karate tournaments between their countries. It was noted that the unification of the different Karate styles was impossible, and so they decided to unify the refereeing.

By 1965 the European Karate Union had been created, with Jacques Delcourt voted in as President. The following year the first European Karate Championships were held, in Paris.

In 1970, the International Karate Union (IKU) was formed by Delcourt in an effort to organise Karate at world level. Upon hearing this, Ryoichi Sasakawa, President of the Federation of All Japan Karatedo Organization (FAJKO), travelled to France to discuss the creation of an international governing body. The IKU was quickly disbanded and a new organisation was formed between the EKU and the Japanese federation, and was called the World Union of Karate-do Organisations (WUKO).

The first WUKO World Karate Championships were held in Tokyo and Osaka on October 10 and 13 1970. Hideo Tsuchiya and Terry Wingrove were among the organisers and the event featured diverse masters such as Gogen Yamaguchi and Chew Choo Soot.

In 1985 the World Union of Karate-do Organisations was officially recognised by the International Olympic Committee as the official board for Karate.

Terry Wingrove and Hideo Tsuchiya helped plan the first Karate world championships under Ryoichi Sasagawa [Pic courtesy of Terry Wingrove]

In the early 1990s, Hidetaka Nishiyama's refusal to align his ITKF organisation with the World Union of Karate-Do Organizations (WUKO) caused the International Olympic Committee to suspend its recognition of WUKO as amateur Karate's international governing body. WUKO tried to unify with the International Traditional Karate Federation (ITKF) in 1990 to form the WKF; however, this attempt failed and the WUKO group left to form the WKF on their own. The World Karate Federation (WKF) is now the largest international governing body of sport Karate with 191 member countries.

It is the only Karate organisation recognised by the International Olympic Committee and claims more than ten million members. The styles recognised by the WKF are Shotokan, Goju Ryu, Wado Ryu and Shito Ryu. The old WUKO eventually became the World Union of Karate-Do Federations in late 2008. In August 2016 it was announced World Karate Federation's brand of Karate would be in the 2020

Summer Olympics. The WUKF is perhaps the second largest world governing body for Karate.

Okinawan Goju Ryu master Tetsuhiro Hokama discussed the Olympics with *The Guardian* newspaper saying: *"My heart is divided 50-50.*

"If you just concentrate on the physical side of karate, that's no good. The mental side is very important. Karate is not really a 'sport' sport."

Morio Higaonna added: *"We have traditional Karate and we have a sport Karate. For the Olympics, sport Karate is OK."*

Terry Wingrove reflected: *"As it sinks in that Karate Do will be in the 2020 Olympics I find it so hard to believe as 48 years ago it was decided to hold the first World Karate Championships in Tokyo in 1970 and as the manager of the Information Dept in FAJKO (then WUKO) in Tokyo I was amazed how fast we did it and how well the various countries accepted the invitation to come to Tokyo with all costs paid for by one man that was my boss and the 'Godfather' of post war martial arts Ryoichi Sasagawa, Japan's richest man and the most powerful man I have ever met. How I wish he could see today the results of all his hard work and millions and millions of dollars and the endless IOC meetings in the 70s we attended pushing to get Karate Do accepted into the Olympics. Eventually when TKD was admitted for the Seoul Olympics it seemed to be the last straw for Karate Do."*

Kickboxing and Freestyle Karate

As Karate, Muay Thai, Tang Soo Do and Kung Fu spread across the world in the 1960s, inevitably people came up with the idea of pitting style against style. Mixed style pioneers like Bruce Lee, and fighting champions like Chuck Norris and Benny 'the Jet' Urquidez, need no introduction in a book like this.

The first kickboxing event in Britain may have been in the early 1970s promoted by Danny Connor and John Smith. Connor had trained in Karate since around 1960 under Martin Stott and they and Roy Stanhope were among Manchester's pioneers. The basic Yoseikan-based Karate they were learning soon gave way to more 'official' styles of Wado Ryu and Shotokan. Connor became something of a godfather of martial arts in Manchester, also enjoying a good relationship with the local Chinese community and its Kung Fu teachers. At some stage he became adept in Preying Mantis Kung Fu and later Taijiquan. Connor was also responsible for bringing over the Taekwondo (and later Muay Thai) experts like masters Sken, Krin and Toddy.

John Smith was a Wado Ryu exponent of a similar vintage to Ticky Donovan, training under the likes of Tatsuo Suzuki in the later 1960s. Smith and Connor, under the British Karate Association, created a style called Bujinkai, based on Wado Ryu and Preying Mantis, and together they hosted what is thought to be the first kickboxing and full contact event in Britain.

Jujutsu teacher Allan Tattersall was also instrumental in promoting some of the first Muay Thai fights in the country. Thai boxer Steve Hateley is quoted: *"Danny Connor was running the first ever fights around 1974 and we were going down. I fought on a couple of their shows, but they were still using the 4-oz tag gloves, and it was just dangerous. The first fight I remember clearly was at Rochdale College when I fought a Karate 4th Dan.*

"I was introduced to Master Toddy by a Jujutsu man, Allan Tattersall, who had promoted the fights at Rochdale. At the time they were doing the Thai Kwon Do, the normal Tae Kwon Do with the leg kicks and knees."

If kickboxing combined the best of Karate, Muay Thai, boxing and Taekwondo, it was perhaps a fusion of Karate and Kung Fu that led to the creation of semi contact points fighting. One of the pioneers of this form of martial arts was Alfie 'the animal' Lewis who coined the phrase 'freestyle Karate.' Liverpool Lau became Liverpool Freestyle and then Mushinkai International.

Lewis blended Shotokan Karate with Lau Gar Kung Fu and boxing and won several WAKO world championships. The WKA (World Kickboxing Association) emerged and from that the WKC splintered along with its sibling group the FSK. Lewis set up an alternative body called the World Martial arts Organisation.

WAKO originated in Europe in 1976 and formulated the rules and regulations for the new fighting sport de facto, acting as the Kickboxing Federations of the World. It was founded by American Kickboxing promoter Mike Anderson, and his friend, German Kickboxing promoter George Bruckner.

WKA was created in the United States as the World Karate Association in 1976 by Howard Hanson, a Shorin-Ryu Karate black belt, and Arnold Urquidez. The organisation was the first non-profit governing body to use an independently controlled rating list, the first to establish a world championship division for women and the first to include countries from Asia. The organisation became one of the major sanctioning bodies for professional Karate. Early stars of the WKA included Benny "The Jet" Urquidez, Don "The Dragon" Wilson, Kevin Rosier and Graciela Casillas.

WKA is based in Massa Carrara, Italy with branches throughout Europe, Asia, Oceania, Africa, and in North America. In 1994, Paul Ingram took over the organisation. From 29 September 2012 WKA had a new management: Michele Panfietti World President and Cristiano Radicchi General Secretary. From December 2016 the management was passed back to Paul Ingram, and the WKA headquarters was transferred back to Birmingham, England.

Freestyle pioneer Alfie Lewis, now a 9th Dan, describes his training: *"I started boxing with my father,"* he explains. It is perhaps boxing that has influenced the Mushin Kai training style. Fighters are expected to do hard road work as well as train in the gym. *"I used to run to school and run home every dinner time. Conditioning was always part of my routine."*

Coming from a mixed race family - black, European and Chinese - Alfie also had Chinese relatives who practiced Tai Chi and as such the doors to China Town were opened for him when they were closed to others. He then trained in Judo and progressed to Jujutsu, training at Skyner's on Catherine Street. As he first ventured down the old stairs into Gerry Skyner's basement, seeing Jujutsu students defending against realistic street attacks like hook punches and throwing opponents onto the old Tatami he couldn't help be impressed by the gritty realism. But even though the training was hard *"nobody was bullied,"* he says.

After boxing, Judo and Jujutsu, Alfie trained in traditional Shotokan Karate. But despite living in Liverpool he was not drawn to Andy Sherry's Red Triangle saying the KUGB was *"run like the Catholic church, too much dogma."* The Red Triangle did not, he says, *"allow students to be a free spirit and expand upon their art."*

An art that did allow him to be more free and open was Lau Gar Kung Fu which he studied along with sampling Hung Gar, Preying Mantis, Pakua, Tong Long and Tai Chi. While complimentary of British pioneers like Steve Babbs, he is dismissive of the skills of the claimed grandmaster of the art, who Lewis says taught *"a bastardised form of Kung Fu."*

Lau Gar comes from the same part of China that the early Karate pioneers looked to – southern China. Lau Gar Kuen is derived from a form of boxing practised at Kuei Ling Temple situated in Kong Sai (Guangxi) Province in west China.

According to the style: *"It was learned from a monk on retreat from that temple by Master Lau Sam Ngan, whom we honour as founder of our style. He is reputed to have earned his name because of a deep scar in the middle of his forehead which resembled a third eye. The style subsequently became popular over a large part of south west China. In fact all of the southern systems of Kung Fu are derived from 5 major styles namely: Lau, Hung, Choy, Li and Mok."*

For ten years Lewis dominated the -84 kg category and won the titles of the WAKO World Champion in 1983 (London), in 1987 (Monaco), 1990 (Venice), in 1991 in London and in 1993 in Atlantic City. One of Alfie's coaches was traditional Karateka Ticky Donovan who, he says, *"ruled the roost"*.

He added: *"Ticky taught me how to be a good coach, how to structure. How to manipulate the mind, he was a genius when it came to psychology."*

The late Steve Cattle of Shotokan taught him how to use proper Tai Sabaki and says he trained with him *"as a good friend every day for a year."* He added: *"Steve Cattle had intelligence beyond belief."*

Renowned as he is for points fighting, it would be a mistake to think he neglects other areas of Karate such as kata. *"I do respect Kata,"* he says solemnly. *"I love strong fast Kata - but I love traditional Kata like Nijushiho. I grew up seeing people like Terry O'Neill. When they did the Kata they WERE the Kata. I saw the best in Britain, what's not to love?"*

Author's note: One of Alfie's team mates was my former teacher Steve Bullough (now 8th Dan), who began in traditional Karate with instructors such as Mike Newton (British Budokan pioneer) before training under Roy Stanhope (British Shukokai pioneer). He also studied Aikido, Judo, boxing and several other arts, founding a style called Bushido Karate.

Karate and Mixed Martial Arts

A Shotokan student in the lifetime of Gichin Funakoshi went on to become the founding father of pro wrestling (puro resu) in Japan which in turn led to the advent of Mixed Martial Arts. Now in recent years Shotokan has been seen in the Ultimate Fighting Championship.

Shotokan student 'Rikidozan' used a 'Karate chop' as one of his finishing moves and defended the honour of Japan against gaijin like Lou Thesz. After Rikidozan was murdered, he was succeeded in Japan by his former students Antonio Inoki and Shohei Baba. Inoki challenged fighters from other martial arts, including Karateka, Judoka and boxer Muhammad Ali in what foreshadowed mixed martial arts.

In the mid 1980s a group of wrestlers who worked for Inoki created the UWF which combined wrestling with Muay Thai and Jujutsu creating what would become shootfighting. In the early 1990s this gave way to the UWFI, RINGS and Pancrase, which saw fighters like Nobuhiko Takada, Ken Shamrock, Dan Severn and even Karate legend Patrick McCarthy.

Shamrock, Severn and Brazilian Jujutsu master Royce Gracie went on to dominate the first few Ultimate Fighting Championships and Shotokan practitioner Lyoto Machida achieved notable success, becoming Middleweight World Champion and proving that Karate was effective against other disciplines.

Throughout the history of Okinawan Karate, the name of Patrick McCarthy is mentioned, whether for his translation of the Bubishi, or for his identifying of Ryuru Ko, or for his numerous other academic achievements. But McCarthy Hanshi is not simply a researcher but a true Karate master. He was one of the first in the world to turn the study of grappling-based bunkai into a true art form. He was awarded his 9th Dan by Okinawan master Kinjo Hiroshi. But he is also a pioneer of what became known as MMA.

McCarthy Hanshi was an early competitor and coach in the UWFI, the forerunner of Pride.

I interviewed McCarthy Hanshi for a martial arts magazine. Asking him how he first started martial arts he replied: *"I first started judo at the Saint John [New Brunswick, Canada] YMCA in September of 1964. Three years later I took up Kyokushin Karate, also in Saint John, under Sensei Adrian Gomes and stayed with him until I relocated to Toronto. Of course, I boxed as an amateur and competed as a collegiate wrestler in school."*

I asked him what it was in particular about Karate that appealed to him. He replied: *"There were many reasons. Bruce Lee had a lot to do with helping me define how/why to embrace such an inner passion. Moreover, Karate has always been a unique way through which to keep fit [although I had let myself slip for many years], pursue my identity and learn exactly who I am, while allowing me to creatively express myself."*

Asked who his earliest influences were in Karate and Jujutsu he replied: *"Some of the most memorable from my formative years [1970s] had been Sensei Wally Slocki, Hanshi Richard Kim, Shihan Bob Dalgleish, Master Tsuruoka Masami, Prof Wally Jay and Prof Ron Forester."*

An interesting early instructor of McCarthy's was Daniel K Pai, of Pai Lum. He explained: *"Master Pai commanded a huge following during the 1970s as the founder of Pai Lum Kempo [a Hawaiian-Chinese based fighting art]. He was a charismatic instructor, a brutally powerful human being [understatement] a remarkably knowledgable and deeply spiritual person."*

Hanshi Richard Kim of the Dai Nippon Butokukai is perhaps his greatest influence. He said: *"I was looking for an instructor who could teach me more about tradition, its value and functional application and my [then] kumite coach, Wally Slocki, recommended that I attend his Oct 1977 seminar in Hamilton, Ontario, hosted by Don Warrener. I attended the week-long gathering and was so taken with him that I made a petition to study under his guidance and was accepted.*

"I've always been fascinated by oriental culture but it was Richard Kim who inspired me to look beyond the physical aspects of the art and understand its historical, anthropological, spiritual and pedagogical aspects. Such studies also made it easier to grasp the application-based methods culminated in kata.

"My principal instructor, Richard Kim, wanted to bring as much recognition to his art as possible, and so he teamed up with the number #2 man [originally] of the JKA, Nishiyama Hidetaka ['the man' at that time], back in the late 1950s after returning to the USA from Japan. In doing so, he fused his application-style practices with JKA-style kata dynamics to create an innovative interpretation of Okinawan Karate.

"By doing so he not only became the IAKF's VP [Nishiyama's organisation] he also strengthened his own position in world Karate

while at the same time popularising his own modified Okinawan-style of karate [Shorinji Ryu]."

Explaining how he came to live in Japan, McCarthy said: *"I first went to Japan in 1985 and spent the entire summer months in Okinawa. As I was not officially associated with any one specific local Okinawan group at that time I was free to visit any dojo that interested me. In spite of the so-called political 'restriction,' which tends to prevent enthusiasts from freely visiting any dojo they want to these days ... such was not the case in a far more political free era of the mid-1980s. Although I literally visited dozens of dojo on the island the most notable were Nagamine Shoshin, Miyazato Eiichi, Nakazato Joen, Yagi Meitoku, Uechi Kanei, Kishaba Chokei & Shinzato Katsuhiko, Hokama Tetsuhiro, Uehara Seikichi, Toma Shian, Matayoshi Shimpo, Nakamoto Masahiro and Akamine Eisuke. As someone interested in more than just physical training, a passion with learning the history, philosophy and culture of this art opened many doors of opportunity allowing me into the dojo and homes of the senior most authorities of the Okinawan fighting traditions. Not long after this I met and married a wonderful Japanese girl and we decided to settle in Kanagawa Prefecture. In the decade I resided in Japan it became a mission of sorts to seek out the best technicians, most knowledgable instructors and well respected personalities of the fighting arts."*

I asked McCarthy Hanshi to sum up his training under Kinjo Hiroshi and whether this was his greatest influence. He replied: *"Hmmm... That's a big question... honestly. Kinjo sensei was, without question, the single most knowledgable person I'd ever met with regards to Okinawa's fighting arts... and described by many as 'A Walking Encyclopaedia.' Much more impressive, however, at least for me, was his remarkable modesty ... even until the day he died at nearly 95 years old he remained a genuinely humble gentleman and maintained that such a demeanour exemplified the character and spirit of the art. He liked to quote his old friend, Chibana Choshin, who said, 'Karate aims to build character, it does not by virtue of practice, however, guarantee it!'"*

I asked McCarthy Sensei how a traditional Karateka like himself found himself at the start of the MMA revolution, competing in the UWFI. He replied, with a smile: *"Oh ... you really did your homework Simon san. In the mid-1980s while residing in Japan I met Gene Pelc, an American businessman in Tokyo. He was passionate about*

Kakutogi [a Japanese word which roughly means combat sports] and had watched me perform at a local demonstration. Through Gene I met Sayama Satoru [the puro resu legend Tiger Mask], the man who established the MMA movement in Japan, then called, "Shooto" [from the pro wrestling term to shoot, meaning a straight shooting contest as opposed to a 'work']. Shooto, in its original form, was a remarkably brutal form of stand-up fighting with clinch-work and ground and pound. Void of many rules and equipment Shooto used a boxing ring, no gloves and seemed to appeal mostly to submission wrestlers of that era. Wanting to preserve an ageing body I decided to try Shoot-Boxing under Cesar Takeshi which favoured using a little more equipment; i.e. gloves, mouth piece, cup etc. In those days [late 1980s] the rounds were 10-mins in duration and terribly challenging on this then 34-year-old body. When Gene organised an opportunity for me to become an in-house trainer for the UWFI I seized it. Those years were wonderfully educational and I literally met and trained with the who's who of Japan's Kakutogi community. Our submission wrestling mentors were Karl Gotch, Billy Robinson, Lou Thesz and Danny Hodge, etc. This set the stage for what would ultimately become Pride Fighting.

"These days I still enjoy watching MMA and do a fair amount of related training myself. As far as rating anyone in MMA ... that's a hard call for me as I am from an earlier era that featured outstanding fighters like Muhammed Ali, Tommy Hearns, Jose Palomino, Marvin Hagler and Ray Leonard, etc. I find myself constantly comparing fighters of today's arena with the greats of the boxing world who were such marvellous technicians. While I have certainly seen some strong competitors in the Octagon I still have yet to find ones with the same technical ability. As such, I am drawn more to BJJ and no-gi grappling as this is an arena where it's all about technique and tactics."

I asked McCarthy Hanshi about his pioneering teaching of two man exercises and flow drills and asked if, in his opinion the likes of Matsumura and Sakugawa trained in this way.

He replied: *"Oh ... absolutely they did! There is no question in the minds of any serious researcher that such is the case. Moreover, anyone who has done their homework will tell you that China [i.e. Fujian Province] was THE PLACE any young Okinawan man went to study the fighting arts during its old Ryukyu Kingdom Period. We also know that 2-person drills are the fundamental base practice for all*

241

functional southern quanfa styles. Understanding this and knowing something about the men who plied the waters between the Ryukyu Archipelago and the Middle Kingdom during those time frames the rest is easy to deduce. Making it even easier to understand are the time capsules handed down in the form of kata, which mirror several well known local southern Chinese quanfa styles; i.e. Yongchun, Monk Fist, etc."

I asked him how his system of Koryu Uchinadi differs from general Karatedo, and he replied: *"May I begin by stating that modern Karate [i.e. the rule-bound Japanese combative sport] does NOT represent the original fighting art culture once extant during Okinawa's old Ryukyu Kingdom. Understanding that the art of self-defence cannot and is not limited by rules and regulations may I subsequently ask how can one even make such a comparison? The totality of my research revealed a wonderfully accommodating fighting art that literally dealt with a phenomenon I have coined with the phrase, 'Habitual Acts of Physical Violence,' aka HAPV. So, I suppose in many ways one could say that I am NOT practising and/or teaching Karate, but rather older and far more original practices NOT limited by rules.*

"I would like to see it become a valuable contribution towards clearing up the ambiguity surrounding what this art truly is. In its purest form I really don't see Koryu Uchinadi as a 'style,' as such. In such a diverse and multifaceted tradition I have succeeded in discovering what I believe is something quite timeless... a human practice which transcends 'style,' culture, age, nationality and gender, etc. and is based exclusively upon common mechanics and governed by immutable principles. Koryu Uchinadi's unique system of application practices is a pathway between kata and kumite. Learned correctly, it can enhance the depth and value of any dojo curriculum without adversely affecting its cosmetic appearance or taking anything away from its cultural heritage. KU can also be learned/imparted as a provocative alternative to conventional methods of physical fitness and stress management.

"Learning how to respond dispassionately to unwarranted aggression requires self- empowerment. Such training promotes an inner-calm and, where conflict exists, helps restore a natural balance to personal and professional relationships."

Epilogue: The Okinawan Karate Kaikan: A New Beginning for Okinawan Karate

In 2017 the Okinawa Prefectural Government opened the doors of the Okinawa Karate Kaikan. This facility will serve to inherit, preserve, and develop Karate's role in traditional Okinawan culture and tell the world that Okinawa is the birthplace of Karate.

It was opened by the Governor of Okinawa Prefecture, Takeshi Onaga, and Minister of the government of Japan, Yosuke Tsuruho.

The opening ceremony was attended by over 1,000 people (governmental authorities, politicians, businessmen and the greatest masters of world Karate). In addition to the official opening ceremony there were held demonstrations of Karate and officials planted a symbolic tree.

The Okinawa Karate Kaikan stands in Tomigusuku City, located in the southern part of Okinawa Island, on hills that are connected to the ruins of Tomigusuku Castle. Its construction cost over 65 billion yen. The 3.8 hectare site contains three main buildings: the Karate Dojo, the Karate Archives, and the Special Dojo, built with red tiled roof that symbolises Okinawan tradition.

On Okinawa's new Karate Kaikan, Higaonna told the *Guardian*: "I'm proud of the Kaikan. It's splendid."

One of the first international courses at the Kaikan was taught by: Isao Yagi, 9th Dan (Bu Mai Moidi Motobu Ryu Gassen Tuidi), Yoshio Kuba 10th Dan (Goju Ryu), Tetsuhiro Hokama 10th Dan (Goju Ryu) and Terry Wingrove 9th Dan (Karate Jutsu).

Yagi Sensei is the successor of Shiroma Kiyonori Seihan (10th Dan) who was in turn a student of Uehara, in turn a student of Choyu Motobu.

Born in 1942 and a former senior high school teacher, Shiroma Sensei met the grand master Seikichi Uehara Sensei at 27 years old and started training with him right away.

Seikichi Uehara Sensei (1904-2004) learned the Ryukyu royal court martial art "Motobu Udun Di" from the 11th descendant of the Motobu family, Choyu Motobu Sensei.

Shiroma Sensei returned to his homeland of Sashiki to open his Dojo under the name "Motobu ryu Gassen Tuite". He was reportedly given the blessing of Motobu Chosei to teach the family art in 2006.

As Yagi Sensei taught the Udon of Choyu Motobu and Wingrove Hanshi taught his Motobu-baserd Karate Jutsu in the Kaikan, Okinawan Karate had perhaps come full circle.

The palace art was back in the palace.

About the Author

Simon Keegan
Karate Renshi, 5th Dan
Jujutsu Renshi, 5th Dan

Simon Keegan is a Karate, Jujutsu and Quanfa instructor who has taught for decades and has an impeccable lineage in the classical martial arts, grading on the mat up to 5th Dan and holding the traditional teaching rank of Renshi.

He has trained under some of the senior Japanese and Chinese masters in the world with his grades recognised by authority of the Japanese royal family and Shogun dynasty.

He trained and graded under Tokyo's Kokusai Budoin, which is presided over by Tokugawa Yasuhisa and had as its first chairmen Prince Tsunenori Kaya and Prince Higashikuni. Members have included Hirokazu Kanazawa, Gogen Yamaguchi, Hironori Ohtsuka and Kyuzo Mifune. He is now a member of Kyoto's Dai Nippon Butokukai, headed by Higashi Fushimi, cousin to the Emperor. Members have included Gichin Funakoshi and Chojun Miyagi.

Simon was born in Liverpool to a martial arts family and studied from an early age. His father David Keegan is a teacher of classical Japanese and Chinese martial arts, and his great uncle Bill Nelson was a blackbelt at two of the oldest Jujutsu schools in the country.

At the age of 16 Simon was competing at national level in Karate while studying in S Bullough's Bushidokan. The Bushido style of Karate was an eclectic mix of styles including Shotokan and Budokan. Simon competed in Karate, kickboxing and Kobudo/Iaido and became his teacher's Uchideshi (a senior student and assistant instructor) in 1997.

He left competition martial arts to focus on classical Okinawan, Japanese and Chinese styles. He trained for 10 years with Kyoshi R Carruthers and later his teacher Shihan P Handyside who became a mentor to him in the art of Shobukan Karate, derived from Japanese Shotokan and Malaysian Budokan which is a softer Chinese influenced style of Karate. Budokan is a main influence on his study. Grandmaster CS Chew trained in the Okinawan styles of Toyama and Shimabukuro as well as in Chinese styles like Pakua.

Studying Chinese martial arts for some 20 years, Simon's studies include Yang style, Sun style (which also comprises Pakua and Hsing-I) and Chinese sword. He trained in a Chinese internal martial arts school for nine years which was presided over by Chinese National Living Treasure Professor Li De Yin and taught by two world champions. Simon was authorised to teach Yang style forms in 2004 and has since developed his understanding of the art under Sifu Steve Rowe who trained directly with Yang style headmistress Ma Lee Yang. Simon competed at European Wushu events and performed sword and Yang style in front of the mayor of Shanghai.

In Japanese martial arts he was awarded 2nd Dan in Jujutsu, studying the Bugei Ju Hapan (18 martial arts including Bo Jutsu, Jo Jutsu, Iai Jutsu, Ken Jutsu, So Jutsu and Kusari Gama etc). Simon established a school called Bushinkai dedicated to teaching classical Japanese, Okinawan and Chinese martial arts.

In 2003 on a seminar with the legendary Mitsuhiro Kondo, one of the masters who introduced Karate and Aikido to Europe in the 1950s, Simon joined Japan's oldest Budo fraternity, the Kokusai Budoin of which he went on to become a regional officer with his grades recognised by the hereditary shogun Tokugawa Yasuhisa.

He also was awarded 2nd Dan in Nihon Jujutsu under the late Shizuya Sato, later attaining 3rd Dan in Jujutsu and Judo.

Simon began studying Goju Ryu Karate and Kobudo and was

graded up to 3rd Dan by Kyoshi Reiner Parsons, also training with headteacher and Kokusai Budoin chief director Tadanori Nobetsu. The style was Nisseikai which combined Okinawan Goju Ryu with Feeding Crane Quan Fa, bringing the art closer to its Naha-Te origins. This is another key influence on his study.

He also began to pursue the old Karate Jutsu and Yawara methods, training with masters like Hanshi Terry Wingrove. Simon was awarded his 4th Dan in Karate and Jujutsu in 2007 and became a member of the International Ju Jitsu Federation (Seibukan) and Karate Jutsu International. He was also invited by Hanshi Wingrove to become a founder member of the English Karate Federation.

Simon was awarded his Renshi title in 2009, endorsed by the national head of the Dai Nippon Butokukai Hanshi Allan Tattersall. Simon hosted Hanshi Tattersall on a number of courses, and would train with him privately taking particular interest in Takenouchi Ryu Jujutsu. Hanshi also taught Simon's father David Keegan and presented him with a hand painted 'Bu' kanji to mark their Renshi awards. Hanshi Tattersall hosted the Bushinkai school's 10th anniversary at his Myoshinkan Dojo which was the UK headquarters of the Dai Nippon Butokukai. To honour the memory of Hanshi Tattersall, Simon was invited to become an official member of the Dai Nippon Butokukai and the Myoshin Ryu.

Simon was awarded his 5th Dan in Shobukan Karate by Shihan Handyside in 2012 and later attained that grade in Jujutsu.

He has demonstrated his arts in Japanese cultural festivals and performed Kata with the London Symphony Orchestra, the first person to ever do so.

This is his third book, having previously written two history books. His Karate, Jujutsu and Quanfa studies continue.

CONTACT DETAILS

BUSHINKAI ACADEMY:

Okinawan and Japanese martial arts
Head teacher: Simon Keegan (5th Dan Renshi)
Email: simonkeeganmedia@gmail.com
Website: BushinkaiMartialArts.wordpress.com

Chinese internal martial arts
Head teacher: David Keegan (5th Dan Sifu)
Email: Taijidave@runbox.com
Website: BushinkaiMartialArts.wordpress.com

SHIKON

Chairman: Steve Rowe (9th Dan Sifu)
Email: Steve@shikon.com
Website: www.shikon.com

KARATE JUTSU INTERNATIONAL

Technical Director: Terry Wingrove (9th Dan Hanshi)
Email: Sensei@cyberbudo.com
Website: KarateJutsu.wordpress.com

HAKUTORA FIGHTWEAR

Contact: John Dang
Website: Hakutora.com

Index of key Karateka featured

Abbe, Kenshiro: 154, 189-194, 209-215
Akiyama, Yoshitoki: 23-31, 93-100, 159
Anan: 100-106
Aragaki, Ankichi: 142-143
Aragaki, Seisho: 77-92, 105-113
Arneil, Steve: 200, 216-217
Asai, Tetsuhiko: 168-170
Ason: 84-93, 101, 105-106
Azato, Anko: 49, 77-83, 88, 90-98, 132
Bell, Vernon: 188-189, 191-216
Brennan, Frank: 199-200
Britten, Jack: 187, 188, 194, 198, 207-208, 214
Chen Gempin (Yuan Pin): 26-31
Chen Wangting: 26
Chew, Choo Soot: 139, 198, 227-237
Chibana, Chosin: 79, 131, 135, 137, 142, 167
Chinen, Teruo: 204
Chitose, Tsuyoshi: 83, 139
Chomo Hanashiro: 98, 102, 127, 135-136, 147
Chow, William: 168-181
Colwell, Ronnie: 187, 198
Connor, Danny: 195, 198, 200.-211, 216, 235
Cummins, Cyril: 198-200, 216
Demura, Fumio: 150, 183
Donovan, David 'Ticky': 198, 201, 216, 238
Egami, Shigeru: 133, 163
Enoeda, Keinosuke: 135, 167, 170, 196-200
Fang Qi Niang: 108, 113
Fujimoto, Hiroshi: 127-129, 203, 218-225
Fujiwara, Katsumi: 123, 129-203, 217, 218
Fujiwara, Ryuzo: 65, 116
Funakoshi, Gichin: 66-68, 87, 96, 132-140, 147-149, 157, 163
Funakoshi, Gigo: 133-135, 148, 163, 169
Funakoshi, Kenneth: 168
Gima, Makoto (Shinkin): 66, 132-134, 147, 164
Gusukuma, of Tomari: 77, 80, 84, 100-103, 132
Gusukuma, Shinpan: 135
Handyside, Phillip: 167, 216, 228

Harada, Mitsusuke: 195, 198, 216
Higa, Hama: 34, 45, 52
Higa, Seiko: 114, 142, 171
Higa, Yuchoku: 142, 167
Higaonna, Kanryo: 84, 89, 106-109
Higaonna, Morio: 172, 173, 203, 235
Higgins, Billy: 200
Hoang Nam: 192, 193, 201, 205, 215
Hokama, Tetsuhiro: 107, 142, 171, 235
Hung I-Hsiang: 37, 56
Ishimine, Bushi: 93, 92, 98
Itosu, Anko: 26, 98, 102-119
Iwah: 78, 84-87, 90, 98, 105, 116
Kanazawa, Hirokazu: 93, 100-105, 135, 142, 166-169, 196-199
Kano Jigoro: 25, 132
Kase, Taiji: 48, 169, 196-199, 216
Kim, Richard: 52, 64, 80, 148, 240
Kimura, Shigeru: 201, 225
Kise, Fuse: 58, 142
Kishimoto, Soko: 90, 142
Kojo family: 44-45. 73-75
Kojo, Kaho: 110
Kojo, Isei: 110
Kondo, Mitsuhiro: 163, 170, 189, 202
Konishi, Yasushiro: 126, 128, 131, 134, 148, 157, 164, 226
Kushanku: 63-73, 76, 78, 85
Kuwae, Ryusei: 81
Kyan, Chotoku: 59, 83-87, 138-146, 228
Kyoda, Juhatsu: 85-86, 115, 135-138, 171
Laville, Pauline (Bindra, Fuller): 197, 209, 217
Lewis, Alfie: 236-238
Mabuni, Kenwa: 65-66, 79, 91, 102, 108-109, 111-118, 127-147
Machida, Lyoto: 239
Mack, Charles: 195, 201, 211, 215
Makabe, Choken: 54, 73
Manning, Michael: 190-215
Masters, Paul: 30, 202
Matayoshi, Shinko: 114-115
Mather, Jim: 181-183
Matsu, Kinjo: 177

Matsumora, Kosaku: 83, 84, 99, 100-101, 121
Matsumura, Nabe: 77, 81, 98, 11, 142
Matsumura, Sokon: 49, 56, 65, 73-96, 98-109, 126
Matsuo Kanenori Sakon: 43, 45, 53,-60, 92, 99, 105, 118
McCarthy, Patrick: 40, 50-52, 65-87, 107-109, 115-116, 239-242
Minamoto Clan: 49, 50, 54, 59
Miyagi, Chojun: 25, 64, 66, 75, 85, 110-116, 127-156, 171-172
Miyagi, Anichi: 172-173
Miyazato, Eiichi: 142, 172, 173, 241
Mochizuki, Hiroo: 163, 170, 189, 196, 215, 224
Mochizuki, Minoru: 133, 135, 138, 152, 162, 180, 188-190, 194
Motobu, Choki: 35, 54, 62, 80, 98, 119-131, 221, 226
Motobu, Choyu: 54-59, 120-124
Nagamine, Shoshin: 100, 137-143
Nakayama, Masatoshi: 135, 163, 166
Naylor, Charlie: 198-215
Nishiyama, Hidetaka: 135, 163, 169, 234
Nobetsu Tadanori: 114, 154, 173
Norris, Chuck: 181-182, 235
Ohtsuka, Hironori: 133-134, 147, 157-160
O'Neill, Terry: 172, 197, 199, 200-217
Oyama, Mas: 8, 195
Oyata Seiyu: 174-175
Parker, Ed: 181
Plee, Henri: 37, 88, 180, 189-204, 215, 233
Qi Ji Guang: 41-42
Ryuru Ko: 85, 89, 105-115
Sakugawa, Kanga 'Tode': 62-76
Sato, Kinbei: 27, 29, 185, 203
Sato, Shizuya: 151-162
Sherry, Andy: 187-217
Shimabuko, Tatsuo: 144
Shimabukuro, Zenryo: 142, 143
Shirai, Hiroshi: 49, 166, 170, 196, 199, 202
Suzuki Tatsuo: 159, 189, 196, 198, 200
Taira, Shinken: 52, 63, 146, 149
Takahara, Pechin: 52-60, 62
Tang Daiji: 109-117
Tani, Chojiro: 127, 129, 139, 198, 218, 220-222
Toyama, Kanken: 102, 126, 135, 138, 140-141, 227

Trias, Robert: 124, 126, 180-181
Uechi Kanbun: 89, 113-118, 127-138, 219
Waishinzan: 84, 85, 105
Wingrove, Terry: 134-149, 164-165, 190-217, 220-226, 237, 245
Yabe, Kentsu: 98, 102, 122, 132, 141, 180
Yagi, Meitoku: 142, 241
Yara, Chatan: 64-65
Yamaguchi, Gogen: 35, 114, 152, 155
Zhou Zi He (Shushi Wa):113-116

Lightning Source UK Ltd.
Milton Keynes UK
UKHW02f1349110318
319128UK00006B/65/P